HUNGRY
HEART

HUNGRY HEART

The Literary Emergence of
Julia Ward Howe

Gary Williams

UNIVERSITY OF
MASSACHUSETTS PRESS

AMHERST

Copyright © 1999 by
The University of Massachusetts Press
All rights reserved
Printed in the United States of America

LC 98-35053
ISBN 1-55849-157-0

Designed by Dennis Anderson
Printed and bound by BookCrafters, Inc.

Library of Congress Cataloging-in-Publication Data

Williams, Gary, 1947 May 6–
Hungry heart : the literary emergence of Julia Ward Howe / Gary Williams.
p.   cm.
Includes bibliographical references (p.   ) and index.
ISBN 1-55849-157-0 (cloth : alk. paper)
1. Howe, Julia Ward, 1819–1910.   2. Women and literature—United
States—History—19th century.   3. Women authors, American—19th
century—Biography.   4. Feminists—United States—Biography.
I. Title.
PS2018.W55   1999
818'.409—dc21
[b]   98-35053
CIP

British Library Cataloguing in Publication Data are available.

For Joy

Contents

Illustrations

Acknowledgments

Many people and organizations helped me make this book.

First, I express gratitude to the National Endowment for the Humanities for a travel to collections grant that made possible my first reading of the Howe Family Papers at Houghton Library. For subsequent support enabling travel to Cambridge, I am grateful to the University of Idaho's Sabbatical Leave Evaluation Committee and to the English Department's Lillian White Fund for Professional Development. Kurt Olsson, dean of the College of Letters and Science, and Douglas Adams, chair of the English department, intervened in a number of ways to provide time, space, and equipment for the writing of the book.

During four years of research the reading room staff at Houghton Library was unfailingly pleasant and helpful. Leo Damrosch, chair of Harvard's Department of English and American Literature and Language, kindly offered me visiting scholar status during the fall of 1995. The master, tutors, students, and staff of Cabot House, particularly Susan Livingston, Louise Bray, and Gene Ketelhohn, extended themselves graciously and in countless ways to my wife and me during our six-month residence among them. So, too, did, Bonnie Creinin, Ann Getman, Roger and Rosemary Zehntner, and Steve and Mary Goldring.

A number of librarians and archivists offered assistance and insight along the way. Thanks to Donald Yacavone, Virginia Smith, and Christopher Steele of the Massachusetts Historical Society; Robert Volz of Williams College's Chapin Library; Joseph F. Fullum of the Boston Public Library; Lynn M. White of Widener Library's imaging services; Michele Clark of Longfellow House; and Aaron Schmidt of the Boston Public Library's print department. I especially value the help provided by Jennifer O'Laughlin of the University of Idaho Library's interlibrary loan office. For permission to quote and reproduce materials, I thank

Leslie A. Morris of Houghton Library; Sylvia McDowell of Schlesinger Library, The National Park Service (Longfellow National Historical Site); the Massachusetts Historical Society; Cristina Palombi of Fratelli Palombi Editori; Wayne Furman of the New York Public Library; and Sinclair Hitchings of the Boston Public Library Print Department.

For conversation, direction, instruction, and opportunities to hear response to earlier formulations of the book's materials, I thank Wayne Franklin, Susan Shillinglaw, Albert von Frank, Karen Hansen, Veronica Makowsky, Dean Grodzins, Margaretta Fulton, Lance Olsen, Bob Orth, Peggy Pace, Meredith McGill, John Hench, Caroline Sloat, John and Julia Gatta, Edna Hesford, Jane Dewey, Susan Belasco Smith, Eliza Richards, students in my graduate classes (especially Jim Robinson), and my daughters, Liza and Emily Williams.

Three people—Walter Hesford, Kenny Marotta, Richard Penticoff— read most or all of the work in earlier drafts and offered knowledgeable and detailed critiques. The book is a great deal better than it might have been had these good friends not given it the scrutiny they did.

Paula Bennett's enthusiasm for the project, particularly the portion of it that found expression in her insistence that I resist generalization about what antebellum women writers were capable of, was an unanticipated and much valued gift. Jim Wallace's interest in Howe sparked mine; thus his early support for my investigation and his careful, generous comments on the manuscript have meant a great deal.

Finally, I thank those at the University of Massachusetts Press and elsewhere whose professional attentions have helped the book take final form: Clark Dougan, Bruce Wilcox, Catlin Murphy, Pam Wilkinson, Marsha Kunin, Ralph Kaplan, and Stephen Bach.

As the dedication indicates, this book is for Joy Passanante, my wife, who not only read it in drafts and offered wise line-by-line comment, but who lived a version of this book's story with me and taught me how to hear a voice like Julia Ward Howe's.

HUNGRY
HEART

Introduction

When Julia Ward Howe's first book of poems, *Passion-Flowers*, appeared anonymously early in 1854, it garnered two kinds of praise from reviewers—praise for the intensity with which its poems expressed obviously personal feelings and praise for the vigorous intellect they exhibited, an intellect of "masculine self-concentration and force." On the one hand, "[n]othing but the profound experience of a rarely endowed nature could give such an air of reality to such impassioned wails of suffering"; on the other, "[w]ere it not for frequent passages which claim to reveal a feminine history, we should not have suspected these poems to be the production of a woman." To all reviewers, the verses seemed unprecedented: "They form an entirely unique class in the whole range of female literature," said George Ripley in the *New York Tribune*.[1]

Indeed, they did. Poems that spoke passionately of the feelings of a woman, but with the authority and independence that the era's codes of propriety reserved for male discourse, were not in abundant supply in mid-nineteenth-century America. And, before long, added to the extraordinary qualities reviewers attributed to the collection was the rumor that the feelings its author had made public arose from difficulties in her marriage. Although the work was published anonymously, it seems to have been an intentional part of what now might be designated marketing strategy that Mrs. Howe's name was attached by word of mouth to the book. Writing to her sister Annie, Howe noted that even before reviews began to appear the "Authorship is, of course, no secret now, and you had best talk openly of it, all of you, as it may help the sale of the Book in N.Y."[2] The *New York Evening Post* coyly observed that the city's lovers of poetry would feel "a special interest in the history of this gifted minstrel, from the fact that it is confidently stated that she is the daughter of a late highly esteemed citizen of New York, although a resident of a neighboring state."[3] Thus the book was always more than just another volume of poems: it invited scrutiny as autobiography, as confession, as transgressive disclosure. "Here is revolt enough, between these blue covers," Howe's good friend Henry Longfellow mused in his journal, and Hawthorne wrote to William D. Ticknor, her publisher, that "the devil must be in the woman" to publish the poems, since they seemed "to let out a whole history of domestic unhappiness." The book ran through three printings in four months before titillation began to fade.[4]

One sign (among many) of the personal cast of the verse is evident from her husband Samuel Gridley Howe's reaction to its publication. Included in Hawthorne's speculations was a line to Ticknor explicitly posing this issue: "What does her husband think of it?" At the precise moment of Hawthorne's query, Samuel Howe was so profoundly disturbed about both the book and its reception that his personal safety seemed to be at stake; he was "in such a state of mind that it would have been unsafe to leave him," his wife wrote to Annie. The fact of its publication and the startlingly frank acknowledgment of domestic dissatisfaction in several poems drove him to a psychological distress she described as "almost crazy . . . a very dangerous state, I think, very near insanity."[5] It was some months before he recovered a semblance of equanimity—and then only as a result of a capitulation on Julia Howe's part that even at this distance in time has the capacity to startle.

This unusually dramatic literary debut—John Greenleaf Whittier gallantly wrote to Howe that *Passion-Flowers* "placed thee at the head of us all"—has attracted occasional notice from twentieth-century scholars, most recently James D. Wallace. In 1990 Wallace called attention to Hawthorne's enthusiasm for *Passion-Flowers* and incidentally to the book's remarkably self-revealing qualities.[6] Julia Ward Howe has been the subject of two book-length studies within the last twenty years—the standard contemporary biography, *Mine Eyes Have Seen the Glory,* by Deborah Pickman Clifford, and a dissertation, *Private Woman, Public Person,* completed in 1982 by Mary H. Grant. (Grant's essentially unrevised work was made available in 1994 under Gerda Lerner's auspices in a series called "Scholarship in Women's History: Rediscovered and New.") Howe is one of the women poets out of whose lives Cheryl Walker constructed a "composite biography" in *The Nightingale's Burden,* and a handful of critics have examined aspects of her work,[7] but for most people Julia Ward Howe remains the woman who wrote "The Battle Hymn of the Republic." In the popular imagination, that is to say, she is a poet in the way that Francis Scott Key is a poet—patriotic, pious, grand, a rhymer in the nineteenth-century manner, given to the conventions of rhetorical flourish, the producer of work devoid of personal identifying marks. Recent anthologies of nineteenth-century American women's poetry reinscribe *this* Julia Ward Howe: if her work is represented at all, it is through "The Battle Hymn" (or through work from later in her life, when efforts on behalf of peace movements and women's suffrage had supplanted the self-expressive passion of her early adulthood).[8]

Jim Wallace's brief, provocative account of the seeds of *Passion-Flowers* stirred the questions that have led to this study. My exploration took shape out of a sense of the disparity between the story Deborah Clifford's biography tells of the early years of Julia Ward's marriage and the story preserved in the huge store of unpublished materials in Harvard's Houghton and Schlesinger libraries. The latter include many of the Howes' letters to each other, those Julia Howe wrote to her siblings, those Samuel Howe wrote to Charles Sumner and other friends, and Julia Howe's manuscripts and private journals. Clifford, of course, drew on these materials, but from the position of a biographer confronted with the task of condensing a very long and rich life into manageable proportions. Julia Ward Howe lived to be ninety-one years old; she died in 1910 and enjoyed intellectual vitality until very near the end of her life. Clifford's comprehensive focus—and perhaps, too, her interest in the work Howe accomplished in her later decades—resulted in an abridged account of Howe's early married years and the period in which her hopes for a literary career gathered force. In any case, my reading of the unpublished materials led me to a different sense of the dynamics present in the early days of the Howe marriage.

Nor could Clifford's work, given its parameters, do justice to the aesthetic complexities of *Passion-Flowers,* or to those of Howe's other pre–Civil War literary productions, *Words for the Hour* and *The World's Own,* both published in 1857. The first of these, another collection of poems, gathers resonance and consequence when looked at as the outgrowth of the altered state of domestic affairs that had been generated by the publication of *Passion-Flowers. And The World's Own*—a blank-verse play featuring a woman propelled by an ethic of revenge—also seems closely tied to the issues Howe had struggled with in the two earlier books. None of this work has been subjected to systematic literary analysis, and many of the associations, speculative or actual, that might be drawn with events in her life have gone unremarked.

Howe's own account of this period in *Reminiscences, 1819–1899,* especially her comments on her early publications, perhaps suggests why these books have received little close scrutiny. Regarding her life from the promontory afforded by eighty years and numerous accomplishments, she had no desire to revisit the painful period leading up to *Passion-Flowers.* Nor would propriety have permitted her to inscribe a version of that period that might have indicated bitterness or even unhappiness. But we need to read this narrative attentively, with an ear for what Toni Morrison (in a recent introduction to *Huckleberry Finn*) describes as "unarticulated eddies that encourage diving into the . . . undertow."[9] Howe's two-part characterization of her first collection of poems as having "dealt partly with the stirring questions of the time, partly with things near and familiar" needs to be heard with equal emphasis given to both halves of that description—despite her obfuscating invitation to readers to recall that "the events of 1848 were still in fresh remembrance: the heroic efforts of Italian patriots to deliver their country from foreign oppression, the struggle of Hungary to maintain her ancient immunities." The volume's "most important" poems, she assures us, focus on these themes and secondarily on the "wrongs and sufferings of the slaves." "A timid performance upon a slender reed," she concludes dismissively, noting further only that "the great performers in the noble orchestra of writers answered to its appeal, which won me a seat in their ranks." Similarly, *Words for the Hour* merits a mere three sentences, the thrust of her recollection turning on the critics' prediction that it would meet with less success than its predecessor. As for *The World's Own,* she reports only that one critic thought it " 'full of literary merits and of dramatic defects,' " a work that "did not, as they say, 'keep the stage.' "[10]

A comparable inclination toward smoothing silence about the more personal sources of their mother's early poetry pervades the early twentieth-century biographical work of Howe's daughters Laura Richards, Maud Elliott, and Florence Howe Hall.[11] Valuable for their anecdotes of jolly family life and the occasional glimpse into a relationship or event that might otherwise have slipped out of memory, these filiopietistic works afford even less in the way of acknowledgment of marital discord or detailed scrutiny of the poetry. We glean more—or at any rate the suggestion that there *is* more to be gleaned—from Louise Tharp's impudent *Three Saints and a Sinner,* a freewheeling sketch of the lives of Howe and the three Ward siblings who lived to old age. Older brother Sam Ward is the sinner counterpointing the relative saintliness of Julia, Louisa, and Annie, and while Tharp often ironizes her controlling novelistic metaphor, especially in sections focusing on Julia, the book by its very design—the multiple biography—delivers its information in fragmented and condensed form.[12]

Mary Grant's doctoral work, directed by Linda Grant DePauw in the history department at George Washington University, broke much new ground. She wisely limited the focus of her biographical study to Howe's earlier years, a decision that enabled her to draw much more substantially than Clifford on materials indicating the manifold difficulties both Howe and her husband encountered as they attempted to build a marriage and family. An important offshoot of her biographical research, a study of Howe's unusual amalgam of progressive feminist thinking and fidelity to many precepts of the "cult of domesticity," was published in Mary Kelley's 1979 collection, *Woman's Being, Woman's Place.*[13] Gerda Lerner's effort of reclamation, which made Grant's entire work available as a book, is certainly praiseworthy. The absence of a seasoned scholarly perspective on the material, however, much reduces the value of *Public Woman, Private Person.* And like Clifford, Grant is a historian, not a literary critic. Thus, the aesthetic qualities of Howe's work—issues of tone, allusion, and nuance in the letters and manuscripts, as well as in the published work—are for the most part neglected. Too, Grant's reading of the source material was (perhaps unavoidably) sketchy. Her study is often factually inaccurate; it overlooks certain significant exchanges of letters, omits discussion of several influential relationships, and undervalues or misreads certain of the manuscript materials, particularly those examined here in chapters 2 and 3.

Yet in her understanding of *Passion-Flowers* as a solution to the depression that plagued Howe chronically during the first years of her marriage, Grant opens the way for a comprehensive reading of Howe's literary emergence. If the manifest subject of some of the *Passion-Flowers* poems is the revolutionary spirit associated with such figures as Mazzini, Garibaldi, Kossuth, and Pope Pius IX, and if two or three of the poems decry the institution of slavery, it now seems undeniable that other issues as well were at stake for the thirty-four-year-old writer, ten years married and mother of four children. *Passion-Flowers* is primarily about herself—her marriage, her intellectual interests, her spiritual life, her heroes and heroines, her frustrations, her compensations. If the book, as she said, won her a seat in the orchestra of poets, its more important personal function was to restore to her a sense of her own identity, pulling her out from a swamp of dullness, emotional starvation, and maternal obligation. And it was exactly the author's rough edges and interior life—those elements shorn away or deliberately submerged in her mellowness-of-age memoir description—that attracted reviewers' interest and praise when the book appeared. These edges, this interiority, have compelled my attention, as well.

MY STUDY DRAWS on letters, diaries, and manuscripts to build a picture of Howe's life from 1835 until 1857. These years delimit the period between the end of her formal schooling at age sixteen and the publication of the third of her first three books. This work is not, and is not intended to be, an encyclopedic biography. Rather, I have tried to understand the biographical matrix out of which the *Passion-Flowers* poems emerged. Intrigued by the drama surrounding the book's publication, accepting the invitation offered by its introductory poem to understand the work as being *about* her "friends and foes," I set out to learn more about the circle of people Howe regarded in some way as her subjects. This task necessitated, first, working to uncover the nature of her troubles in a marriage to a man whom—if we are to believe their protestations—virtually all her friends and relatives considered an appropriate match for her.

I was, in a sense, unprepared for the richness of detail, the complexities of relationship and emotion I found preserved in Howe's private writings and in her husband's exchanges with Charles Sumner. As will be obvious, the letters became as engrossing an object of analysis as Howe's published work. The circumstances she found herself in, though doubtless not unique, were at least uncommon; there is little in the general store of information about nineteenth-century marriage conventions (despite substantial increases in its inventory over the last two decades) to help us grasp the situation of a woman who finds her husband's best friend an ongoing rival for his affection. In addition to the myriad other deprivations antebellum American women with intellectual aspirations were obliged to accept when they married (or even when they did not), Howe evidently had to learn to live with the consciousness that her husband would answer her reluctance to mold her life entirely to his by withholding his emotional attention and deflecting it toward his younger, unmarried, deeply devoted companion in philanthropic endeavors.

This book begins, however, with an effort to establish that Howe's experience was notable in another way—in the amount and quality of the education she acquired as an adolescent and young woman. As Barbara Miller Solomon has documented, despite enhanced interest between 1790 and 1850 in creating the means for American women to receive schooling, those in a position to benefit from the new opportunities remained a very small fraction of the total population.[14] Even for those able to attend an academy, numerous cultural disincentives inhibited them from pursuing their interest. Mary Kelley notes: "[I]ntellectual aspirations and ambitions on the part of females generally were regarded as gratuitous, perhaps abnormal. Even for daughters of prominent families intellectual accomplishment was more symbolic and ornamental than functionally purposeful."[15] Although she encountered this attitude from members of her family, Julia Ward was nonetheless provided with first-rate tutors, a privilege of which she took full advantage. Her level of achievement, particularly in the study of languages and European literature, was matched by only a handful of other women in the country. I emphasize this aspect of Howe's experience, as well as her hypersensitivity to perspective-enlarging influences, to explain both the allure and the potential problem that this highly accomplished young woman posed for Samuel Gridley Howe.

The decade between the Howes' marriage in 1843 and the construction of *Passion-Flowers* can be divided into four segments. First, the Howes spent the fifteen months immediately following their wedding in Europe, mainly in Rome. The excursion (Julia's sister Annie was with them the entire time—her other sister, Louisa, for a little under a year) was intended to combine the pleasures of a wedding journey with visits to schools, prisons, and other institutions in which Samuel Howe, director of the Perkins Institution for the Blind, took a professional interest. Their first child was born in Rome in March 1844; they returned to South Boston in August of that year. The period in which Julia established herself as a resident of Boston, bore three other children (1845, 1848, 1850), and struggled to organize her life so as to accommodate her passion for study and writing constitutes a second phase. That period ended—in defeat, it might be said, at least as far as the organizational struggle was concerned—around 1850, when it was determined that the Howes would return to Rome, Samuel to recover from overwork, Julia to be relieved temporarily of some of the burdens of motherhood (although the two younger children accompanied them). Samuel returned to the United States after three months; Julia enjoyed almost a full year of near-complete liberty from the demands of domesticity. The fourth phase encompasses the period from Julia's return (a new understanding forged regarding her degree of responsibility to her husband's vision of connubial commitment) through the assembling and printing of her first book of poems. Chapters 2 through 4 present a narrative of this decade, chapter 2 looping back to examine the beginning of Samuel Howe's friendship with Charles Sumner in 1838 and chapter 3 including a summary/analysis of a never-published four-hundred-page prose work in which (I argue) Julia Howe first struggled to conceptualize the strangeness of her marital situation. Chapter 5 offers a reading of the *Passion-Flowers* poems that draws on the complex of tensions, needs, compensations, and sources of energy set out in the "biographical" chapters. Chapter 6 traces the Howes' distress in the difficult aftermath of Julia Howe's entrance into public life, presenting *Words for the Hour* and *The World's Own* as the means through which she eventually reached a perspective sufficient to enable her to live more or less amicably with her husband.

Lest it appear from this abbreviated account of the book's contents that, so far from being the chief focus of attention, Howe's published poetry has become nothing but grist for a biographical mill, I want to identify the scholars whose work has encouraged the approach I take. Many feminist historians and critics—Annette Kolodny, Nina Baym, Paul Lauter, Emily Stipes Watts, Mary Kelley, Cheryl Walker, Susan K. Harris, Susan Coultrap-McQuin, Alicia Suskin Ostriker, Paula Bennett, among others—have helped me modify or unlearn some older paradigms for understanding nineteenth-century literature. In contemplating Julia Ward Howe's work I have tried to think in the spirit called for and practiced by three terrain-mappers whose work I particularly admire—Joanne Dobson, Judith Fetterley, and Adrienne Rich. Dobson's

1993 essay, "The American Renaissance Reenvisioned," describes the lenses through which we will view a re-imagined history of the period as built "on the assumption that women's experience *counts.*" She encourages an approach to midcentury texts that "focuses on the interconnections of literature and culture, of literary evaluation and power," one that observes (among other things) writers' engagements with social and political issues, their representation of ordinary life, and their "embodiment of female subjective experience."[16] This approach is in accord, I believe, with Fetterley's recent suggestion that those interested in nineteenth-century American women writers "may need . . . to revitalize modes of criticism no longer fashionable."[17] I confess that I do not know whether the critical mode practiced in this book will strike readers as fashionable or un-, or whether its premises are useful for approaching the work of other antebellum women poets, but I heartily hope that it will be seen as enabling Julia Ward Howe's work to be understood in the terms Dobson proposes.[18]

Fetterley notes the potential strategic pitfall in Jane Tompkins's efforts to recover ideological contexts as a means for understanding the power of women's texts over their early readers: works reclaimed in this way may seem to have historical but not contemporary thematic significance. Yet I wonder if the "passionate involvement" Fetterley records as her students' responses to such texts is not in fact the more common reaction. In the case of Howe's verse, although its apparent surface-level conventionality sometimes impedes the initial perception of its force, her willingness to regard as her central poetic subject an array of emotions that women of her time frequently masked has deeply interested students with whom I have studied her work. Readers readily see parallels between contemporary situations and the situations that evoked Howe's creative resources. Phyllis Rose has observed, "We are desperate for information about how other people live because we want to know how to live ourselves."[19] Nineteenth-century American women's poetry often preserves this sort of information in an especially potent form; poems can, as Adrienne Rich affirms, "uncover desires and appetites buried under the accumulated emergencies of our lives, the fabricated wants and needs we have had urged on us, have accepted as our own."[20]

Many of the opinions and perceptions Rich presents in *What Is Found There: Notebooks on Poetry and Politics* have resonated sharply for me while writing about Julia Ward Howe—not least, Rich's distaste for the extent to which speculative biography is displacing serious writing about poets and poetry. "We have seen," she notes, "an obsession with intimate details, scandals, the clinical or trivializing reduction of artists' lives."[21] Hoping not to be seen as guilty of perpetrating this kind of commodifying reduction, I have tried to keep before me the mode in which Rich introduces biographical considerations in her discussions of contemporary poets. And I have proceeded with the confidence that Julia Ward Howe's life is a striking, as-yet-unappreciated example of what happens when (Rich's words) "an undomesticated woman refuses to hide her sexuality, abnegate her maternity, silence her hungers and angers in her poetry."[22] My title is a piercing phrase from a letter that Howe, wrestling with the demands of mothering a six-month-old infant and another not quite two, in what she felt was an emotional vacuum, wrote to her sister Louisa in midwinter 1846:

> Dearest Wevie, what is this problem? are we meant to change so utterly? is it selfish, is it egotistical to wish that others may love us, take an interest in us, sympathize with us, in our maturer age, as in our youth? are our hearts to fade and die out, with our early bloom, and, in giving life to others, do we lose our own vitality, and sink into dimness, nothingness, and living death? I have tried this, and found it not good—so methinks, I will not hold it fast. But then again, what shall I do? Where shall I go to beg some scraps and remnants of affection to feed my hungry heart? it will die, if it be not fed.[23]

That hunger, I believe, found at least temporary appeasement in the crafting of a mode of poetic discourse that enabled expression of her discontent. If expression brought other difficulties, other hungers, it brought also the self-assurance that empowered her to cope with these and that prepared her to be the formidable champion of women's rights that she became in later life.

A word about modes of reference to the principal characters in this narrative. My standard identifying term for Julia Ward Howe is "Howe," except in references to the period before her marriage (where she is "Julia" or "Julia Ward"). However, when it is necessary to distinguish between her and her husband in passages referring to both, I sometimes refer to her as "Julia" and to Samuel Gridley Howe as "Chev," the nickname used by Julia and her sisters. Since neither Charles Sumner nor any of Samuel Howe's male associates used this nickname in letters (where he is always "Howe"), I refer to him occasionally as "Samuel." In notes, wife and husband are identified as authors of letters by the initials "JW" or "JWH," and "SGH." The goal has been to afford Julia Howe, at every possible point, the courtesy of reference we extend, for example, to Henry Longfellow or Margaret Fuller, by using their surnames, recognizing however that describing her life before marriage and her intimate family interactions after marriage sometimes calls for an unambiguous distinction between husband and wife.

ONE

"The Thought of What I Have Undertaken Weighs upon Me"

Early Writing and the Decision to Marry

J ULIA WARD, the young Julia Ward: who was she? What details do we call upon to draw a picture of the twenty-two-year-old woman who, in 1841, looked out the window of the Perkins Institution in South Boston and watched a man almost twenty years her senior ride up on a black horse?

"I left school at the age of sixteen," Howe, many years later, ironically noted, "and began thereafter to study in good earnest."[1] What had gone on before that? Her mother had died in 1824 from puerperal fever three days after giving birth to her seventh child; Julia Ward, born 27 May 1819, was five at the time, the third of the surviving six children and the oldest of the three girls. Her father, a wealthy New York banker, had established his immediate and extended family in a row of substantial houses on Bond Street near Broadway. And he had established himself as an extremely cautious and protective father, seriously religious, determined to exercise careful control over his childrens' associates. Her brothers—Sam, Marion, and Henry—had been students in Joseph Cogswell's progressive Round Hill School in Northampton, Massachusetts.[2] Sam, the oldest, having completed a Columbia degree in two years, was in 1836 just back from four years of travel and study in Germany, having brought with him an enormous collection of European literature.

The elder Samuel Ward's intent had been to educate his daughters at home. But after some experimenting with in-house governesses and tutors, he sent his bright eldest daughter, beginning at age nine, to schools near the Bond Street house. Memorization was the skill most in demand. Julia Ward, immediately placed in a class of older girls, studied chemistry, moral philosophy, history, geometry, and penmanship. Although it was unusual in the 1820s for females to have the chance to study such subjects, none of this labor ignited her. She was, she said later, "somewhat precocious for my age." She remembered memorizing many pages of Paley's *Moral Philosophy* "in a rather listless and perfunctory manner"; remembered liking chemistry but not being afforded the chance to perform any experiments; remembered the excellent charts used in history instruction; remembered learning to write a good hand. She spoke French from early childhood, and while in school she also learned Latin, Italian, and some German (13–14). Languages and music were her passions.

At about the time that her father built a library for her brother Sam's books, he also invited Joseph Cogswell to live with the family as a tutor to Julia and her sisters. This was a felicitous moment for Julia. She had begun to study German in school, but Cogswell was able to take her along much more quickly. Cogswell had known Goethe—had persuaded him to donate copies of his books to the Harvard Library—and under Cogswell's tutelage Julia Ward became proficient enough to read the great German writer fluently.[3] Few women in the United States at that time had such an opportunity. The books in Sam's collection afforded her a breadth of vision unavailable to most young women; they included not only all of Goethe's works, but also works by Jean Paul, Matthias Claudius, Herder, Balzac, and George Sand. She read these hungrily, feeling consciously the degree to which they pulled her out of the constricted world she otherwise occupied. "I did not desire to be counted among 'fashionables,' " she recalled, "but I did aspire to much greater freedom of association than was allowed me. I lived, indeed, much in my books, and my sphere of thought was a good deal enlarged by the foreign literatures . . . with which I became familiar" (48–49).

It needs emphasizing that this informal education, which she sought avidly, elevated her far beyond the level of learning available even to upper-class women of her day, and above that of many men as well. Nancy F. Cott, Susan Phinney Conrad, Mary Kelley, Barbara Miller Solomon, Linda K. Kerber, Christine Bolt, Nina Baym, and Patricia Okker, among others, have documented the premises underlying the education of females in early nineteenth-century America and the many disincentives that confronted women seeking more than their culture deemed appropriate in the way of higher learning.[4] In general, only women from families of some means had access to any sort of out-of-the-home schooling in the 1820s, and the curricula at so-called dame schools and female academies, however apparently rigorous, were essentially intended to prepare women to educate their children and perform other domestic responsibilities. Colleges did not admit women until 1837, and it was at least two decades after that before women in significant numbers began to be able to take advantage of the opportunity. During Howe's youth, women who aspired to be educated became so through the help or dedication of family members. Catharine Sedgwick relied on her father's tutelage; Eliza Lee Follen's mother dedicated herself to providing her daughters with a thorough education; Sarah Josepha Hale received the equivalent of a college education from her mother, older brother, and husband; Lydia Maria Francis relied on her brother Convers's extensive library; Elizabeth Peabody learned from her mother until, as William Ellery Channing's secretary, she had access to his collection of European Romantic writings; Margaret Fuller's father was determined that she be educated as if she were male; Elizabeth Drew Stoddard read the great eighteenth-century English writers in the library of a friend. The number of women educated in this way was, it hardly needs saying, small. Howe's hunger is especially noteworthy, given her father's conservatism and the supposition that she would eventually marry within the family's social and economic circle.

The constraints imposed by her father were the result not of social exclusivity but of his deep anxiety that his children not be exposed to untoward moral and religious influences. Always a pious man, Mr. Ward became, after his wife's death, an ardent Low Church Evangelical, exercising tight control over the family environment and over Julia in particular. When at one point she objected to such a tight rein, he let her know that he had always felt that she possessed "a temperament and imagination over-sensitive to impressions from without" (53). He was distressed when he read a translation of *Faust* and learned that his daughter, too, had read "this wicked book" (59).[5] Not without cause did Howe feel like "a young damsel of olden time, shut up within an enchanted castle" or recognize her father, "with all his noble generosity and overweening affection," as her "jailer" (49). Opera was another forbidden fruit. At age seven she had seen two Rossini operas performed by the

Garcia troupe, but thereafter such productions, as well as any theatrical performances, were denied her.[6]

For all the circumscription Julia experienced in her father's house, there was nonetheless plenty of literary and intellectual stimulation available to her. Her father's position as one of the city's eminent businessmen and cultural leaders brought people of education and wide experience to the Ward drawing room. William Cullen Bryant, Fitz-Greene Halleck, Washington Irving, John L. O'Sullivan, Richard Dana, and Charles A. Davis were all guests of the Wards. The family entertained Mrs. Jameson during her 1835 visit to the United States. (Julia, sixteen at the time, had already read her *Diary of an Ennuyée* and, soon after, her accounts of European art.) A particularly important friend was Charles King, brother of one of her father's partners and editor of the daily newspaper the *New York American*. Howe considered him the patron of her early literary ventures because he printed several of her poems in his paper. In part no doubt because of this rich environment, and perhaps also because her mother had written and published poetry, Julia Ward grew up persuaded that she would eventually produce an important literary work, "the novel or play of the age" (57). This vision made her studious, driving her to equip herself in a way that later struck her as both remarkable and inexplicable, given the difficulties facing a female of that time in finding guidance toward a literary career.

Sam's return from Europe meant not only access to his books, but the comfort of his active support for her intellectual ambitions. She helped him with translations, and he served as her champion at several points in skirmishes with their father.[7] Sam was, in general, a force in enlarging the tightly focused mental space of the Ward household. "He brought into the Puritanic limits of our family circle," Howe wrote, "a flavor of European life and culture which greatly delighted me" (68). He also brought friends, among them Charles Sumner and Henry Longfellow, the latter already gathering the momentum that would make him, within just a few years, one of America's most adulated poets. Julia instantly identified him as a potential soul mate, writing in July 1838 to her sisters: "I am so very glad to have seen this gentleman, he is so modest, yet so full of information and intelligence, so different from the stupid young men of whom our society is composed."[8] Some of Longfellow's letters to Sam from this period show that he took his friend's younger sister seriously as a poet, even to the degree of showing her work to William Ticknor's wife and offering suggestions about particular phrasings.[9] And Longfellow, too, sought her assistance with translations.

Julia Ward's aesthetic acumen is revealed in a pair of anonymous reviews published in the 1830s. The first, written when she was seventeen and working closely with Cogswell, is a review of Lamartine's *Jocelyn* (1836). This piece appeared in the *Literary and Theological Review*, a journal edited by another of her father's friends, Leonard Woods. It suggests remarkable breadth of reading in both French literature and European culture: Julia authoritatively distinguishes Lamartine from his poetic predecessors and draws on differences between styles of pre-Renaissance Italian painting to illustrate the nature of the distinction. She clearly sets forth the grounds for the aesthetic judgments she renders, and she shows herself capable of severity in the judgments themselves.[10] Unsurprisingly for a girl raised in a religious household, she finds the chief value of *Jocelyn* in its picture of the virtuous heroism of the title character:

> His enthusiastic piety, the spirit of devotion and humility in which he sacrifices happiness to duty, his universal benevolence and philanthropy, diffusing itself alike over all men, his deep and unchanging love, form one of the fairest modes of excellence which ever suggested itself to a poet's imagination.

This opinion leads her to conclude that the surest way for a "monument of literary renown" to resist the encroachments of time is that it be built on "the sacred ground of truth and moral excellence" rather than on "the mere force of intellect"—a sentiment underscored in her own inclination toward religious subject matter in her early poems.

The review attracted comment from those who knew it was her work. It was distinctly not the kind of thing her culture expected a young woman to produce. Julia Ward's Uncle John undoubtedly spoke for many of the males around her when, after showing her a favorable notice of her essay in a daily newspaper, he said: " 'This is my little girl who knows about books, and writes an article and has it printed, but I wish that she knew more about housekeeping" (20).[11]

The second piece, a review of John Sullivan Dwight's *Select Minor*

Poems of Goethe and Schiller (1839), appeared three years later in the *New York Review;* Cogswell was one of the editors of the journal. The tone is more expansive, the evidence of confidence in her own judgment even clearer. The review demonstrates broad familiarity with the works of both poets, knowledge of other translated versions of the poems included in the volume, and the assurance of someone capable of appreciating the nuances of the poems in their original language. The piece begins by recognizing the inadequacy of even the finest translations to provide the experience offered by the originals. Poems are flowers: each climate produces its peculiar blooms, and those of one region cannot survive in another. Translations, then, are *pressed* flowers: "[T]hough the hues of the one, and the scented breath of the other, are lost in the process, yet they retain enough of their form and color to reveal their nature to those who otherwise would scarcely have been aware of their existence." Schiller, she felt, was well served by the translations Dwight had secured. Many of Goethe's poems, however, had not emerged with their distinguishing gracefulness intact: "We have seen much better versions of some of them, than these." Still, Dwight is praised for making the work available (closer acquaintance with "the two greatest bards of Germany," she avers, will favorably influence America's own poets), and the collection offers the occasion to speculate on the particular cast of mind of each writer. Goethe "attained a wider range of thought than Schiller, and though he attained neither his intensity nor his power, yet in variety of style, in playfulness, in flexibility of mind, he is far his superior." On the other hand—and here we sense the continuing influence of her religious milieu—"children of another generation will see, that though Goethe was possessed of a more extended and universal intelligence, Schiller's was the nobler and higher nature."[12]

The essays are remarkable not just for the authority and range of the evaluative voice but for Julia Ward's determination to publish them. Longfellow, then Smith Professor of Modern Languages at Harvard, wrote to Sam Ward almost in disbelief: "Is it true, that yr. Sister Julia wrote the Rev. of Göthe and Schiller? It is very good."[13] Although much writing by American women had found its way into print by the 1830s, as Nina Baym and others have demonstrated, Julia Ward's work is striking for someone of her age, class, and marital status. In the first place, for an unmarried woman to be "literary" was to invite opprobrium and to put at risk her desirability in the marriage marketplace. Intellectual effort, it was thought, would unsuit her for the work God had intended for her. Moreover, publishing the fruits of her intellectual labors compounded the violation, putting her on the counter, as it were, for the delectation of the prurient multitudes. Lydia Sigourney's husband wondered, "Who wants or would value a wife who is to be the public property of the whole community?"[14] In the second place, much of the writing published by women in the early part of the century was explicitly directed toward an audience of females or children.[15] In her reviews—protected, of course, by the screen of anonymity—Julia Ward speaks without reference to gender, either hers or that of her supposed readership. It is a tacit assumption that her reflections and assessments will carry the sort of impersonal authority automatically conferred on the male literary critic. During this historical moment, among writing women whose efforts are known, only the work of Margaret Fuller, Elizabeth Oakes Smith, Elizabeth Ellet, Lydia Maria Child, and Elizabeth Palmer Peabody (ranging from six to thirteen years older than Julia Ward and all the beneficiaries of strong and extensive male intellectual communities) exhibits similar confidence and scholarship.[16]

AN IMPORTANT influence in the late 1830s was Julia's friendship with Mary Ward of Dorchester, Massachusetts. Mary was not a relative; the two met in the summer of 1837 in Newport and began an avid, intimate correspondence. Both were daughters of bankers (Mary's father was also the American representative of the London Baring Brothers firm), and both were intellectually inclined. Mary's brother was Samuel Gray Ward, soon to be a member of Emerson's Concord circle and, like Julia's own brother Sam, happy to open a wider sphere of thought and experience for his sister. Mary's interest in books and ideas attracted Julia; these were pursuits her younger sisters—close though they were in other ways—did not share with her. Their friendship intensified when Mary became engaged to Julia's brother Henry. Trips to Dorchester to visit Mary became a regular part of Julia's life, and Mary grew to be not only her most important confidante during this time, but another means by which Julia Ward's intellectual range expanded. Mary had been part of Margaret Fuller's first group of women students during the winter of 1836–37, when Fuller began teaching German, Italian, and French literature in Boston. Although Julia had had the enormous benefit of her brother's books and the private tutelage of one of the country's most respected educators, she had not enjoyed the chance Mary had to work with other young women under the guidance of someone like Margaret Fuller. Visiting Mary meant gradual exposure to Unitarian and Transcendental thinking, a wide-spreading intellectual terrain at once frightening and enticing.

Six letters from Mary to Julia and two from Julia to Mary are preserved in the Houghton collections. The first three of Mary's and both of Julia's date from 1839 and deal mainly with social preoccupations. In the first, Mary casts herself as an introvert, dazzled and smitten by the attentions the New York woman of letters has deigned to bestow on her (Mary extravagantly praises Julia's review of the Goethe/Schiller translations). The subject of the next two letters is Julia's romantic interest in an unnamed person: Mary discreetly advises against marriage until Julia has given the matter a good deal more thought.[17] Julia's letters mainly provide details about a party she and her brothers had planned, but one records the sharp distinction she was beginning to draw between Boston and New York. Boston is "an oasis in the desert, a place where the larger proportion of people are loving, rational, and happy. I long for its green pastures and still waters, its pure intellectual atmosphere and its sunlight of kindness and truth."[18] Just over two months later, however, the world of parties, summers in Newport, and intellectual stretching melted when Samuel Ward Sr. died. From this loss, compounded a year later by the sudden death of her brother Henry from typhoid fever and the 1841 loss of her sister-in-law (Sam's wife, Emily Astor Ward) in childbirth, ensued a profound depression, a time Howe later described as devoid of light or comfort. The religious doctrines in which she had been reared asserted themselves "with terrible force," and for a time she threw herself into revivalist and benevolent activities in the hope of somehow offsetting her sense of irreparable loss. She also poured her grief and guilt into a body of poems.[19]

There is a two-year gap between the 1839 letters and the next preserved letter from Mary, the tone of which, predictably, is quieter, more mature. Mary's loss has been severe as well, her imagined future vanishing with the death of her fiancé. Her sense of closeness to Julia has intensified. Here, she continues to serve as adviser in questions of romantic attachment, but she also overtly assumes an educative role, determined to draw her friend away from what she sees as an unhealthy absorption in debilitating religious ideas. She advises her not to attend further Bible classes, to keep clear of all extremes, and she encloses a Channing sermon explaining Unitarian doctrine. She states plainly:

> I want you to step out of the religious atmosphere in which so much of your life has been passed and for a moment, at least, to look abroad upon the church Universal towards which the spirit of the age and of the best and most enlightened men of the age, is so strongly tending. That you will ever adhere to all that is holy and true in your particular church I believe but for God's sake let us seek to separate the chaff from the wheat—purge away the old heaven of bigotry and intolerance and God grant that the truth may indeed make us free.[20]

This new world made Julia Ward uneasy initially. However high the value she placed on Mary's friendship and conversation, the prospect of deeper involvement in Boston intellectual circles was unnerving[21] and a possible source of misunderstanding within her family. A letter to her sisters written during an 1842 visit suggests, despite the antic tone, how her interest in Mary's world was a potentially touchy matter:

> I have had hardly the least dash of Transcendentalism, and that of the very best description, a lecture and a visit from Emerson, in both of wh[ich] he said beautiful things—and tomorrow, don[']t be shocked, a conversation at Miss Fuller's, wh[ich] I shall treasure up for your amuse-ment and instruction—I have also heard, don[']t go into hysterics, Dr Channing once—it was a rare chance, as he does not now preach once in a year. His discourse was very beautiful—

Yet in the same letter she testifies feeling to the warmth with which Boston culture has received her. The enjoyment she experiences is "not gratified vanity, wh[ich] gives at best a momentary and feverish plea-sure"; rather, it is the gratification arising from

> finding a circle of society composed of warm hearted, intelligent people, not cold, carping critics, people who are disposed to make the best of you, who have sense enough to perceive your good qualities, and charity enough to overlook and be sorry for your faults.[22]

Another service Mary performed for Julia Ward was to suggest unam-biguously that the religious poetry written after the deaths of her father and brother should not be published. The poems, Mary wrote, "would not universally interest because they express but a very partial view of the truth of one religion, and that one of a stern, painful, ascetic character to which the whole spirit of the times is opposed." More important, she argued, the sentiments no longer expressed the current person; they were of the Julia Ward of over a year ago, then in the painful grip of a religion of penance, the product of a deeply suffering mind. The portrayal of a God of fear, of the world as outcast and condemned, and of Jesus as bequeathing intense suffering as his only legacy is no longer her friend's religion:

> in an excited state of mind you strove to make it so, but nearly lost your reason in the attempt: your judgment and your conscience is opposed to it, if I do not mistake, and if so, you will not wish to give as food to others what has proved pernicious to yourself.[23]

A coordinate perception came in the form of a letter from Margaret Fuller, to whom Mary had apparently shown the poetry. We know from an earlier Fuller letter that at her first introduction to Julia Ward, during a chance meeting at Washington Allston's studio in 1839, she had been unimpressed.[24] Yet in responding to her poetry, Fuller exemplifies the spirit Julia described to her sisters. The likelihood that the work (now lost) expressed sentiments agreeable to Fuller is slim; Fuller makes sure to distinguish herself from those to whom the "rites and signs" of the church "still bear their mystic significance," and she suspects that some may see little in it beyond "the technics of Trinitarianism." Her admiration and praise are nonetheless readily given. The poetry is "the record of days of genuine inspiration . . . when the spiritual harmonies were clearly apprehended and great religious symbols reanimated with their original meaning." She expresses surprise that the Julia Ward of her acquaintance can have lived this life: "I saw, in her, taste, the capacity for genius, and the utmost delicacy of passionate feeling, but caught no glimpse at the time of this higher mood." She says she would like to see the work published.[25]

At length, due perhaps mainly to Mary Ward's determination that her friend recognize the limitations imposed by her hard-line Calvinist beliefs, Julia began to move away from zeal and rigidity.[26] Her *Reminiscences* recounts moments of "enlargement"—for example, her reaction to the image of a subjugated-but-not-conquered Satan at the end of *Paradise Lost*. It struck her as impossible that Satan's strength should rival God's in staying power, and so, she wrote, "I threw away, once and forever, the thought of the terrible hell which till then had always formed part of my belief."[27] This kind of "emancipation" led to others:

> I soon welcomed with joy every evidence in literature which tended to show that religion has never been confined to the experience of a particular race or nation, but has shown itself at all times, and under every variety of form, as a seeking for the divine and a reverence for the things unseen. (62–63)

Her growing seriousness about her poetry led to discussions about it with other members of Boston intellectual society, particularly Longfellow. Her visits to Mary meant increased opportunity to seek Longfellow's advice and support, which he gave unhesitatingly, and which she repaid by helping him with translation projects. In Julia Ward's early 1840s letters to her sisters, Longfellow's name is constantly linked with that of Charles Sumner, suggesting the degree to which he, too, was a player in her period of "enlargement."

In 1840, Charles Sumner was twenty-nine years old. Since his admission to the bar in 1834, he had practiced law unenthusiastically, teaching occasionally at the Harvard Law School. Three years earlier he had met Longfellow, then in his early years as a Harvard professor; the two had become close friends immediately, but then Sumner had left Boston to fulfill a childhood dream of travel in Europe.[28] In May 1840 he returned, having met and charmed most of the influential people in England, France, and Italy, as well as having educated himself thoroughly in European languages and literatures. Through Longfellow, Sumner became acquainted with the Ward sisters. Some of the letters exchanged during Sumner's sojourn abroad suggest that he (or his friends, on his behalf) considered one of the sisters a possible marital match, but whether or not this is true, he, with Longfellow, frequently visited Julia Ward whenever she was in Boston. It is reasonable to assume that she found the company and conversation of the well-traveled Sumner liberating, although the role he soon began to play in her life—one of the major strands in the story this book tells—makes her earliest response to him difficult to discern. In addition, during that summer Julia's attention was focused elsewhere, as a letter from Sumner to Longfellow makes clear: "*Miss Ward* (the sister of yr friend) is engaged to *Kirk*, the fiery, Parisian, well-dressed, orthodox parson."[29]

Sumner and Longfellow were part of a group of Boston/Cambridge men that also included Longfellow's Harvard colleague Cornelius Felton, Sumner's law partner George Hillard, and (when the original fifth member, Henry Cleveland, grew ill) Samuel Gridley Howe. The "Five of Clubs," as the group styled itself, met monthly for dinner, literary conversation, and general camaraderie. Sumner introduced Samuel Howe to the group, although he was well known to all of them before he was made an official member. Indeed, Samuel Howe was well known generally in Massachusetts. Trained as a surgeon at Harvard, he had first distinguished himself in 1824 by sailing to Greece to offer his services, like his hero Byron, in the effort of the Greeks to repel the Turks. He had become a hero there, not so much as a soldier (although he did sustain injuries), but rather as an organizer and fund-raiser. He made sure both military and civilian populations received supplies; he planned and executed improvements to the harbor at Aegino; and he tended to the wounded and sick. He had returned to Boston in 1831 bearing the title "Chevalier of the Order of St. Savior," immediately shortened by his friends to "Chev."[30]

Casting about for a new challenge, he had taken on the direction of the New England Asylum for the Blind and had left immediately again for Europe to study methods of educating the blind and to hire teachers. Back in Boston in 1832, he threw himself passionately into this work, determined to demonstrate that blindness was not the absolute deterrent to becoming educated that popular wisdom of the time held it to be. His experience raising money for Greece had served him well in providing a sound financial base for his work at the Asylum (renamed the Perkins Institution when, in 1839, it moved to larger quarters in the old Mount Washington Hotel in South Boston). More than for his fiscal successes, though, he was an object of attention in the late 1830s for his success in working with Laura Bridgman, a girl whom scarlet fever had left both blind and deaf. The strides Laura had made under Samuel Howe's committed tutelage were widely known, and his deep dedication to her education had brought him enormous respect. Charles Dickens, during his 1842 visit to the United States, asked to be taken to the Perkins Institution and subsequently featured Samuel Howe's work with Laura in one of the chapters of *American Notes* (1842). It was during just such a visit to the Institution, an excursion organized in the summer of 1841 by Longfellow and Sumner, that Julia Ward was introduced to the man she was to marry.

The picture of Julia Ward that I have set out thus far, it has to be said, would—if they could read it—surprise her brothers and sisters. This serious, studious, extravagantly religious, literary-minded girl-woman, though she certainly existed, was not the Julia her family and friends knew best.[31] It was not that she was secretive about her intellectual passions, but rather that they were contained and usually subsumed in an apparently quite different persona, of which the chiefly visible characteristics were animation and a delight in the comic.[32] Despite, or perhaps because of, the sober atmosphere that prevailed in the Ward household after the death of Julia Cutler Ward in 1824, all the children, as they grew up, but particularly Julia and her brother Sam, derived pleasure from small violations of decorum, breaches in the conventions and restrictions imposed by the patriarch. In *Reminiscences* Howe remembered in herself "a certain over-romantic and imaginative turn of mind" (43) that frequently interfered with her studies. Her daughters were perhaps alluding to the same inclination when they described her as having "singularly diverse" strains of blood: "All through her life Saxon and Gaul kept house together as peaceably as they might, but sometimes the French blood boiled over."[33] This facet of her character, kept more or less in check while growing up, emerged forcibly in the early 1840s after the double period of mourning for father and brother and her submersion in Calvinist self-abnegation. In the winter of 1842 Julia and her younger sisters relinquished the house their father had built, moving in with Sam, and the Ward household again became a locus of jollity that was frequented by Sam's Boston friends whenever they were in New York. In Boston, too, Julia Ward's high spirits were noticed and much appreciated. George Ticknor had known the elder Samuel Ward and made a point of welcoming his daughter into the Beacon Hill circle over which he and his wife presided, thus guaranteeing her acceptance by the highest reaches of Boston society. It was at a Ticknor party in February 1841 that she first made the acquaintance of the "Chevalier."[34]

Samuel Howe was widely regarded as handsome. A woman told his adult daughter Laura Richards that when in his twenties and thirties he rode down Beacon Street on his black horse, " 'all the girls ran to their windows to look after him.' "[35] Not much information survives about his early romantic interests. Harold Schwartz suggests that part of his motivation to go to Greece in 1824 was disappointment in love—"an affair with a girl [Sophia Hyatt] whom he could not marry, probably because he could not afford to."[36] Several years later, at age twenty-eight, Samuel wrote to a friend that he was beginning to think of himself as "late": "I should have been married long ago, I think, had it not been for the recollections of S____. My mind has never been able to master my bitter regret for her loss; though to others and in society I showed it not, it has not been the less severe." The severity of the loss notwithstanding, this letter also exhibits a characteristic frame of mind that—then and later—tended to substitute work-related resolve for emotional disappointment: "romance and feeling have nought to do with the matter-of-fact business of this sordid world, where so few look out for anything but their own interests."[37] This attitude may help explain his indifference to those girls who ran to windows, as Richards suggests: "Absence of self-consciousness was one of his strong characteristics, and I doubt if he ever knew or thought why the pretty girls looked after him, even if he noticed that they did, which seems improbable."[38] Schwartz notes only one other interlude of romantic attachment prior to Samuel Howe's being captivated by Julia Ward, a brief engagement in the summer of 1834 to a Boston lady named Mary Ann Marshall.[39] Otherwise, the slate is blank; Samuel Howe's letters after his return to America are "completely devoid of any references to women" (104). He wrote to Sampson in 1831, "I have not yet numbered thirty years, and I feel like a man of fifty. . . . Not that I am old physically, but I feel old and time-worn within."[40]

Julia Ward had just turned twenty-two in the summer of 1841, when Longfellow and Sumner drove her, Louisa, Annie, and Mary Ward to the Perkins Institution. Samuel Howe was away when the group arrived, but before long—as Julia Howe recounts the moment in *Reminiscences*—Sumner glimpsed him through a window, riding up to the building on his black horse. It is tempting to linger over this moment, to let it resonate while its emblematic possibilities register: Samuel Howe—internationally famous war hero, decorated for his service to Greece, now in midlife equally renowned for his philanthropic work—galloping into Julia Ward's young life in a manner that would make the strongest possible romantic impression. Although by this time he was just a few months shy of his fortieth birthday, Dr. Howe on this summer day exhibited none of the time-weariness of which he had complained to Sampson a decade earlier. To Julia—sitting with Laura Bridgman, deeply impressed by the doctor's achievement in having drawn the girl into communication—he was "a noble rider on a noble steed" who "made upon us an impression of unusual force and reserve" (82).

It is hardly surprising that she would find him attractive. Boston had for several years represented for Julia Ward a strongly agreeable alternative to the fashionable world and "stupid young men" of New York, and here was a man who seemed to embody two of Boston's most salient characteristics: high seriousness and passionate commitment to the alleviation of social evils. These are, at any rate, the aspects of his personality Howe emphasizes in the pages of her *Reminiscences* that follow his first dramatic appearance. If we look there for reflection below the surface, for an explanation of the attraction that goes beyond awe and admiration, the gleanings are few. Aside from the facts of his achievements, she highlighted only one consideration: the contrast she felt between her life as "student and . . . dreamer" and his "superiority of experience," which afforded him "the practical knowledge which is rarely attained in the closet or at the desk" (84–85). A sense, then, of complementarity—one supplying what the other might lack—may have enhanced for her the allure of this man who, as she also pointedly noted, "was my senior by nearly a score of years" (84).

In fact, no letters or other indications from this summer indicate that the impression Samuel Howe made on Julia Ward *was* substantial. We naturally infer that it was, from her account of it and from the fact that they married a year and a half later. Yet we find in a letter from Mary Ward written six months after this excursion—the same letter in which she includes a Channing sermon—advice about how Julia should handle the love protestations of several other men.[41] When Julia was next in Boston, in late January 1842, Samuel Howe was away traveling in the south, and all Julia's news in letters to her sisters was about whom she danced with at Boston's *fête* for Charles Dickens; she recorded no chagrin at the fact of the doctor's absence.[42] This is also the period of her growing interest in Transcendental ideas—her first attendance at an Emerson lecture and a Fuller Conversation, her increasing openness to Mary's urgings toward a wider conception of religious truth, the period of her indirect interaction with Fuller regarding her poems. Men were also still on her mind, but not *one* man particularly, or the memory of a single dramatic encounter. This was the situation until June, when Samuel Howe journeyed to New York to meet Dickens on the last leg of his American tour.[43]

This moment must be accounted the true beginning of Julia Ward's relationship with her future husband, or at any rate the moment when interest on both sides became deep. The signs of this mutual attraction are two long letters Samuel wrote to her after he returned to Boston.[44] She had clearly charmed him and Cornelius Felton—in person during two evening parties and in a (now lost) letter to the two of them. The doctor, driven to write in a mode commensurate with her eloquence and wit, begins by complimenting her as a masterly player on the soul's chords, capable of "draw[ing] forth from it a thousand varying notes of feeling!" His tone is excited, his diction elevated and extravagant. Julia is a "*Mechante* Musician," plucking heartstrings with her pen, taxing her correspondents' highest intellects, exciting "uproarious mirth." In an ornately developed metaphor, she is "young Music," and he and Felton are "[e]xulting, trembling, raging, fainting . . . [d]isturbed, delighted, raised, refined."

As if to demonstrate her muse-like powers of inspiration, he then spins a fairy tale, purportedly a dream that occurred as he fell asleep rereading her letter. In it he is the loving subject of a Prince who has ordered him to go on an undefined mission to a foreign land. Though vague, his charge has an altruistic cast: he is "to go steadily and trustingly on, stopping not for pleasure, turning neither to the right hand nor to the left for any fear or any obstacle, but only when an opportunity offered of doing some good to the people through whose country I might be passing." Counselors advise him to take a friend "for sympathy and support," but the intrepid traveler determines to go alone. The going gets tough, at which point an indistinct but angelic form appears. This being fades in and out of focus, but eventually assumes human shape and—this is most important—"appeared to be animated by the same spirit that I was, and, perchance, was bound on the same errand." As soon as the traveler moves toward the figure, however, it vanishes, "crying gaily, 'thou art too late!'" The dream ends when the traveler stretches out his hand to grasp the figure's garment and the dreamer finds his hand clutching the just-expired candle on his bedstand. "So,

Miss Julie, you have burned me most dreadfully," he jokingly concludes the dream narrative.

This supposed illustration of Julia Ward's inspirational power is in fact a pretext Samuel Howe uses to characterize himself and attempt to describe, indirectly, his sense of who Julia is and how she might become attached to him. Who is each, then? The traveler's charge in life is to do philanthropic work, and he sees in the mysterious form an ally, perhaps the "friend" recommended to him at the outset by the wise counselors. This is an unexceptionable image of a nineteenth-century marriage, but two other elements of the picture could unnerve a prospective "ally." First, pleasure is explicitly prohibited as a goal of his life quest. Second, although the traveler imagines that the apparition will be a "companion" in the great work, his personal need for association arises at first as a yearning for "a friend to protect" or "a little child to grasp by the hand and guide and guard"—a relationship in which the companion will be his dependent and inferior. The dream's end strikes a discordant note, since the angel form derides the traveler's hopes and the real Samuel awakes feeling "burned." Yet it is clear from the balance of the letter that, despite the jarring terminus of the fantasy, the doctor had begun to imagine Julia as exactly the soul mate the apparition seems at first to be.

He thanks her for the words she has written about Laura Bridgman. She has, he says, expressed "in two lines what I have stumbled over whole pages to set forth; you embody what has been a vague yet firm belief of my own, but which is for the first time reflected to me from another mind." This excitement over their congruence on this matter expands as he approvingly quotes and embellishes Julia's thoughts on religious exclusivity. Her belief that no sect is "comprehensive enough to embrace the varied attributes of humanity, the wide religion of nature" leads him to rail against the intolerant:

> We ask for aid and encouragement to the feeble yet God-like aspirations which we think are within us; and they tell us we shall be surely damned unless we believe we are utterly unworthy to be saved; we think we have found a path to Heaven, and they shout and say we shall certainly bring up in Hell unless we travel on their turnpike, and pay toll at their gate.

United with her, then, in hostility to the evangelical sensibility, he delivers a rhapsody about seeing God in every sight, hearing Him in every sound, finding surer proof in all living things of His existence than in Holy Writ. He ends by apologizing for the homily, but pleads help-lessness because her words "stirred up a flame of religious feeling" about which he hopes to speak more with her soon.

Taken as a whole, the letter tries to construct a being "animated by the same spirit . . . bound on the same errand" as its author. A couple of its features, however, acknowledge that the real Julia Ward may diverge somewhat from the would-be architect's plans for her. The most obvious is the apparition's light dismissal of the traveler's move to join her. In the same light vein, the doctor calls it "an awful thing" for Julia to be "bewildering and burning innocent wictimes [victims]." The interac-tion suggests his awareness of (and distress at) elements in Julia's person-ality that may not quite accord with his devoted-helpmeet vision of her. The other feature is a glimpse of a particular kind of exchange between the two that might reasonably be viewed as a forecast of later, more pointed examples of the same thing. Samuel writes: "You seem to have got a strange idea that I did not like you in the Allegro. . . . You threaten me with the Penseroso, and say you will inflict it until I am tired, and cry out for a little of the Diablerie of other days." He gallantly protests that he likes her in "any and every strain" and that for her to try to talk to him in any mode until he is tired of it would involve her in a lifelong task. Yet we need to register what this glimpse suggests of Julia's reading of her new suitor. She has evidently caught a whiff of disapproval at her antic self, to which she responds with a vow to be so completely the opposite of that self that that, too, will become a source of torment. In other words, she offers to reform, but in such a way as to make him con-tinually aware of her annoyance at having been chastized in the first place. Whether he understood Julia's response in exactly this way is not clear from the letter, but the passage does show his consciousness of what could be called Julia Ward's volatile sensibility—hardly an ideal trait in a philanthropic coworker.

This kind of tension appears even more clearly in the other long letter from the summer of 1842. Again, the general tone is light, the stance this time one of comic, beleaguered defensiveness in the face of Julia's volley of sarcasm and jibes. Yet the tendency of this letter, much more directly than that of the earlier one, is toward instruction. The doctor's rhetori-cal energies are engaged in an effort to find inoffensive ways of proffer-ing "a word of friendly counsel." Responding to her fear that she has been "half spoiled," for example, her would-be mentor first deploys wit:

"[I]f it be so I am very glad I did not know you before the change took place: I am sure you would have *quite* spoiled me." This is followed, however, by some fairly sharp criticism, its point all the more penetrating for being inappropriately, condescendingly embedded in a love letter. "You are not spoiled," he informs her. Rather, "you exercise some qualities of your nature to the detriment, not only of others, but of yourself." The quality uppermost in his mind is her inclination to tease him; he accuses her of "scatter[ing] shot around continually, hit or miss, friend or foe, no matter who suffers so you have the fun of firing." Since his blend of jocular counterattack and didacticism is difficult to convey in brief quotations, I reproduce a sizeable piece of the letter:

Now I am not a non resistant, nor do I hold the doctrine of an illustrious member, & Vice President of the American Peace Society—Charles Sumner: I believe that nature implanted destructive impulses within us for the purpose of being exercised; & the Scriptures confirm me, for even the meek Jesus severely upbraided the hypocrites, & whipped the profaners of the Temple. But nothing in nature can be abused with impunity; we must keep the propensities in abeyance to the higher sentiments, or (woe betide us) we are nourishing whelps within us, which, like the horse-leech, cry "give, give"; which fatten & grow with every gratification; which yelp louder, & closer at our heels as we go on in life; untill, at least, like him of old who fed his hounds on human flesh, we are swallowed up by them. Did you ever remark, to take the lowest punishment which nature inflicts for a violation of her laws, how she makes undue indulgence of a propensity to impair personal beauty? Passion, it is true, may sometimes be commanding & even sublime: but not when it struggles up of its own accord from the depths of our nature; it must be summoned up by a high sentiment; and, acting under its command, it becomes beautiful by its very energy; (oh! how beautiful have I seen towering indignation) but the beauty of passion fades away, shade by shade, as it is commanded by a motive of lower ranks, until nothing is left but its naked deformity. What beauty, what sublimity is there in that truth which Babbage demonstrated so clearly, that every whisper makes its impress on the air, and remains written there, an everlasting record to our weal or woe: and how equally true is it that every emotion of the mind makes its impress upon the countenance, and gradually moulds it to beauty or deformity. Think you not that the countenance of Voltaire was once beautiful, when it reflected kindly feelings, & that it gradually changed under the thousand sarcasms which it was made to point, untill it became the very impersonation of scorn? There, I have read you a sermon, & paid you off for Tacitus, & slain Turks, and all the numerous discovered & undiscovered jests & jibes indulged in at my expense; &

done it too from a not low motive, & in face of not a little fear; but, who would not lend his ever so humble aid, to remove a spot from the sun, though he ran some risk of burning his fingers in the operation; especially were he a Persian, & an advocate of the Sun.

"Sermon" is, in fact, an apt term to describe his speech. Despite his efforts to ironize the impulse behind its delivery and to mock his own heroism, the letter still does seek, at bottom, to try to remove a spot from the sun. Its goal is to further Samuel Howe's construction of Julia Ward as "little child" who needs guarding and guiding.

We might speculate that his impulse to mold her behavior was as strong as it was because of the strength of his attraction to her. He was, patently, smitten. The letter ends sweetly: "I will not allow any one but you to be amused at my expense: but you, you may laugh at me, scold at me, do any thing, so you forget not I am very truly yours, 'Gentle Doctor.'" At about the same time, Sumner wrote to Longfellow in Europe that their friend had described his New York jaunt as "the pleasantest he has made for more than seven years," adding, "Felton says that the 'inadvertent captivation' which he has experienced is very strong. . . . I think Howe very much touched by the Fraulein Julia's various charms." A month later, again to Longfellow, Sumner reiterated this news, noting that in addition to admiring her, Howe "appreciates her character very justly." Sumner predicts that the next time they meet, if Julia receives Samuel kindly, she will "excite a declaration" that it will be difficult for her to resist.[45]

Yet among Sumner's several descriptions of the relationship in romantic terms is this different, quite revealing perception: "Howe is more restless, if possible than you or I—how it would delight me to see his perturbed spirit find repose at last on such a bosom!" This restlessness is mentioned in many exchanges among Sumner, Longfellow, and Howe during this period; all three frequently express their ardent longing to get married, to find somebody, to leave the lonely state of bachelorhood (widowerhood in Longfellow's case). Thus, while Julia Ward's charm and intelligence undoubtedly struck Samuel Howe forcefully, it is fair to suggest that at least part of the propellant motion arose from a feeling that simply *to be married* was the chief consideration. According to Longfellow, in fact, Felton was going around making the suggestion that Longfellow, Sumner, and the "Gentle Doctor" should each simply marry one of the three Ward sisters. Samuel Howe evidently seconded this notion; Sumner reported that his friend had designated Louisa for him, promising Sumner that she would be "a marvellous woman" because of her "beautiful head,—a true woman's head—full of benevolence & the social feelings with a very good intellect, highly cultivated."[46]

But paramount in Samuel Howe's consideration of Julia Ward as a mate was the question of her tractability. How likely was it that she could become—was inclined to try to become—the being "bound on the same errand"? His interactions with her after the first flush of infatuation passed appear to have been designed to answer this question. He had sent her a report he had published in May on Laura Bridgman, and she had commented sympathetically—a fact he undoubtedly found encouraging. When she next visited Dorchester, in the fall of 1842, he took her to the Institution to see Laura again. He had asked Julia to bring a particular bracelet, shaped like a snake, as a way of giving Laura an idea of snakes. He left her alone for a while with Laura, then asked her to sing for the male pupils. Afterward, he served cake in his quarters and gave her flowers, before driving her back to Dorchester. This visit seems obviously orchestrated so as to allow the doctor to observe the New York belle at work, so to speak—to test her mettle as a collaborator in the great project he had undertaken and to advance his modeling of her as that helpmeet. The account comes from a letter Julia wrote to her sisters.[47] She offers no comment on anything she describes, except to note that she had been, on this occasion and others when her suitor had been present, "very good, a little too amiable for my own taste—but no matter." "The Dr," she also notes, "calls me child." These two notes suggest that she understood the visit as an examination of sorts and that she felt under obligation to put on her best face in order to pass it—but also that she was not entirely happy about the need to do so.

That she would tolerate this treatment tells us a good deal about the power differential in their relationship and perhaps something about Julia Ward's general powerlessness in the face of social/familial pressure. It seems clear that the relationship's future was for the gentleman to decide, based on his estimation of the goodness and amiability she was able to muster. Her effort to exhibit these qualities, it appears from this letter, was urged and encouraged by her family—particularly, doubtless, by her father's brother, Uncle John Ward, who after the elder Samuel's death saw it as his inherited patriarchal responsibility to hold tight reins on her temperament. Samuel Howe—famous, handsome, passionately committed to righteous causes—was by a substantial margin the most impressive suitor Julia Ward had attracted, and it was certainly time for her to marry. Implicitly, beneath a façade of free choice, the machinery of family opinion operated to propel her toward him, and she apparently saw no point in resistance.[48]

EVIDENTLY, IN HER FALL 1842 visit to Boston, her amiability was not quite up to the mark. The doctor visited New York twice more before late February 1843, and what we glean of these visits—from two Sumner letters and one letter from Julia to her brother Sam—is evidence that Samuel's affections were not fully committed to Julia and that he had begun to regard the Ward sisters as more or less interchangeable. On 8 December Sumner wrote to Francis Lieber: "Howe feels as cool towards New York & all therein, as a North wind." On 6 January he noted that during his friend's most recent excursion he had "transferred his allegiance from the Diva Julia to Louisa the Lovely," pronouncing her "the most incomparably sweet creature he has ever known." Julia, writing to her brother in early February from Dorchester (where she had probably gone to be near her supposed suitor), reported that he had left for New York without seeing her. "The object of his visit is not to be mistaken, I find it quite a matter of pleasantry among his friends, and his making the trip at this time proclaims quite publicly who it is that he goes to see."[49]

It is pardonable, therefore, to register a degree of astonishment at the fact that, on 21 February, Julia Ward and Samuel Howe announced their engagement. The doctor wrote to Sam that he had offered Julia "what both you & she knew very well she possessed"—his heart—and that she had accepted it. Julia also wrote to her brother to confirm the engagement, and to her he replied the following day, warmly, that he cordially approved and considered Samuel Howe exactly the man he'd have chosen for her. Yet he makes clear, as well, that her "very interesting announcement" was unexpected. If it is a "happy omen for the future of all of us," a moment when after "years of clouds & darkness we once more see the light of hope dawning upon us," he cannot help adding that they were all "somewhat taken aback with surprise—though our amazement by no means equals our gratification."[50]

Cordiality is also the keynote of two letters Sam wrote to Samuel Howe soon after. Cordiality, that is, is the text; something less affable is the subtext. The first, of 4 March, is a jovial account of his sister's homecoming from her Boston stay.[51] She is "the old bird" (the family's affectionate name for her) nearly torn apart by the clan of eagles to which she has returned. The noise, Sam says, "would have startled your sensitive nerves." He vows, to universal agreement, that she will never return to Boston, now that they have recaptured her. He reports that she seemed flustered by the fact that she had left her coat and hat flung over the chair, but someone "wicked[ly]" points out to her that since the Chevalier is not there, she can safely leave them lying until after dinner. In another way, too, her return called for an adjustment from her:

> [I]t was very funny to see the little difficulty that our truant warbler found in tuning her throat to a pitch in concert with ours. We were the same laughing & screaming set of madcaps & the intensity of our phrensies was heightened by [her] presence.

The letter emphasizes in several ways the temperamental differences between the Wards and Samuel Howe, and it records the subduing influence he exerted on Julia.[52]

In the second letter, Sam pretends the engagement is an elaborate hoax that Chev and Julia have decided to perpetrate on their friends.[53] He notes that the frequent exchange of letters between the two has given rise to an "evil"—namely, public reports; "for, strange as you may think it, it is rumored here that you and Miss Julia *are engaged!* and some people maintain it is not a comedy—." He advises the doctor to visit New York and give the stories the lie "before you lose all character for moroseness, celibacy, and mysogyny [*sic*]." Although both letters are genuinely friendly and extend warm offers of hospitality, they also bespeak ambivalence, perhaps even masked hostility. This submerged uneasiness rose to direct expression less than a month later when Julia asked Sam to answer a deeply upsetting letter she had received from her betrothed.

Julia had assured Sam in her 21 February letter that Chev's "true devotion" had, in her words, "won me from the world, and from myself," adding, "I am perfectly satisfied to sacrifice to one so noble and earnest the day dreams of my youth." The two had evidently disagreed about the optimum length of their engagement—she preferring two or three years, he two or three months—but she had capitulated, since her prospective husband seemed "determined to have things his own way" and since "the Chevalier's way will be a very charming way, and is, henceforth, to be mine." This spirit of renunciation was evidently not enough for the Chevalier, though, for in early April he wrote expressing "doubts and fears" (Sam's words) about various aspects of his bride-to-be's character. This letter is not preserved, but its tenor and some of its specifics are clear from Sam's reply.[54]

Sam describes finding Julia in tears reading Chev's letter and says that he agreed to intervene only out of a conviction that a misunderstanding had occurred. A modification of "individualities" is needed, producing a "system of reciprocal concessions." Sam assures him that after Julia's return from a recent visit to Boston, her character was more altered than he believed could be achieved by "the alchemy of any man's love." Chev's fears are "unfounded and groundless"; he has let himself be tormented by a phantom of his own creation.

> My sister's disposition & characteristics will be naturally modified by her union with you—the love she gives you and the changes that love has already operated are undeniable proofs of this, which I should hardly think could have escaped a man of your penetration. So, hereafter, whatever further modifications may be desirable will gradually & surely occur like organic changes.

One of the specific concerns, Sam's letter reveals, is Julia's determination to continue writing poetry. Sam advises Chev to cherish her inclination toward intellectual occupations; they strengthen the mind, refine the taste, divert attention from "scandal & romances," and "render the woman a fitter companion for the man." "A woman cannot have too many qualities," he suggests. If Julia drew beautifully, Chev would certainly be proud to exhibit her album; "why should not a fondness for history & philosophy be also an attribute of the mother of one's children—or poetry be welcome when it gushes from the 'wellsprings' of a nature imaginative yet reasonable, aspiring though gentle?"

Another part of the letter suggests that Samuel Howe's list of expectations was precise and extensive. Sam says:

> You have obtained quite enough to ensure the whole of what you desire & I urge you to await the result with that calm confidence which distinguishes unhesitating & disinterested devotion. The church service contains some of those provisions for which zealous & inexperienced apprehension incites you to stipulate.

He reminds his future brother-in-law:

> There is a spirit of rebellion in human nature which is equally aroused by
> suspicion or over exaction—Love has given you authority, let its influence
> work invisibly—and do not strive to accelerate the approach of the not
> far distant day, when every thought & desire will be stamped by your
> wishes, by insisting upon a formal renunciation of tastes & impulses
> which so far from being rivals will one day become your cherished
> friends.

Although Sam's effort throughout is to allay anxiety and to heal the
breach of trust that prompted Samuel Howe to write, it is hard to miss
the undercurrent of annoyance in his reply. There is no reason to suppose that Sam had not been serious, six weeks before, in calling the
doctor the man among all his friends he would have chosen for Julia. Yet
the Chevalier's on-again, off-again behavior both before and after the
engagement was announced, and his belatedly expressed antipathy to
exactly the interests and accomplishments that distinguish his bride-to-
be from other women, must surely have caused Sam to question his
earlier judgment. He struggles to keep his tone even and positive, yet he
cannot resist pointing out an "inconsistency" in the position he has
taken—lauding at first "the treasures of [Julia's] heart" and concluding
by suggesting that if the heart is not wholly bestowed on him, it is not
worth having. And in the following paragraph, impatience and sarcasm
invade his rhetoric:

> Do you regard it as a *small* evidence to the contrary that a young maiden
> reared in the midst of tenderness & luxury & lacking no desirable com-
> fort of a worldly order—accustomed for years to the books, the repose
> and the speculations that excite your apprehension, should have freely &
> nobly consented to share your lot and forsake her friends & native city?
> Or how can you reconcile the admiration you avow for her intellectual
> powers if you imagine them to be inadequate to foresee the respon-
> sibilities and cares that the wife assumes?

On balance, however—given that Sam's obvious goal in writing was to
effect a reconciliation—we have to conclude that the Ward family approved the union, whatever reservations they may have harbored. Another letter from about this time, to Julia from her younger brother
Marion, seems to indicate that *her* sense of the rightness of this marriage
has wavered.[55] Since we have no text from Julia, it is difficult to be sure

exactly what kind of advice Marion was offering. He may have been encouraging her to embrace her reservations or, equally plausibly, trying to impress on her how deeply a rejection at this point would wound the Chevalier. Samuel Howe had evidently written to Marion ("a most sad note") asking that he intercede on his behalf with Julia. Marion, not knowing what Julia has said (but apparently assuming that she had decided *not* to marry him), pleads with her to "pause long before you take your final resolution." He urges her to consider the yearnings of her soul, rather than her intellect, and to remember "the shadow which you may cast over the whole future existence of another instead of the golden light of which he had caught a bright glimpse." Worried that Julia's impulsive nature would mislead her and give her cause for regret, he asks her to "judge rightly and truly not for Wevie's [Louisa] but for the Gentle Doctor's sake, and for your own."

DESPITE THIS rich collection of epistolary material, little of it is from Julia Ward. Trying to determine why the engagement was finally settled and to describe her most personal feelings about the prospect of marriage to Samuel Howe are to some degree matters of speculation. That he impressed her through his history of bravery in the Greek revolution; that his work with blind children and his recent success in helping Dorothea Dix bring attention to the plight of the insane moved her to admiration; that he cut a dashing figure; that he dazzled her with intelligence, charm, and wit—all this we could assume, even if it were not testified to by her daughters' accounts of their relationship and by her own account in *Reminiscences*.[56] She did, obviously, seek to attract and keep his attention. But Samuel Howe was not the first man she found interesting or considered marrying. Tharp emphasizes an attachment Julia Ward formed, or hoped to form, when she was barely fifteen with a young man of a different social class. "How hopeless is my passion," she wrote to a friend of her father's, "returned as I am assured it is, with all the ardor of youth; why must we both be unhappy from the difference of our station?"[57] There had been the "fiery, Parisian, well-dressed, orthodox parson" Edward Kirk in the summer of 1840, and she had also (before his marriage to Anna Barker) been much intrigued with Samuel Gray Ward, Mary's brother. Longfellow, too, by taking her seriously as a poet, had distinguished himself within the crowd of eligible gentlemen, and Mary's letters intriguingly mention others who registered sharply on

Julia Ward's emotions. The clearest indication of a strong—indeed, indelible—attachment other than the "Gentle Doctor" is a poem Howe wrote not quite a month after she married him. This appears in a notebook dated 1843, titled "Life is Strange and Full of Change":

The Past Lives

Hide thee behind the hill, beneath the wave,
Oh thou whose fearful beauty haunteth me,
Fly from this earth, for the heart hath no grave
Deep, wide, and sure enough to bury thee.

Strange was the chance that bore thee to my sight,
Stranger, the power that carried thee away—
All heaven was centred in thy genial light
All heaven departed with its fading ray.

Love found me half unconscious, half afraid,
He lured me onward in the guise of play;
I followed him, then turned to seek, dismayed,
The blissful quiet that was gone for aye.

Say, was it guilty, or was it innocent,
That mingling of my spirit's life with thine?
We touched not, spake not, but our thoughts were blent,
Our souls were wedded in one look divine.

Not for mine own, but for another's peace
I plead, for his who slumbers at my side;
Let then thy daily resurrection cease,
Nor come, at night, to claim another's bride.

May 20th[58]

Whose memory it was that provoked this poem is impossible to unearth. The point is simply to note that, in addition to the many predictable adjustments marriage certainly meant, Julia Howe was also privately occupied in trying to lay to rest a handsome ghost whose daily (and nightly) visits disturbed the general peace.

However, even had there not been potential or actual rivals for her romantic attention, her consciousness of the paternalistic, authoritarian side of Samuel Howe's character is evident at several points. We remember her noting that he called her "child" when she visited the Perkins Institution the previous summer. In her 21 February letter to Sam, partly quoted above, her insistence that she is happy to sacrifice her youthful dreams has something of the aspect of willing herself to believe that she is so. She avers, rather too extravagantly on this first day of her engagement, that the past "is already fading from my sight; already, I begin to live with him in the future, which shall be as calmly bright as true love can make it. . . . He will make life more beautiful to me than a dream." She remarks in this letter on the Chevalier's determination to have things his own way; calls him (albeit lovingly) "very presumptuous" and "impertinent" for his insistence that she remain in Boston until he can accompany her back to New York; and characterizes herself as "the captive of his bow and spear."

Most telling is a letter to her sisters, undated but probably written the same day as her letter to Sam.[59] She narrates an exchange with her soon-to-be husband that is intended to be comic, but that also underlines the power dynamic in their relationship. She has expressed her intention to try to please him "in every thing," to which he responds, " 'what? . . . even to the paring of a nail?' " Embarrassment at the state of her fingernails drives her "instantly" upstairs to cut them very short—"at which he was much pleased." In a more serious tone, Julia goes on to acknowledge that she "cannot write very gaily," feeling "quite tamed and sobered in spirit."

> The thought of what I have undertaken weighs upon me, and I fear to be at home, lest the pressure of old associations, and the thought of parting should be more than I can bear—but the wind is tempered to the shorn lamb, and the Chevalier is an angel of light—so all will be well—

Why, exactly, at this precise moment, he is this angelic figure for her, we can finally only guess. But her other image is more than a little disconcerting. "The shorn lamb"—the phrase is striking, and the brave hope that "all will be well" is quietly touching.

TWO

"Sumner Ought to Have Been a Woman"

Learning to Live in a Triangulated Marriage

THE PRESENT IS DEAD

Fancies and frenzies all have passed away,
A wide but level space comes to my mind;
Methinks the soul is ebbing from the clay,
So little of itself remains behind.

I feel my varied powers all depart
With scarce a hope they may be born anew,
And nought is left, save one poor, loving heart,
Of what I was—and that may perish too.

God! spirit! come to me, in any form;
Afflict, arouse, alarm, awake my soul!
I will not dread the lightning or the storm,
Becalmed at sea, the bark nears not its goal.

And thou, my husband, in whose gentle breast,
I seek the godlike power, to keep and save;
Thou to whom I unkind, or fate unblest
These fragments of a scattered being gave,

Come nearer to me, let our spirits meet,
Let us be of one light, one truth possessed;
Tis time, our blended life on earth is sweet,
But can our souls within one heaven rest?

I am content to live, content to die,
For life and death to me are little worth;
I cannot know, through all eternity
A grief more deep than those I know on earth.

June 4th[1]

THIS POEM'S extraordinary quality centers on its date of composition—4 June 1843, exactly six weeks after its author had become Mrs. Julia Ward Howe. The Howes, accompanied by Julia's sister Annie and the also newly married Horace and Mary Peabody Mann, sailed for Europe within a week of their 23 April wedding, and when Julia Howe wrote these lines, she and her husband were comfortably established in London, recipients of a shower of invitations and other expressions of kindness from England's most highly regarded families, whirled into the very vortex of the London social season. Two days before, they had been guests of the Duchess of Sutherland at Stafford House, one of London's most sumptuous palaces. There, in addition to being warmly welcomed and given a tour of the family's private picture gallery, they had been served cake baked in honor of the christening of one of Victoria and Albert's children and sent to the duchess on Her Majesty's order. One might imagine that the thrill and splendor of these new experiences would, for a while anyway, offset the invasion of depression these obviously personal lines describe.

We can take it as a sign both of Howe's essential seriousness and of the intensity of her investment in her marriage that they did not. The poem articulates the state of mind of someone nearly sunk in despair, conscious that personality itself is threatened (it is one thing for "powers" to dwindle, another for soul to ebb away and heart to die). Yet, interestingly, it is not an accusatory utterance, or at least one that attributes blame elsewhere: it does not imply that her husband's controlling nature has forced her to relinquish things that are important to her. A listless passivity is the central sensation, its causes not clearly traceable. It may derive from Howe's sense of having entered the relationship a "scattered being"— perhaps an oblique reference to the not-quite-laid-to-rest earlier love that is the subject of "The Past Lives," written two weeks earlier. Her effort to rejuvenate her spirits, however, takes the form not of a renewed pleading with the former lover's ghost to back off, but rather of a plea first to God and then, more to the point, to her husband to "come nearer." Her anxiety seems to arise from a vague fear that the two of them do not quite occupy the same spiritual or emotional region. "Blended" life is sweet, yes, but—something is missing, an absence she believes can be remedied by feeling that she and her husband are possessed of "one light, one truth." Without that feeling, the prospect for her is bleak. The poem's last two lines pessimistically foresee no relief even in eternity.

What caused Howe to feel such a sense of distance from her new husband? Although some of the poem's language suggests that the issue might have had to do with religious matters, this seems unlikely. Her evangelical sentiments had by this time been replaced by a belief in the universality of the spiritual impulse, probably very close to the pantheistic rhapsody in the Chevalier's first long letter to her the year before ("I feel Him in every sensation; the world is full of Him; my soul is full of Him, every being around me is full of Him"). Nor did the grief arise from a feeling of having to take a back seat to his philanthropic zeal, a complaint she voiced later in their marriage. Although in a diary she kept during a trip to Dublin later this summer there are one or two murmurs at the inconveniences imposed on her by his eagerness to explore every educational establishment in their vicinity, the level of discontent is mild, nothing like that articulated in "The Present Is Dead." Her letters to Louisa from London indicate that she may occasionally have felt eclipsed in society by her famous mate, or have experienced slight jealousy at the amount of attention he received from attractive women. But such feelings would not have led to despair.

The explanation I have reached is difficult to document. It rests on hints, scraps, scissored letters, truncated expressions, a sense of a fuller interchange in texts that no longer survive and quite possibly never existed as actual texts in the first place. For its clearest articulation we must leap ahead fifteen months to a letter written in September 1844 from Samuel Howe to Charles Sumner. He tells his friend: "When my heart is full of joy or sorrow it turns to you & yearns for your sympathy; in fact as Julia often says—Sumner ought to have been a woman & you to have married her: but I should not agree to this in any monygamic land, for Julia is my love as a wife."[2] Suggested in this jocular remark, I believe, are the roots of the malaise behind Howe's 4 June poem and, more generally, a plausible explanation for at least one of the forces that eventually propelled her into a decision to publish *Passion-Flowers*. The story of the decade between her marriage and the publication of her first book is one of fairly constant difficulties between wife and husband— due mainly, I believe, to Howe's gradual grasping of the fact that her husband's commitment to her, though unshakeable, was emotionally deficient. Sumner, though perhaps not the cause of Chev's distance, became for Julia more or less the focus of it.

However much Julia Howe in later years admired Sumner, welcomed him into their family, and found common cause with him in his political efforts, she always retained some degree of reserve in relation to him. Her remarks about him in *Reminiscences* (168–73) open with this observation: "I little thought when I first knew Mr. Sumner that his most intimate friend was destined to become my own companion for life." The quiet distinction between "companion" and "intimate friend" is surely not accidental. The sketch of Sumner follows a dozen pages of extravagant praise for Theodore Parker, and the contrast in tone as she moves into anecdotes about Sumner is marked. Whereas Parker is characterized in terms of the "luminous clearness of his mind, his admirable talent for popularizing the procedures and conclusions of philosophy, his keen wit and poetic sense of beauty," all these leading her to see him as "one of the oracles of God," Sumner is "a man of great qualities and of small defects," lacking "the sort of imagination which enables a man to enter easily into the feelings of others." "This deficiency on his part," she continues, "sometimes resulted in unnecessary rudeness." Sumner's weakness for ad hominem argument is noted, as is his lack of a sense of humor. She recounts inviting him to dinner once to meet a distinguished visitor and being told, " 'I do not know that I wish to meet your friend. I have outlived the interest in individuals.' " She notes that she wrote in her diary: " 'God Almighty, by the latest accounts, has not got so far as this.' "

Tracing the triangulated relationship suggested in Samuel Howe's letter is complicated by the fact that the language of 1840s America gave those involved in this relationship—to the degree that it is homoerotically inflected—no terms, no phrases, no concepts with which to understand the sensations they experienced. Thanks to the careful work of many historians and sociologists in recent years, we have a clearer picture of how *late* nineteenth-century Americans regarded the phenomenon of intense same-sex affection, but we still know precious little about how an antebellum male whose strongest emotional impulses focused on those of his own sex might have conceptualized this fact to himself, or have been understood by his closest associates.[3] Moreover, any late twentieth-century discussion of such matters is at every turn threatened by an impulse to import intellectual constructs that often distort the fragile facts as much as they illuminate them.[4] Yet despite these barriers to understanding, an attentive reading of correspondence during the early years of Samuel Howe's involvement with Julia Ward suggests that

Sumner's sense of having lost his most intimate friend to marriage put all three of them under duress. We sense Sumner's accumulating depression as well as his determination to mask it from his friend, Samuel's guilt at abandoning Sumner as well as his own nostalgia for the closeness of their relationship, and Julia's grief and anger at the suspicion that her husband's love for Sumner rivaled his affection for her.

The Charles Sumner–Samuel Howe exchanges resemble what Donald Yacavone, in an insightful study of the correspondence of male abolitionists, has termed the "language of fraternal love." Appropriately, Yacavone reminds us of the need to avoid distortion by not mistaking this language for homoeroticism: "preoccupation with elemental sex," he notes, "says more about the twentieth century than about the nineteenth."[5] Yet there also exists the possibility for distortion of another kind in presuming that expressions of intense affection exchanged between nineteenth-century men are entirely *free* of sexual meaning. As Michael Quinn notes (and exhaustively documents), "the line separating emotional attachment from romantic love is often unclear—even to the person who experiences the emotion."[6] Although I will not argue that Sumner was homosexual, in the late twentieth-century understanding of that term, or suggest that the two were physically intimate in a sexual sense, I do believe that this mode of discourse may have offered Sumner a means of veiling deeper feelings for Samuel Howe, and he for Sumner, that were perhaps both inexpressible and incomprehensible. It was left to Julia Howe (as we shall see in chapter 3) to discover a way to articulate these meanings. In the meantime, we must backtrack a bit to the beginning of the men's friendship, tracing it through the period of Chev's courtship of Julia, then observing its nuances during the Howes' first year of marriage.

CHARLES SUMNER and Samuel Howe had met in 1837, at about the same time that Sumner had become attached to Longfellow.[7] Sumner was twenty-six, Samuel thirty-five. The two had participated in an effort to defuse anti-Irish sentiment during a riot in Broad Street that summer. Shortly thereafter, Sumner had departed for Europe, and during the time he was away he evidently did not correspond with his new acquaintance; epistolary energy was channeled into his letters to Longfellow.[8] These letters are long and affectionate, reciprocating what he felt emanated from his poet-friend's words ("Yr letters seem warm as a lover's heart. I can almost feel the heat as I break the seal").[9] At this period Sumner does not seem to have regarded Samuel Howe as another potential intimate, but during the year following his return, their friendship deepened. By the time Samuel had occasion to write to Sumner—while on fund-raising tours of Southern states in the winter of 1841–42—the two had become quite close. In several letters he suggests that in spite of himself Sumner has become his "alter ego"; he feels he ought to be writing instead to Horace Mann but can think of nothing to say to him ("he is so awful good & high I have nothing that is fit for him to read: a compliment to you"); and he reminisces sentimentally about evenings the two of them have spent together "in sweet converse," wishing they could again " 'make a night of it' . . . as we have done, oft & again in interchange of thought and feeling." By May 1842 their attachment was intense enough to provoke humorous comment from other members of the Five of Clubs. Hillard wrote to Longfellow that Sumner was "quite in love with Howe and spends so much time with him that I begin to feel the shooting pains of jealousy," and Felton wrote to Sam Ward that the "wags of Boston" were calling them "the 'Dioscuri, or Immortal Twins,' like Pleasure and Pain, if you see one, the other is sure to be near."[10]

Another running theme in letters exchanged among this circle of friends is Sumner's difficulty in finding a female to whom he might attach himself. His biographer David Donald notes, "Available women did not interest Sumner,"[11] and indeed, the letters do document his continual tendency both to lament his single state and to find reasons not to become involved with women he knew. "The truth is," Francis Lieber wrote him, "you don[']t wish for love, but delight in amatory cro[a]king. . . . How else is it that you are always, not once, smitten with women out of reach?" Sam Ward speculated to Longfellow that Sumner would "never abstract himself enough from his abstractions to fall in love," adding "I think a woman would have hard work to please him."[12]

Just three weeks after Hillard posted his remark about Sumner's affection for Samuel Howe, the New York farewell parties for Charles Dickens provided an occasion for Chev to meet Julia socially again—the reunion that sparked his long letters of serious courtship in the summer of 1842. Sumner, although he did not accompany his friend on this excursion to New York, was very much attuned to his infatuation, writing almost immediately to Longfellow:

> Howe fell in love with Dickens & with Julia Ward. He describes his jaunt as the pleasantest he has made for more than seven years; & Felton says that the "inadvertent captivation" which he has experienced is very strong. They passed two evenings with what they called "the Society of Bond St", till *one* o'clock sounded!—Howe thinks Julia's head very remarkable, but with too much *destructiveness*. . . . I think Howe very much touched by the Fraulein Julia's various charms.

In this same letter Sumner reports, perhaps coincidentally, that the recent demise of the *New York Review* has meant that an article Julia Ward had written on Spanish Gypsies would not be published. His reaction to this turn of events is oddly gleeful: "From curiosity I should like to see her article; but on other grounds I am glad that the doors of publication are closed upon her." Perhaps this is simply an expression of happiness that his good friend's possible future wife will be discouraged from becoming a bluestocking (a path vehemently satirized in the popular press and considered a major social liability for a man should his wife choose it),[13] but it is certainly tempting to read it, too, as an outcropping of antipathy toward the woman who might steal his dear friend's heart. Despite his effusions of delight to Longfellow that Samuel Howe's perturbed spirit would find "repose at last on such a bosom" and several florid outbursts of longing for a devoted wife of his own, to other correspondents he was less sanguine about what the future would hold. To Lieber, for example, Sumner expressed how deeply he would miss his evenings with the doctor:

> Bachelors both, we drive & ride together—& pass our evgs far into the watches of the night in free & warm communion. His seat is a summer retreat, & I pass one or two evenings of every week with him. I think, however, he will be married very soon. What then will become of me?—It is a dreary world to travel in alone.

Even if we credit him with genuine and deep pleasure at the prospect of his friend's happiness and read his self-pity as mostly a joke and a pose, it is also true that at some level he did clearly feel despondent in contemplating Samuel Howe's eventual desertion.[14]

What was everyone *really* feeling in that summer of 1842? After

Chev's first visit to New York in early June, he pleaded with Sumner to return with him in a month; it was at that point that he began to talk of Sumner's possibly marrying Louisa. But Sumner begged off, melodramatically lamenting that his dreams were over, the chambers of his heart "dark & stifled." The doctor meanwhile was writing the first of his two long letters to try to communicate his paradigm of the ideal life companion, the partner-in-philanthropy vision that he sensed somehow evoked derision from Julia. She, for her part—whether out of coyness, inexperience, ambivalence about the rather daunting man, or uncomplicated instinctual high spirits—had determined to project a saucy persona, mocking the Chevalier's war experiences and zeal. This stance, we recall, provoked him in his second letter to express concerns about her propensity to "scatter shot around continually." (Interestingly, in that letter Charles Sumner's pacifist disapproval of the exercise of destructive impulses is introduced as the context in which Samuel Howe evaluates Julia's behavior.) Sumner, meanwhile, was characterizing Chev's attraction to Julia not as the discovery of the love of his life, but rather as a solution to the problem of his restlessness—a formulation that may reveal Sumner's need to find a nonthreatening explanation for his friend's defection more than it provides insight into Samuel Howe's actual feelings. In sum: a man in love but nervous both at his future wife's insouciance and at the prospect of deserting his closest friend; that friend seeking ways to solace himself at being deserted; and a woman, much younger than either man but in full possession of her sharp wit, joyfully deploying the strategies of the mating game but ill-equipped to read the complexity of her partner's situation.

We know the vagaries of the Howe-Ward courtship through the following fall and winter, but what can be said about Sumner's position relative to the two of them during this period? Late in August, after the two men made a trip to New York, Sumner reported to Longfellow a conversation he had had with a female friend of Julia's. In response to hearing that Samuel "was very much struck with Julia Ward's head," the friend wondered "if he were not very much struck with her in all ways." Weirdly echoing Robert Browning's Duke of Ferrara ("My Last Duchess" was published in 1842), Sumner replied that the doctor was "certainly pleased with her, but that, as the Pres'd't of the Phrenological Soc., he would like to have her head in their collection—perhaps, I might have added that he would like it for his *private cabinet*." This is intended humorously, of course, but one does nevertheless register Sumner's image of a decapitated Julia. In the same letter he describes the three Ward sisters collectively as "bland and lovely," but when he particularizes the description, Louisa and Annie are "bright, beautiful & soft . . . meek, gentle," whereas Julia is "self-poised, clever & *at times* quite engaging."[15]

Later in the fall, during the trip to Boston in which Julia again visited the Perkins Institution, a letter to her sisters characterizes an unusually playful Sumner one evening at a party at Felton's house; the lawyer is pictured ambushing Mary Ward and Julia under a curtain, calling them his "dear wives," describing the moment as the commencement of his domestic bliss. This is the same letter in which Julia's sense of being under scrutiny emerges, causing her to assure her sisters that she's been "very good, a little too amiable for my own taste." In her narrative the doctor and Sumner are paired in their inclination to infantilize her ("The Dr calls me child, Sumner calls me dear child"), and it is possibly significant that she was unwilling to allow Samuel Howe to read this letter before he added a note of his own in the corner. Sumner in these brief glimpses appears as a trivializer of the romantic impulse and as someone finding opportunities to criticize Julia and to reinforce his friend's sense of her youth.

Two letters from Sumner to Lieber, September and December 1842, offer further evidence of a subtle antagonism between Sumner and Julia Ward. In the first, he says he has heard that Julia is telling people he has no heart. He remarks that if he ever sees her again, he will call her to account for this condemnation; meanwhile, he asks Lieber to tell her she is wrong, he *does* have a heart, and that "it is not my fault if all its throbbings have been in vain." The second letter describes his trip with Samuel Howe to New York to greet Longfellow on his return from Europe. The three of them, of course, visited the Wards, but this was the moment when the Chevalier's interest in the eldest sister seemed either to have been transferred to Louisa or to have simply faded. Sumner reports dismay in some quarters at this turn of events, but as for himself, he says: "I am not sure that [Samuel Howe] is not a very wise man." When in January 1843 the doctor began to pay court to Louisa, Sumner's report to Lieber, while not exactly exultant, reflects a certain excitement. Sumner presumably continued to hope with one part of his brain that his friend would find a reposable breast; Louisa's, perhaps, seemed less threatening than Julia's. A melancholy note from Sumner written near the time of his friend's engagement suggests, however, that whether it was Louisa or Julia, the preeminent fact from Sumner's point of view was loss:

> Where are you? I never see you; I never expect to see you more. Like two ships that have sailed together over many seas, we are at last parting company; Western breezes are floating you away to Happy Isles, while I, weltering on stagnant waters, can scarcely discern your pennan far off against the sky. I sit alone in my office, finding as much comfort as possible in books.

AFTER THE doctor announced his intention to marry Julia, Sumner wrote two letters, one to Sam Ward and one to the lady herself. If I am right that Samuel Howe's drive toward marriage posed problems for Sumner that could scarcely be thought about, let alone articulated, these letters inevitably strike the ear as masterworks of ambiguous expression. To the brother, Sumner wrote on 21 February:

> My dear Sam, I cannot forbear letting you know, even at this early hour, how much I have sympathized with Howe in his love for your dear sister. His joy knows no bounds. He thinks himself unworthy of her, I think them worthy of each other. God bless them both!
>
> There are few who know, as well as I do, the strength and beauty of Howe's character. To energies the most manly, he joins sympathies & feelings, equalling those of woman in gentleness & delicacy. He is the true Christian hero, never tiring, never shrinking, where any duty is to be done, or any good to be accomplished. You know well the perseverance, constancy, devotion, & self-sacrifice which have marked so much of his past life. I know no one, of whom the world thinks so much, who thinks so little of himself.
>
> He well deserves the happiness that he has now obtained; & most richly will he repay it by the ever-gushing affections of his warm & faithful heart. His love, like his whole nature, is generous, overflowing. But, my dear Sam, why do I write this? Out of the fullness of the heart the mouth speaketh; & I could not refrain from giving you joy, as I have most earnestly rejoiced with Howe, on his most happy love! I hope you will not think me too bold or hasty in these words of sympathy.
>
> I feel sometimes that I am about to lose a dear friend; for the intimate confidence of friendship may die away, when love usurps the breast, absorbing the whole nature of a man—as the nourishment that supports a tree gradually retires from the distant branches, absorbed entirely by the trunk. But Howe's nature is too generous, I believe, for such a fate. His

heart is large enough for her to whom he has given it, & for his friends besides. Him I shall not lose, then; & have I not gained a friend in Julia? I trust she will let me be the friend to her, that Howe will say I have been to him.

One sign of the conflicting impulses behind this letter's effusions is Sumner's rhetorical question midway through: "why do I write this?" The question suggests the oddness of the letter, or at least of some aspect of it. We cannot attribute this oddness to the letter's overtly stated intent. It is not unusual for a good friend of both parties to express his happiness to the brother of one of them, particularly when the brother is also an old friend and the letter-writer is in a sense the medium through which the betrothed couple have become acquainted. Longfellow wrote a similar letter to Sam Ward on 6 March, rejoicing in the event and assuring him that he "may safely look forward to a serene and happy life for [his] sister."[16] But the difference between the two letters is instructive: Longfellow's does not include two paragraphs of adoring description of the bridegroom.

The specific terms of the praise Sumner lavishes on Samuel Howe are also remarkable. His first impulse is to stake a claim to privileged knowledge, underscoring his own intimacy with the about-to-be-married man. Samuel Howe is then lauded, interestingly, for his androgyny: he is both manly and womanly, both strong and beautiful. Sumner seems especially sensitive to his friend's feminine characteristics, the "sympathies & feelings, equaling those of woman in gentleness & delicacy" and the "ever-gushing affections of his warm & faithful heart." In light of Sumner's note written out of the depths of loneliness a week or two before this moment ("I never see you; I never expect to see you more"), the line about his friend's love being "generous, overflowing" seems permeated with irony and pain. It is at this point that Sumner pulls himself up into self-reflection, perhaps suddenly conscious of the degree to which his motives in writing may not be clear—or may be *too* clear and yet not directly acknowledged. After apologizing for possibly overstepping some boundary, he begins to speak less obliquely about what surely has been on his mind, the prospect of losing closeness. It is a frightening consideration, and his efforts to solace himself do not lead unequivocally to assurance. He asserts the largeness of his friend's heart and the certainty that he will not sacrifice their friendship, but the interrogatory mode in a key clause ("have I not gained a friend in Julia?") is significant in its irresolution, as is the uncertainty in the statement, "I *trust* she will let me be the friend to her, that Howe will say I have been to him" (my emphasis). Truly, if in a sense Sumner did not intend, "out of the fullness of the heart the mouth speaketh."

To Julia herself he wrote:

> Howe has told me, with eyes flashing with joy, that you have received his love. May God make you happy in his heart, as I know he will be happy in yours! A truer heart was never offered to woman. I know him well. I know the depth, strength, and constancy of his affections, as the whole world knows the beauty of his life and character. And oh! how I rejoice that these are all to mingle in loving harmony with your great gifts of heart and mind. God bless you! God bless you both! You will strengthen each other for the duties of life; and the most beautiful happiness shall be yours—that derived from inextinguishable mutual love, and from the consciousness of duty done.
>
> You have accepted my dear Howe as your lover; pray let me ever be   Your most affectionate friend, Charles Sumner
>
> P.S. Sir Huldbrand has subdued the restless Undine, and the soul has been inspired into her; and her "wickedness" shall cease.[17]

Some of the same notes are sounded here, particularly the assertion of his own special intimacy with "dear Howe" and a desire to be thought of as her friend. There is in addition his reflection that in plighting their troth, the two have acted out of both love and *duty*—the latter, perhaps, a dictum internalized and authorized by cultural uneasiness about the bachelor state, but probably also something Sumner needed to assure himself of, to soften the emotional blow. In most ways, though, the letter is unexceptionable as an expression of congratulations and happiness; in fact, it would hardly merit attention were it not for the likelihood that its central message, encoded, is in the postscript.

La Motte-Fouque's 1811 romance *Undine* tells of a water-sprite raised as a human girl by an elderly fisherman and his wife, who do not suspect her real nature. The child at age eighteen is full of high spirits and affection, but is also impulsive, willful, imperious, and subject to jealous fits and flashes of anger. Sir Huldbrand is a traveling nobleman who happens on the couple's lakeside cottage and is detained there by a severe storm, during which Undine disappears and requires rescuing by the visitor. Days pass, and Huldbrand falls in love with the volatile creature;

the two are wed by a priest who passes by the cottage. Sumner's reference is to Undine's explanation, on the day after the wedding, of her origins and purpose: offspring of a mighty prince of waters beneath the Mediterranean, she has received a soul by "the most intimate union in love" with a human being.

Although Sumner's rendition of the myth gives Sir Huldbrand credit for subduing Undine and obliterating her "wickedness," in the story itself it is more clearly Undine who woos Sir Huldbrand. Of the wedding night, we are told that whenever Huldbrand falls asleep, he is "disturbed by strange and horrible dreams of phantoms, who endeavou[r] with horrid grins to disguise themselves as fair women, or else of fair women whose faces suddenly bec[o]me the masks of dragons."[18] Though Undine's nature later proves to be anything but dragonlike, it is obvious in La Motte-Fouque's telling that she engineers the marriage for her own secret purposes and that, however ultimately admirable her purposes and she herself are, her first relations with Huldbrand are capricious and duplicitous. In short, it is difficult to read Sumner's remark in any way that renders it a compliment to Julia Ward.[19]

Sumner also wrote a note directly to his friend, ostensibly of congratulation, which has not survived. Samuel Howe's response on 22 February suggests that Sumner did not bother to suppress his feelings of abandonment; the doctor wrote that the note had made him as nearly sad as he could be at that moment and that he could take consolation only in the fact that the "extremity" of Sumner's distress must soon force him to seek sympathy from a woman. He ends by assuring his friend of his hope that the appropriate one will soon surface, but in any case, "in hope or fear, in fortune or adversity, in joy & in sorrow, I am, forever will be, your affectionate Howe." In this and in several other notes to Sumner during the spring and early summer, Samuel Howe's sentiments are propelled by a triple impulse—to celebrate his joy in ecstatic terms, to wring his hands over the sad fact that his best friend is still standing out in the cold, and to assure that friend repeatedly of his continuing devotion to him. "I am so very happy," he wrote on 29 March, "that I am really frightened: what does it mean? is it not some illusion? I do not deserve it: I never saw any thing like it before; no one ever did, for as for all the happiness they tell you about in novels, it is humbug." And on 13 May, posted from Liverpool:

[Y]our forebodings are not realised—the torrent of affection which is continually flowing from my breast toward the new object of my love diminishes not by one drop the tide of feeling which ever swells within my bosom at the thought of thee dear Sumner: I love thee not less because I love her more.

There is, on the other hand, a sense of silence on Sumner's part. Perhaps this is so only because, if he wrote truly personal letters in this period, they have not survived. Those that do exist are businesslike and relatively unemotional. Late in March he wrote to his brother George that his "dear friend" was soon to marry "the cleverest & most accomplished woman I know," but aside from a brief note from the happy husband on 3 April in which Sumner is affectionately addressed as "you miserable cold hearted anthracitic wretch," we find little indication of Sumner's state of mind.[20]

In May, however, Longfellow told Sumner that he, too, would soon be married, and this development provoked two letters. In the first, Sumner feels he must apologize for seeming to have received Longfellow's happy news with indifference. That was not the case, he says; he rejoices in his friend's joy. Yet the impact of the now doubled loss was clearly severe, and though he promises Longfellow not to mar his joy with any "gloomy suggestions about myself," he cannot resist adding, "Howe has gone, & now you have gone, & nobody is left with whom I can have sweet sympathy. My days will pass away, 'rounded by a sleep.' You cannot fathom the yawning depths of my soul." The other letter also testifies to Sumner's inclination to see his friends' marriages as desertions of himself. He mocks his self-pity and says he's "half-ashamed of the semi-dismal tinge of this note," but he nonetheless foregrounds his own solitude and characterizes Longfellow as sailing toward happy isles "where I cannot follow."[21]

WE NEED TO remember that Samuel Howe's extravagant protestations of happiness in his letters to Sumner are issued against the dark backdrop described in the previous chapter—his own deep-seated anxiety about whether the step he is taking is the right one, as well as Julia Ward's consciousness that in marrying this man she is agreeing to sacrifice her dreams. Just at the moment that Chev is rhapsodizing about the intensity of his love for his bride and joking with Sumner about the impossibility of his friend really understanding these feelings,[22] Julia is mourning the departure of her powers and her husband's emotional distance. It is hard to avoid wondering whether the near-manic quality of Samuel Howe's effusions may have arisen out of a need to reassure himself and whether they may have been, in some sense, expressions of deflected emotion, the true object of which was the friend left behind. In mid-June, he wrote:

> You complain of your lonely lot, & seem to think your friends will lose their sympathy with you as they form new ties of love, but dearest Sumner it is not so with me and in the days of my loneliness & sadness I never longed more for your society than I do now in my joy & in the whirl of London life: hardly a day passes but [I] think of you & long to have you by my side.

This letter also testifies to the existence of some level of animosity between the wife and the friend. Sumner has complained, evidently, that Julia does not like him; Chev says Sumner wrongs her in thinking so, because "she often says anyone who knows Sumner must love him." We are probably justified in reading this assurance, as Sumner no doubt did, skeptically.[23] At the top of this letter, which is partially scissored away, is the warning (in Samuel Howe's handwriting): "Reader! Sumner has no right to show this, so stop here." This note, in the context of the textual excisions, suggests that during this period there were two levels of communication between the friends—a more-or-less public one and another intended to remain just between the two of them. Both men shared some of the other's letters with their respective local circles (Sumner with the Five of Clubs, Chev with Julia and Annie), but from the scissorings and other hints—the injunction at the end of several letters to "burn this," for example—we can infer that not all components of the exchange were intended to be read by others.

In one midsummer letter, Samuel Howe seems to speak openly about this agreement: he directs Sumner to "write fully," sending his "private" letters through Baring's; he need "fear not" as long as he marks them private. This letter is signed "Forever your own Brother."[24] Since most of what remains of this correspondence has been fairly well sanitized, we move into speculative territory when we try to describe the nature of their private exchanges. One undated fragment of a letter from Samuel Howe, however, seems to offer a glimpse into their more personal sense of each other. This fragment has been preserved with other letters he wrote from London and Dublin; its paper and content suggest it was part of the 2 July letter. The fragment is distinct, first, in its marked difference in tone from the "public" letters. A good portion of it is devoted to complaining about having to endure the company of one of his wife's cousins as they traveled to Dublin. The narrative of the cousin's socially inappropriate gestures as the group passed through the grounds of famous houses is full of the kind of spiteful, gossipy remarks that one makes only in private and to one's most trusted friend. Its primary distinction, however, is in its frank characterization of Sumner's importance to the writer:

> I must have a friend—one dear friend & you are he: Mann—I saw much of—saw him something as I used to see you, tried to love him as I did you, but my frightened heart came back to me; you are my only friend— you and Julia; may I [preserve?] you as long as I live, may you live to sigh for me when I am gone, for I shall go before you.

This testimony of deep affection, unambiguous and obviously heartfelt, bespeaks a level of emotional involvement that the new Mrs. Howe might well have found distressing, had she been aware of its intensity. While her husband in other contexts made no secret of his warmth of feeling for Sumner, and although Julia here seems to be granted equal status with Sumner in Chev's small pantheon of friends, there is imaginably, in this proto-Lawrentian formulation of the situation, something beyond what a wife might find tolerable. Perhaps her growing consciousness of the degree to which Sumner was a rival for her husband's love—might she have read this letter, or an earlier one like it, before it was posted?—explains the specific anguish apparent in "The Present is Dead."

As 1843 progressed and the spatial and temporal distance between the two men increased, Samuel Howe's surviving letters begin to reflect a lessening of intensity. Writing toward the end of August from Baden-Baden, he had trouble remembering when he had last spent an hour "hobnobbing across the Atlantic with my dearest friend." Travel notes constitute the bulk of this and other letters penned as the party made their way (Julia pregnant and easily fatigued) toward Rome. A quickly penciled note from Geneva in mid-September to reassure Sumner ("no time to say a word by this packet but that I love you and yearn for your society") is offset by a chatty, relatively impersonal letter from early October, in which Howe comically describes the impediments of journeying with women. Julia read this letter and added a sweetly sardonic note about her husband's alleged difficulties, concluding by advising Sumner not to marry—"for great are the miseries of femininity, and we are all malae bestiae."[25]

The light tone, the showcased intimacy between husband and wife, and a reiterated insistence on the contrast between single and married men, as well as on the pregnancy, all contribute to an image of the Howes happily intertwined. It is possible to imagine that under the jovial tone of his mock complaint there lurked an element of genuine frustration. Such a mode of travel, he suggests, however much it may do for the heart, is an inefficient way to get a solid sense of the political and social institutions.[26] And he may well have missed his friend more than he acknowledged. He concludes by urging Sumner not to give away his heart until Samuel returns—"then let me have it." Still, on the whole, the letter does not suggest the particular intimacy of the summer, and although later in the month he wrote apologetically of his sparse communication ("I am loving you all the time & occasionally speak out on paper"), the letters beginning in late fall 1843 are mainly given over to rhapsodies evoked by Julia's pregnancy. Samuel Howe was clearly thrilled at the prospect of parenthood (or at least at the prospect of Julia's becoming a mother). What he had to say to Sumner underlined the impossibility of his friend's understanding either these feelings or the intensity of the husband-wife bond:

> Long before Julia, (with blushes & with hesitation) had avowed to me her condition, had she felt within her breast a flame of affection for her infant, which will never be quenched but with her life. Since then, how much have we rejoiced together; how have we tasted in advance the bliss of parental love; how have we formed plans for its future; how have we felt the force of this new life which rivets our souls together for aye!

He goes on to recall a period, presumably from the preceding spring, when he had expressed to Sumner a fear that his happiness would fall drastically short of his expectations. He now minimizes this dark interlude ("only a moment") and predicts not only joy in his marriage but renewed capacity for philanthropic action as a result of his now fully engaged affections. Although he encourages Sumner to write often, he leaves no doubt that the news he particularly awaits is that of Sumner's "prospects of happiness for the future."[27]

News reached the couple in December that Sumner had been seriously ill. Although Sumner's letters from this period are resolutely upbeat, he was in the early stages of a condition that, by May of 1844, his doctors were calling tuberculosis. Overwork undoubtedly contributed to deteriorating health—Chev instantly named it the sole cause—but it is probable that working too hard was a symptom of another kind of malady: depression. Sumner had suffered severely at the loss of his two closest friends. And despite their continued vehement protestations of undying love for him (and Longfellow's insistence that he accompany him and Fanny on their honeymoon), these letters through the fall were bringing home the ineluctable fact that a married man simply could not provide him with unambivalent, sustaining emotional support. The effort, conscious or unconscious, to internalize this perception seems literally to have made Sumner sick.

Samuel Howe's letters from early 1844 seem to reflect no particular solicitude about the state of Sumner's health. In fact, one might almost read some passages as contrived to rub salt in the wound—supposing the doctor knew the wound existed. He repeatedly reminded Sumner that father-love had subsumed every other feeling, including (he says explicitly) his feeling for Sumner.[28] If on the one hand he recalled old times when Sumner and he used to talk familiarly late into the night, on the other he used such memories merely as a bridge into rhapsodies about the delights of marriage. A letter written 2 February images the Sumner of the previous year—"your straps unbuttoned, your waist band also, your feet in my red slippers, a glass of ouvrietta in your hand, your sweet smile on your lips"—as a lead-in to lamenting Sumner's current lonely state:

> If I, unworthy sinner that I am, enjoy this much of happiness, how much more would you, whose affections are warmer, whose nature clamours louder for sympathy, whose heart is more tender, ah how much more would you dear Charlie enjoy & be enjoyed in such a relation than myself! Do you know how I feel when I think you alone, unloving, unloved—as if I had got into paradise & left my best friend outside.

And yet there is also in these letters—exemplified in part in the passage just quoted—a strange sense of *guilt* over having defected from a relationship that satisfied his friend more than himself. Samuel Howe seems uncomfortably aware that his defection may have something to do with Sumner's illness. He acknowledges that his own happiness, great though it is, is less than perfect because it must exist in the context of Sumner's unhappiness. He knows the cause is *not*, as some of their friends have joked, Sumner's incapacity for love: "you have more of love in you than any man I ever knew, and if you but bring your affections to the right focus, you may make it set fine to any heart you fix it upon." *Bring your affections to the right focus*—as if the problem with Sumner is not the absence of impulse, but rather the inappropriateness of its object. He concludes this letter with a sharply drawn picture of Julia and himself, the two of them laying plans to get Sumner to fall in love:

> You used to say I did with you what I pleased; you will see how much more I will do with such an ally as she. If you see her, more beautiful than ever, with her arms around my neck before, *qui que* se soit, her large eyes flashing light & love, & happiness, and mine glowing with more than I can show, you will forswear what you are, become as one of us, & make us still happier in witnessing that happiness we have so longed for in you.

Sumner evidently received these letters as unambiguous signs of his friend's continuing deep affection for him, calling them "warm love-letters" and passing them unselfconsciously along to Longfellow. Indeed, they *are* love letters, whether we read them at face value, signifying Chev's genuine desire for his friend's happiness, or as signs of his effort (for Sumner's own good) to distance Sumner emotionally, emphasizing his own blissful state as a way of encouraging Sumner to forswear what he is and become like Samuel Howe.[29]

By April, Sumner had begun an enormous project, the editing of eighteen volumes of Francis Vesey's Chancery Reports for use by American lawyers. His schedule required him to complete one volume every two weeks, a task Longfellow called "Herculean." Longfellow also noted in his journal that Sumner at this period appeared "rather sad" and "weary with the great Ixion wheel of life," a state perhaps caused by the task or perhaps one for which the task was intended to be a distraction. To Longfellow's efforts to cheer him by pointing to the opportunities life offers for memorable words and acts, Sumner replied he had once dreamed of that, but that all such "illusions" had long since vanished. His letter of congratulations to his absent friend on the birth of Julia

Romana is subdued, offering "the cold felicitations of a bachelor's bosom, unconscious of the fountains of delight which well in a father's soul" and urging him to remain in Europe another six months. By June the symptoms of tuberculosis were manifest, and although he spent the Fourth of July with the Longfellows, two weeks later he was bedridden, off-and-on delirious, and too weak to complete the writing of a letter. His doctors at one point declared him beyond the possibility of recovery.[30]

In early August, however, just as the Howes were embarking for home, Sumner's condition began to improve. On the sixteenth he was sufficiently well to write again, a letter he intended as a welcome home, but which became instead an account of his illness and a sober reflection on his ambivalence at having regained his health. It strikes the contemporary ear as the most revealing of his preserved letters:

> For such a signal recovery another person would feel unbounded gratitude. I am going to say what will offend you—but what I trust God will pardon. But since my convalescence I have thought most often whether I have any just feeling of gratitude that my disease was arrested. Let me confess to you that I cannot find it in my bosom. If I had been called away it would have been with the regret that I never had enjoyed the choicest experience of life—that no lips responsive to my own had ever said to me—"I love you." But my life has had too many shadows. My childhood & youth passed in unhappiness, such as I pray, may not be the lot of others. From earliest boyhood I have been laborious beyond the example of any I know. You have not seen me in this mood. During our special intimacy I have been blasted by another unhappiness, which unmanned me, & took from me all interest in labor. As this passed away the genius of labor again acquired his influence, then comes this illness, which strikes at my life. Why was I spared? For me there is no future, either of usefulness or happiness.

Sumner ends by expressing consternation that he has said so much of himself and by urging his confidant to burn the letter. Yet his decision to send it has to be regarded as a sign of his desire, now that they are to be in close proximity again, for his friend to know more of him than he had overtly communicated before. What exactly is its message? Did Samuel Howe understand what Sumner meant by "too many shadows" or by that other unspecified "unhappiness" that blasted him during his "special intimacy" with his dear friend? What sense can we make of it at this distance in time?

David Donald's two-volume work is still the regnant biography of
Sumner, but if we turn to it for answers to questions like these, we may
find ourselves frustrated. Donald does offer an intriguing perspective,
one perhaps not fully intentional, on certain facts of Sumner's youth and
early manhood. He suggests that Sumner's family life offered little in the
way of emotional sustenance and that his primary preoccupation as a
child was finding ways to impress his "unlovable" father. Entry to law
school in 1831 brought him under the tutelage of Joseph Story; about this
meeting Donald notes: "Never had Sumner encountered anybody so
captivating as the little pink-faced, cherubic professor who combed his
pixie-like wisps of curling blond hair on his forehead as he talked to his
students." Donald claims that Story's influence "shaped not merely
Sumner's professional career, but also his pattern of thought, his outlook
on life, and even his gestures and mannerisms." During the years in
which this influence held sway, Sumner occasionally lived with the
family and instructed Story's son in Latin. Donald quotes William Wet-
more Story's later remark about his tutor: "It was in vain for the loveliest
and liveliest girl to seek to absorb his attention. . . . He would at once
desert the most blooming beauty to talk to the plainest of men."[31]

Sumner did not, in fact, marry until he was fifty-five years old, and
the experience was short-lived and traumatic. In Donald's account of
the alliance with Alice Hooper—entered into immediately after the
death of Sumner's mother and lasting less than a year—the question of
Sumner's possible homosexuality is overtly raised. It was alleged at the
time—first through word of mouth and eventually in the newspapers—
that Mrs. Sumner, twenty-five years younger than her husband, sued for
divorce on grounds of impotence. Donald notes that some of Sumner's
college classmates, at that point, recalled "that Sumner had always been
known to be impotent and that at Harvard they had nicknamed him
'The Stag' because of his alleged deficiency." Donald also quotes a letter
to a man who had just been hired as Sumner's secretary: " 'Please ask
Charley confidentially if his wife left him because he *could not perform
the functions of a husband* owing to continued secret ____. This is what
Madame Rumor says.' " Donald observes in an earlier footnote: "As a
young man Sumner frequently spoke of his 'love' for male friends like
Longfellow and Howe. Perhaps it ought to be explained that the word in
nineteenth century usage did not imply an overt homosexual relation-

ship, of which I have not found the slightest evidence in Sumner's entire career."[32]

The point is not whether Sumner's intense attachments to his male friends were ever manifested in physical expression, but whether his feelings (and their apparent impact on his health) might have been understood by both Howes as a threat to their marital intimacy.[33] Sumner himself may have thought them to be so, because, despite doctors' warnings, as the day of the Howes' return approached he hastily planned an excursion to Newport and western Massachusetts. Did he wish to postpone the reunion? Did he wish to place himself in a position in which his old friend could visit him alone? On 27 August Sumner dashed off a note to apologize for his sudden departure, mentioning his "shattered constitution" and his fear that when the two did meet again, Samuel Howe would find him "but half a man." Sumner went on to contemplate the career now stretching "beautifully in a well-defined vista" before the doctor and concluded by nostalgically contrasting his current solitary journey westward with the one on which he had accompanied his friend fifteen months earlier, the "bridal journey" that took the Chevalier to his betrothed. Samuel Howe immediately rode out to Pittsfield to see his friend and a few days later wrote to offer his services as a companion on the continuation of Sumner's excursion (an offer of company Sumner accepted as "a greater pleasure than I can imagine, except that of the 'girl of my heart' ").[34]

It was in this context that Chev conveyed Julia's conviction that "Sumner ought to have been a woman, and [Samuel Howe] to have married her" (11 September 1844). Such a remark—frequently repeated, he indicates—signifies at the very least Julia's understanding of the depth of feeling between the two men. Whether she felt threatened by it is less clear: in another letter to Sumner written later the same day, the doctor reported (oddly echoing the plot turnings in *Undine*) that he and Julia were talking much of Sumner and had "arranged what we call 'Sumner's room' . . . we long to have you in it." We have, of course, only one party's assurance that the longing was shared.[35]

Indeed, we are afforded little direct access to Julia Howe's thoughts during the previous year. When it was determined that Louisa would join her sisters in Rome, Julia had no further occasion to write personal letters. What does remain from this first year and a half of marriage are a number of poems in notebooks, most describing sights or characteristic people ("My Donkey Driver in Wales," "The Ladies of Llangollen," "A Dream of Holy Week," "The Roman Beggar Boy," for instance), but a few recording what seem to be private ruminations.[36] One, written in Dublin, was evidently inspired by her husband's negative reaction to some poems she had shown him. Noting that she "is not moved by common themes" but rather "sings of silent joys and pains, / Of wondrous thoughts that come to her," she asks that he "list with patience to her strains, / And let Love be interpreter." Another, written in October in Vienna, again laments the loss of the former lover whose memory had provoked "The Past Lives" five months earlier.[37] At the turn of the new year came a poem in which Howe attempted to lay to rest the sorrows of the previous year:

> The thought has vanished
> That came, and came, to make me mad;
> The thought has vanished,
> And I, methinks, am almost glad.
>
> . . .
>
> For I have conquered,
> The serpent grief has lost its fang,
> Yes, I have conquered,
> And did not perish with the pang.
>
> Am I then happy?
> Oh! what should come to bring me woe?
> I have forgotten, God has forgiven,
> And this is all I know.

Although the poem bespeaks resolution of a sort, the putting aside of the question of happiness is not an especially salutary note, and the permanence of even that level of emotional stability is called into question by a pair of poems written later that spring:

> THE DARKEST MOMENT
>
> Tears, come to my relief!
> Despair, thou art not grief—
> A groan is not a sigh;
> Shadows depart, but truth cannot pass by.
>
> Tis no unreal want
> For which my soul doth pant,

That highest sympathy
Which God Himself to man will not deny.

Hope died as I was led
Unto my marriage bed;
Nay, do not weep—twas I
Not thou, that slew my happiest destiny;

For thou hadst quickly flown
Had thy kind heart but known
That, in thy pure embrace,
As pure a soul had lost on high its place.

THE DAWNING OF LIGHT

Husband, I do thee wrong;
Noble art thou, and strong;
And in thy blue eye gleams
As clear a flame as fed my early dreams.

We are not born alike,
Yet may our spirits strike
As bright and warm a spark
As comes from stony flint, and iron dark.

Often I turn away
From thee, to weep and pray;
I cannot rise on high,
My sad soul looks to God, and asks him why.

He says: "ye are not akin,
Your union was a sin;
Your natures meet and jar,
And thus, the order of Creation mar.

I weep, and not in vain—
I pray, and turn again;
thou art so good and true,
Regret departs, and love is born anew.

Then am I drawn to thee
By strongest sympathy;
Then grows the demon faint,
I kiss thy feet—thou art my house hold saint.

I do not love another,
Man is to me a brother;
The perilous passion's glow
Thank God is quenched, nor more shall work me woe.

When once I know my sphere,
Life shall no more be drear,
I will be all thou wilt;
To cross thy least desire shall be guilt.

Then, husband, smile on me,
Smile, and smile tenderly;
Pure angel that thou art,
Build up again the ruins of my heart!

The first paints a bleak picture of her state of mind regarding her marriage, the bleakness intensified by her apparent conviction that *she* is to blame for her unhappiness by not telling her husband of her impurity. The second poem, though seemingly arising from a more balanced, hopeful view of their union, nonetheless does not flinch from confronting their deep differences. As a couple they are, she says, a blot on the order of Creation, and however faint the "demon" grows as she contemplates her husband's angelic qualities and the rebirth of love, it clearly is not routed for good. Happiness is dependent on her coming to know her "sphere" and on learning not to cross her husband's desires. She counts on him to help rebuild what are still, despite her optimism, the "ruins" of her heart.

If, as these poems seem to suggest, Julia blamed herself for their differences, what evidence is there that her husband's affection for Charles Sumner had any bearing on the growing uneasiness she felt about her marriage? We may need to recall the poem quoted at the head of this chapter, written just a few weeks into their marriage. At that point—a year before the moment described above—Julia Howe attributed her unhappiness not so much to any putative deficiencies on her own part as to a sense that she and her husband occupied different emotional spaces. The solution then was for *him* to "come nearer," to help revive her poor, loving heart. Distance from home, and the clear excitement and tenderness he felt during his wife's first pregnancy, may for a period have enabled him to do that. Even so, he missed no opportunity to let his friend know how frequently he thought of him, missed him, desired his company, loved him. If Sumner's absence made him seem a less palpable intrusion—and caused Julia to seek other explanations for the obvious distance between her and her husband—the correspondence between Samuel Howe and Sumner during this year preserves an intensity of feeling that must be kept in mind in trying to understand Julia's state of mind. As we shall see, the mea culpa explanation proved unsustainable as time went forward, and Julia Howe discovered that no matter what she did to merit her husband's smiles, his deepest emotional energies were invested elsewhere.

THREE

"The Internal Fire That Consumes"

The 1840s, Motherhood, and the
Necessity of Writing

❧

I
N JULY 1843, a month or so pregnant, Julia Howe wrote to her
sister Louisa: "I am not good with children—for their sakes, I
should almost be willing not to have any."[1] Her first child was born
in March 1844, eleven months after her wedding. This child was the
oldest of six, all but one of whom lived to adulthood. At the time she
published *Passion-Flowers* in 1854, she was mother to four: Julia Romana
(nine), Florence (eight), Henry (five), and Laura (three). Any suggestion
that she did not love these children deeply would belie the truth, yet the
private communications of husband and wife to their separate confi-
dants during Howe's childbearing years point up sharp differences in
their ways of understanding what it meant to have children. If her first
pregnancy had helped diminish the emotional distance from her husband that she had felt during the wedding journey, the pregnancies that
lay ahead often marked the couple's periods of deepest estrangement,
and the pregnancies would become, for her, a grim emblem of the way
marriage impeded her intellectual and aesthetic development.

The point is illustrated by setting Howe's early anxiety in the context
of her husband's enthusiasm. We remember his rhapsodic certainty that
his young wife, even before telling him of her first pregnancy, had "felt
within her breast a flame of affection for her infant, which will never be
quenched but with her life." In that same letter—remarking delightedly
that Julia had been "working upon a baby frock" instead of "going to
operas or . . . writing poetry"—he had assured Sumner that

> [n]o true woman ever considered it a burden to bear her infant within
> her, to nourish it with her own blood, & to furnish every fiber of its frame

from her own flesh; hardly has she become conscious of the existence of her infant, when an intense and absorbing love for it fills her bosom. . . . I doubt not that most of her day and night dreams, are about it; she labours for it every day; she paints it to herself as most beautiful & most excellent; she selects for it a name; she plans its education, she foresees its career in life, she tastes the sweets of a mother's love without any of its bitterness.

Two weeks after Julia Romana's birth, the new father again described his thrill, not so much at the pleasure he himself took in parenthood (for as soon as Julia began to recover strength, Chev left to spend a month in Athens), but at the evidence that the birth of their daughter had changed his wife irrevocably. In the reference to a "wife who lives only for her husband," we glimpse Samuel Howe's reason for putting such great stock in motherhood:

How beautiful—how wonderful is nature! Only a year ago Julia was a New York belle—apparently an artificial, possibly to some a heartless one; now she is a wife who lives only for her husband, & a mother who would melt her very heart, were it needed, to give a drop more nourishment to her child. To see her watching with eager anxious eyes every movement of her offspring; to witness her entire self-forgetfulness & the total absorption of her nature in this new object of love, is to have a fresh revelation of the strength & beauty of woman's character, & new proof of their superiority over us in what most ennobles humanity—love for others.[2]

Private letters from Julia Howe do not exist from this period, since both her sisters were with her in Rome. But while there is no reason to suppose that she did not experience at least some of the feelings her husband attributed to her, we may also reasonably wonder how careful a reader of her real moods, or how accurate a reporter, he was. Marion Ward had visited the couple briefly in Paris in September and had remarked that Samuel Howe was less attuned to his wife's situation than Marion thought he should be, consumed instead with exploring educational institutions and other reform efforts. Brother Sam, too, seemed surprised that his brother-in-law would send him details about their progress across Europe and omit mention of the new mother's condition and health. The brother raised concerns that, by rights, ought to have been the husband's (and, Ward implies, ought to have moved him to delay parenthood until returning to the United States): the increased difficulty Julia would experience in traveling home with an infant and the "months of pain" she would suffer because of her small frame.[3]

The many letters Julia Howe wrote over the next ten years describing her feelings for her children leave no doubt that she took her role as mother extremely seriously and derived pleasure from it.[4] Yet these same letters bear testimony as well to very different feelings epitomized, perhaps, by a remark in a letter to Louisa not long after the birth of Louisa's first child:

> [F]or heaven's sake, do not undertake another baby immediately. I, for my part, am quite satisfied with my pair of monkies, and devoutly hope for an exemption from similar pangs in future. It is a blessed thing to be a mother, but there are bounds to all things, and no woman is under any obligation to sacrifice the whole of her existence to the mere act of bringing children into the world. I cannot help considering the excess of this as materializing and degrading to a woman whose spiritual nature has any strength.[5]

This divergence of perception is of course predictable in a culture as rigorously constructed regarding gender roles as the Howes' was, and it is, in its general drift, already so familiar as to be unremarkable to those who study antebellum America's married women writers. Yet this divergence offers a window into the more pervasive general discord that marks the early years of their marriage. Samuel Howe's desire to project so-called natural feelings regarding motherhood onto his wife suggests his habitual indifference toward her feelings on all matters. As it became clearer to him that, while he may have found a more-or-less cooperative partner in the task of creating a family, he had not found a soul mate "animated by the same spirit," he withdrew increasingly from the domestic circle. His emotional refuge, in addition to his friendship with Sumner, became his work and the numerous political causes he espoused in the 1840s. The building of this all-too-recognizable marital relationship, the steps Howe took to make it bearable for herself, and the close relation that developed between her feelings about married life and her literary dreams are the subjects of this chapter.

Although Howe had had ample chance to consider the conditions under which she would be living after their return from Europe, the reality of life in a drafty wing of her husband's school was hard to bear.

Her account in *Reminiscences* of this period of adjustment, though partly tempered by embarrassment at how poorly her upbringing had prepared her for domesticity, still displays a biting edge in describing the scope of the adaptation:

> The change had already been great, from my position as family idol and "the superior young lady" of an admiring circle to that of a wife overshadowed for the time by the splendor of her husband's reputation. This I had accepted willingly. But the change from my life of easy circumstances and brilliant surroundings to that of the mistress of a suite of rooms in the Institution for the Blind at South Boston was much greater. (150–51)

Part of the problem was inexperience in hiring and overseeing servants, part of it was being required to carry out these duties under the scrutiny of her husband's sister Jeanette (who had been his housekeeper prior to his marriage and who still lived in the Institution). Howe also felt cut off not only from her family, but from Boston society as well: getting into town from the site of the Institution meant a two-hour omnibus journey, since the doctor did not maintain a carriage. Even when she undertook the trip, she sensed that her status vis-à-vis those who had warmly welcomed her on earlier occasions was subtly changed. Formerly a "petted visitor," she now encountered Boston "with its consideration cap on, pondering whether to like or mislike a new claimant to its citizenship" (150).

More private issues were also troubling the waters. Probably foremost among these was the strain of having to live around the clock with the doctor's professional responsibilities. Their wedding journey had been in part a trip to investigate schools and prisons, and Howe (despite Marion's sense that her husband was ignoring her) had accepted this, most of the time, with reasonably good grace.[6] While abroad, however, she had had as consolation the diversions of her sisters' presence and the spectacle of Europe, as well as her husband's devoted attention a good deal of the time. As soon as they returned, the doctor plunged furiously into institutional work and the writing of a long report about prison architecture. He was also elected to the Boston School Committee, a position that demanded a huge amount of his time. Howe saw little of him, and that little in an environment that prevented real detachment from professional concerns.

On top of this adjustment, Samuel Howe's relationship with Sumner gave rise during the late summer to a different sort of family distress, focusing on Sumner's decision to involve himself in Louisa Ward's romantic affairs. Sumner, during his own European sojourn five years earlier, had become friends with the sculptor Thomas Crawford. Louisa had met Crawford in Rome, and the two had begun to discuss marriage, but the Ward brothers and Uncle John were uneasy about Crawford's ability to, as Samuel Howe put it, "so far wean himself from his exclusive devotion to his art as to administer the daily & hourly food of love, without which her soul will pine & die." In a late September letter, Sam Ward asked his brother-in-law to be an agent of delay in the affair. Meanwhile, however, the doctor had asked Sumner's legal help in altering an antenuptial agreement he had made with the Ward family regarding control of Julia's property. Thus the doctor and Sumner were at this moment allied against the family (Julia seems to have been in her husband's camp on this issue), and Sumner took the opportunity to try to impress on Samuel Howe the worthiness of his friend Crawford. On 25 September Sumner melodramatically described Crawford's downcast state at the family's (and Louisa's) coldness toward him: "The visit, which was to have crowned him with joy, covers him with mortification, fills him with dejection, & unnerves those energies which he hoped to exert in his art." Sumner blamed Louisa for allowing others to sway her affection for Crawford; he told Samuel Howe she needed to "interrogate her inmost nature" and then speak for herself. The others must "stand aloof"—yet in the next sentence he encouraged his friend to "aid" Crawford by "invigorat[ing] L[ouisa] to a conscientious and independent examination of her heart."[7]

Chev evidently passed Sumner's letter to Julia, who discussed it with her sister and showed parts of it to her brother Marion. Marion was furious, considering Sumner's presumption the greatest insult he had ever received and implicitly blaming Chev for having involved his friend in what should have been a private family matter. For Julia, though she was probably more confident about Crawford than her family was, the central issue was neither Crawford's feelings nor the possible obloquy that might sully the name of Ward: it was whether Louisa genuinely loved the man. In terms that it is difficult not to associate with Julia's sense of her own situation, she wrote to Louisa to urge her to follow her heart, but pleaded, "do not be led, a victim to the altar . . . do not marry Crawford if you do not love him—rather, dare any thing, and do any thing." This position, of course, would not have eased the tension between Julia and Sumner, and to the degree that Chev, too, was Crawford's champion, it may well have been a matter of discord between husband and wife. Sumner kept his distance from the Howe domicile, despite the talk about "Sumner's room" and despite Chev's occasional notes protesting (disingenuously, perhaps) that Julia's regard for him was high.[8]

To her New York family, however, Julia was her husband's staunch defender. Chev's legal challenge to the antenuptial agreement was only the most recent instance of strain between the parties, which dated at least as far back as his waffling between Julia and Louisa and his "doubts and fears" letter to Sam Ward in the spring of 1843. The crisis precipitated by Sumner's interference in the Louisa-Crawford matter seems to have affected the doctor's health. In November Julia asked Louisa to tell their brother that Chev's "fever" had subsided and to beg him to "avoid with the greatest care the mention of any thing that might renew it." Her letters to her family often include some such defensive statement about her husband, and while her impulse to do this might be taken in part as reflecting a desire not to be seen as having made a foolish match, there is no doubt that they also reflect genuine respect and love for him, and pleasure in her married state.[9] Whatever difficulties her new circumstances posed for her, it would certainly be a mistake to see Julia Howe, or to imagine she saw herself, as a woman unhappily locked into a marriage to Bluebeard. During this period in particular, her letters suggest that Chev tried to be responsive to her dissatisfactions and to take steps to alleviate them—by coming home earlier in the day, for example, or by devoting evenings to reading aloud together or by arranging for one of her poems to be published in a book he prepared for the blind.

And yet, and yet . . . sometimes in the very passages one might cite to illustrate relative satisfaction, there is the sense that life is grimmer than she can acknowledge directly. Here, for example, are the sentences in which she tells Annie about her husband's support regarding her poetry: "Think of my gratification, yesterday, to find that Chev had had my little 'Roman beggar boy' printed in a new book wh[ich] he is publishing for the Blind. I was so much gratified!" The sentiment seems straightforward, but the likelihood is high (since the rest of the letter is playful) that its intent is ironic. Almost as soon as she returned from

Europe, Howe had begun thinking about how she might establish herself as a writer. In the fall, planning to assemble a collection of poetry, she asked Annie to send copies of poems she had published in John L. O'Sullivan's *United States Magazine and Democratic Review,* and letters from the spring of 1845 frequently include a request for Annie to track down and send old manuscripts and notebooks. In these requests, there is often a sense of the clandestine, a notion that this activity must proceed without her husband's awareness. During this time she wrote a play called "The Life and Death of Little Red Riding Hood," in which she invested great hope: Annie was to consign it to Joseph Cogswell, her old tutor, who would sell it in New York for Howe for fifty dollars. The investment of hope was not only in her literary future, but in the money she hoped to make from it (earmarked for her summer wardrobe); her disappointment when it was returned was severe, partly because "I cannot do any thing with it here. Chev would immediately find it out, and would be displeased." Samuel Howe's effort to publish a single poem, and in a collection intended only for the blind, conceivably might not have thrilled his wife—might, indeed, have struck her as verging on hypocrisy.[10]

Husbandly opposition to Howe's literary interests was a source of fairly constant tension, the letters indicate.[11] Although she devised ways of working around his disapproval, it is probable that she found it irritating to have to do so, particularly in light of the warm praise and support he bestowed on two other women at about this time. Neither was a poet, but both were working (or hoping to work) in areas that mainstream Victorian culture regarded as outside the sphere of appropriate female effort, engaged in tasks that rendered their femininity suspect. One was Florence Nightingale, the other was Dorothea Dix.

The Howes had met the future Lady with the Lamp in England on the last leg of their wedding journey, while spending several days with the Nightingale family at Embley. Howe's brief account of this visit in *Reminiscences* focuses on a private meeting Florence arranged with the doctor early one morning before the family breakfast. She sought his advice as a philanthropist: would it be a "dreadful thing," she asked, if she were to study nursing and devote her life to that profession? He replied that it would, on the contrary, be "a very good thing." Howe notes tersely, "So much and no more of the conversation Dr. Howe repeated to me" (138), but she obviously saw the moment as pivotal in

Nightingale's rise to prominence.[12] Chev insisted they name their second child Florence, a position that upset Julia but to which she acquiesced so as to keep peace.[13] Later, he evidently taught his daughter, when asked who Florence Nightingale was, to reply, "My godmother."[14]

Samuel Howe's working relationship with Dorothea Dix began in 1842, at just about the time he became infatuated with Julia Ward. It is not implausible to imagine that Dix—or perhaps a less tightly wound, more refined version of her—was what the doctor fantasized his future wife might be: the helpmeet, the partner in philanthropy. Dix, a year younger than Samuel Howe, had found her vocation the previous year as a result of a visit to the East Cambridge jail; there, she had been appalled to discover that the indigent insane were confined with prisoners in horrifying conditions. Her outrage spurred her to further investigations, and eventually she turned to Dr. Howe, recently elected to the Massachusetts legislature, for help in securing relief.[15] He had taken up the cause in a series of letters to the *Boston Daily Advertiser & Patriot* and had drawn in Sumner as well. In January 1843 he presented her passionate "Memorial to the Massachusetts Legislature," which he called a "red-hot shot into the very hearts of the people," and followed through by arranging independent corroborative studies of the conditions Dix had observed. The very week Chev and Julia became engaged, he had pushed through legislation to address the plight of the indigent mad in Massachusetts. He wrote Dix: "When I look back upon the time when you stood hesitating and doubting upon the brink of the enterprise you have so bravely and nobly accomplished, I cannot but be impressed with the lesson of courage and hope which you have taught even to the strongest men."[16] By 1844 Dix's attention had begun to focus on prisons. The doctor convinced his Boston Prison Discipline Society to publish an essay Dix wrote in support of the Pennsylvania system (keeping prisoners isolated from one another), and he continued to rely on her to help him gather data for a report he was preparing on prison architecture. A letter to her from June 1845 includes fulsome praise for her achievements, especially for the fact that she overcame "the whisperings of maiden delicacy" in order to follow her conscience.[17]

TAKING THESE various difficulties and annoyances together, it is not surprising to find Julia confessing to Louisa, about a year after their return, that the period had not been a happy one for her. One solace,

which was at least occasionally effective, was to consider that in settling into marriage and domesticity she was "fulfilling the destiny of
women . . . learning to live for others." She professed to Louisa—also
now married (to Crawford) and on her way back to Rome, pregnant—
that in following "the guiding of Providence," they had acted more
wisely than they might have done had they marked out an idiosyncratic
or "eccentric" course of their own. This sort of reflection surfaces occasionally in letters of the mid-1840s, the most poignant instance of it
directed to Annie shortly before her marriage in June 1846:

> Marriage, like death, is a debt we owe to nature, and though it costs us
> something to pay it, yet are we more content, and better *established* in
> peace when we have paid it. A young girl is a loose flower, or flower seed,
> blown about by the wind—it may be cruelly battered, may be utterly
> blighted and lost to this world—but the matron is that same flower or
> seed planted, springing up, and bearing fruit unto eternal life.[18]

When such considerations failed to console, she relied on patience and
on the "strong and hopeful nature" she felt God had given her. Theodore Parker's sermons provided gratification.[19] And she turned to her
babies. A letter to Louisa early in 1845 describes her daily routine with
Julia Romana, "in all of which," she notes, "I have some fatigue, and
much pleasure. The dear little creature's smiles would repay one for a
great deal more trouble." A short while after Florence's birth in late
summer, Julia assured Louisa that she was well and doubly happy in her
two girls, surprised and delighted in the comfort Florence afforded.[20]

But it is difficult, on balance, to believe that any of these sources of
solace provided sustained relief from a life marked more sharply by
stretches of isolation and dejection than by placidity. Despite her best
efforts, Julia Howe was more often unhappy than not in these years, as
letter after letter testifies:

> 4 April 1845 (#422): [I]t is a delightful, but a terrible thing to be a
> mother—the constant care, anxiety, and thought of some possible evil
> that may come to the little creature, too precious to be so frail, whose
> life and well being, the mother feels, God has almost placed in her hands.
> If I did not think that angels watched over my baby, I should be crazy
> about it.
>   July 1845 (#431): [Life after Louisa's departure] was very desolate—but
> now I am getting used to it, and make myself very busy, which is the only
> way to tame oneself down into indifference.

October 1845 (#437): I am not well able to write—writing, sewing, any thing that requires attention causes me at once to feel giddy, and faint. I cannot even make Dudie's [Julia Romana] little clothes, or work on my worsted work, for it makes me feel ill—my eyes, too, have been very weak, so that any employments have been limited to knitting bands for Florence, and reading, now & then, some book with a large print.

[December 1845?] (#334): I am trying to press all the bitterness out of my heart, and to live in a more gentle and loving spirit. I am grown very hard & selfish, but then, it is so long since any one loved me. I say to myself, love begets love, and so determine at least to spread a little of its genial sunshine around me, and to make some sort of a Paradise out of the world I find a desert.

15 December 1845 (#438): It is a wretched, stormy evening, and Chev is in town, upon business with the prison discipline society. I am all, all alone, and shall creep, when my letter is finished, to the bed where my little Fofo and I sleep. Being so much alone, I think I shall find myself compelled to return to some of my old pursuits, and to take to myself dumb companions, since I have no speaking ones.

31 January 1846 (#449): I still live the same subdued, buried kind of life which I used to live when you were with me, but with some ameliorations. My voice is still frozen to silence, my poetry chained down by an icy band of indifference, I begin at last to believe that I am no poet, and never was one, save in my own imagination.

Spring 1846 (#440): What I feel is a premature *old age,* caused by the strong passions and conflicts of my early life—it is the languor and indifference of old age, without it's [*sic*] wisdom, or it's [*sic*] well-earned right to repose.

Two letters in particular, especially when set side by side, encapsulate the melancholy dynamics of the Howe marriage in this period. Both were to Louisa. The first, not precisely dated, was written probably in November or December 1845, soon after Julia's return from her first visit to Annie after Florence's birth.[21] New York had provided a brief respite from the constant demands of two children; Annie's maid had taken entire charge of Florence, and Julia had been at leisure to enjoy her sister's company. Returning to South Boston meant reassuming more or less full responsibility:

When you become the mother of two children, you will understand the value of time, as you never understood it before—my days and nights are pretty much divided between Julia and Florence. I sleep with the baby, nurse her all night, get up, hurry through my breakfast, take care of her while Emily gets her's, then wash & dress her, put her to sleep, drag her

out in the wagon, amuse Dudie, kiss, love, & scold her etc etc. . . . I have
not been ten minutes, this whole day, without holding one or other of the
children, and it was not until six o'clock this evening, that I got a chance
to clean my teeth—at meal-times, I have to sit with Fofo on one knee,
and Dudie on the other; trotting them alternately, and singing Jim along
Jose, till I can[']t Jim along any further, possibly.

These tasks themselves, though challenging for her, were not without
their emotional rewards. It was the having to perform them in South
Boston that brought her low—that, and her husband's ignorance of the
kinds of stress imposed by this regimen. On this evening, Sumner had
joined them for dinner,

> and he and Chev have been pitying *unmarried* women—oh! my dear
> friends, thought I, if you could only have one baby, you would change
> your tune. What a foolish mistake these impudent men make. They
> think that a woman's happiness is ensured, when she becomes tied for life
> to one of them—God knows, one's wedding day may be worse than the
> day of one's death—one's husband may prove any thing but a comfort
> and support.

Then, about three-quarters of the way through the letter, her tone
strikingly changes. She mentions that Chev has read what she had
written thus far,

> and was much grieved at what I have said about S[outh] B[oston],
> wherefore I take it all back—indeed, I am going to have a comfortable
> winter, and shall hope to enjoy myself as much as my maternal duties will
> allow. Poor Chev—he is afraid you will think me discontented, and
> indeed, I hope I am not. I should be very ungrateful not to be satisfied
> with so kind a husband, and such beautiful children.

Irony is not quite the appropriate term for this abrupt about-face.
Though we can sense the tongue in the cheek, there also seems to be
some genuine regret at having distressed him. Evidently contrite—and
determined to be maternal and conspicuously compliant—she closes
with a few lines of gossip and affectionate anecdotes about daughter
Julia's expressions. The letter, however, continues in Samuel Howe's
hand, this part addressed to "Crawford & Co":

> Julia has gone off sleepy & tired & had me fill up the blanks in her letter.
> I would not have you judge her feeling by what she says just now because
> she is a little homesick from N.Y. & it is very dark stormy blue devil

weather; generally she is as happy as she is busy & so busy a body you never saw except it be a mother of four children at a birth who are all to be attended to at once, & it *is* rather hard nursing four at a time you know. We are getting on pretty well, but looking forward to the time when we shall be better.

It would be hard to find a better illustration of his inclination to circumscribe or rewrite his wife—not, I think, out of meanness, but rather from (as Julia says) grief. Yet we note that his despondency results not from what the letter reveals about Julia's burdens, but only, apparently, from the fact that she has called life in South Boston "lonely and dull."

The other letter was written about two months later, on 15 February 1846.[22] Howe's freedom of expression suggests that she was confident that this communication would remain private. Here, her "hungry heart" is near starvation:

My babies are all the poetry and beauty that I can see in life. If I had them not, I should quietly die of inanition. Dearest Wevie, what is this problem? are we meant to change so utterly? is it selfish, is it egotistical to wish that others may love us, take an interest in us, sympathize with us, in our maturer age, as in our youth? are our hearts to fade and die out, with our early bloom, and, in giving life to others, do we lose our own vitality, and sink into dimness, nothingness, and living death? I have tried this, and found it not good—so methinks, I will not hold it fast. But then again, what shall I do? Where shall I go to beg some scraps and remnants of affection to feed my hungry heart? it will die, if it be not fed. My children will, one day, love me—my sisters have always loved me—my husband? May God teach him to love me, and help me to make him happy. For our children's sake, and for our own, we must strive to come nearer together, and not live such a life of separation. We must cultivate every sympathy which we have in common, and try mutually to acquire those which we have not. He must learn to understand those things which have entirely formed my character—I have come to him, have left my poetry, my music, my religion, have walked with him in his cold world of actualities—there, I have learned much, but there, I can do nothing—he must come to me, must have ears for my music, must have a soul for my faith—my nature is to sing, to pray, to feel—his is to fight, to teach, to reason; but love and patience may bring us much nearer together than we are.

Remarkable here, beyond the wail of anguish ("living death"), is Howe's determination. She is deeply unhappy, and for reasons very close to those articulated three years earlier in "The Present is Dead," but she is not defeated. Despite her sense that she has changed a great deal more than he, and her insistence that he must come now farther into her world if life is to improve, she does not therefore excuse herself from the necessity of continued hard work. "*We* must strive . . . *we* must cultivate every sympathy . . . try *mutually* . . . "(my emphasis). Even had this happened, however—and the epistolary evidence suggests it did not[23]— it is still dubious whether Howe would have found what this letter centrally, passionately, cries out for: those elusive "scraps and remnants of affection" that were evidently beyond her husband's capacities.

WHAT DO WE know about Samuel Howe's private emotional life during these years? The gleanings are sparse, and we need therefore to guard against giving undue significance to the few glimpses that remain. We know he was often ill with ailments somehow arising from or affected by stress (Julia's November 1844 request that her brother not say anything to Chev that might cause his fever to recur is one of several similar instances). We know that he occasionally made efforts, though not clearly on his own volition, to spend more time with his lonely wife. We know he took delight, at least occasionally, in his children (but also that he grieved when his second child was not male). We know that his stance on prisons brought him into conflict with an important faction of Boston's political power structure. His philanthropic work no doubt afforded him significant gratification (Julia's phrase for it in one letter is "intoxicated with benevolence"),[24] but Longfellow's journal for 19 October 1845 tells us that his doctor-friend was "in a nervous, morbid state. He has no enjoyment in social intercourse, being painfully conscious of the passing of time, as if life were slipping from under his feet. At the Asylum a bell rings every quarter of an hour—a constant memento mori; and wherever he goes he hears this melancholy bell." He was also under attack beginning in 1846 for the fact that the religious instruction he had given Laura Bridgman was nonsectarian, rather than explicitly Christian.[25]

His relationship with Sumner remained his most important attachment outside marriage and work, and he seems to have tried to connect Sumner to himself in as many ways as he could. Residual tension over the Louisa Ward–Thomas Crawford matter kept Sumner from visiting South Boston often, and so the doctor contrived other ways of spending time with him. When Samuel was elected to the Boston School Committee, he worked to get Sumner into the group as well, and when that failed, he arranged for his election as a trustee of the Perkins Institution. Sumner's support was enlisted in the battle over prisons, too. A note he left for Sumner in his Court Street office in April 1845 indicates how closely Samuel Howe tracked his friend's emotional oscillations: "I could not stay quietly at home & enjoy my domestic happiness," he wrote, "for thinking of you alone, & melancholy, at your office; so I came over to seek you out, to try to console you in my poor way."[26] After Sumner's first major speech—"The True Grandeur of Nations"— Samuel Howe countered with unconditional support the vehement hostility Sumner provoked: "I could never love you more than I did yesterday morning, & yet, at night, I was far more proud of your friend-ship than ever before." Longfellow's journal during this period leaves the impression that Sumner was spending a good deal more time in Cam-bridge than with the doctor, but notes to Sumner from Samuel Howe ("Ever yours, rough without but faithful within . . . more than you think") show that the level of intensity did not diminish, at least on Samuel's side, despite his disappointment at not managing to draw Sumner more fully into his domestic scene.[27]

In the spring of 1846 the family purchased a house near the Institu-tion, "a cottage under the hill, looking upon the sea," as Longfellow described it; Julia dubbed it "Green Peace." The move there brought her a surge of exhilaration, and Chev's health and spirits were improved, too. She was able to write to Louisa, "my heart no longer aches with the thought that I have given up all else on earth to make one man happy, and have yet utterly failed to accomplish it." Life was not without its trials—little Florence still slept with her and "flooded" the bed several times nightly, and Julia Romana's rough behavior toward her sister had begun to be a problem—but generally the summer of 1846 was a time of armistice, even joy. In July the family traveled to Brattleboro, Vermont, so that the overworked doctor could take the "water cure," and the little vacation was a great happiness for everyone. Julia wrote to Louisa: "I shall always remember Brattleboro as a sort of refuge from pain and sickness, if I am ever ill, I will drag myself thither, and wash, and be clean."[28]

This more stable state of affairs continued through the fall, despite Samuel Howe's increasing involvement in politics. In September he and Sumner both delivered inflamed speeches protesting the return of an escaped slave, thereby publicly committing themselves to the cause of abolition. The "Conscience Whigs" importuned Sumner to stand for election to Congress as their representative, and when he could not be persuaded, the doctor was drafted as the candidate. He lost—a relief to Julia, who had not looked forward to spending a winter in Washington. She had, however, been stirred by Sumner's speech. Samuel reported to his friend that she was "completely surprised & carried away," astonished at his self-possession and fervor. Yet when Sumner's public commitment led to the drawing of political lines and increasingly sharp attacks from ideological opponents (a source of serious personal pain), Julia's sympathy for him was tempered by a feeling that he ought to have been able to predict and prepare better for the emotional cost. However much he may have deserved her admiration, there is still a sense of reserve whenever either refers to the other in letters. And though Julia could report to Louisa in December that Chev was talking to her more and taking some interest in her thoughts and pursuits, his political activities afforded reason to continue to spend long hours in Sumner's company.[29] Julia Howe's response at this point to the conditions of her marriage is surely one of the more engrossing stories to be told about a nineteenth-century American writer.

The Laurence Manuscript
"Not . . . a Moral and Fashionable Work"

Sometime during the winter of 1846–47 Howe began a long narrative work, ultimately over four hundred manuscript pages, never published and probably never completed, on which she worked (I believe) for about a year at this point and may have returned to later, during her second trip to Rome and after settling again in South Boston.[30] Information about it, apart from what the manuscript itself reveals, is scanty. The earliest unequivocal reference in Howe's letters is from May 1847, a letter to Louisa. She apologized for having sent no letters for months, citing her "studious, meditative, and most uncommunicative frame of mind" and mentioning that although she had written much poetry during the winter, "it is of a kind wh[ich] I do not readily show." She did, however, enclose four stanzas of a poem entitled "Eva to Rafael,"[31] and she offered to send more of her characters' "correspondence," should Louisa be interested. "I have made quite a little romance about them, but have kept it for my own amusement, the cold praise and ardent criticism of the Club not being at all to my taste." It is important to note Howe's reserve about this work, distinct from her determination to publish or at least share her poems. These "are poor enough, but they have this merit, that they are written out of my own soul, to God, and to the few souls that I love."[32]

Eva and Rafael's story, viewed in the context Howe eventually created for it, is not the central narrative, but rather an intact (mostly prose) piece set within a larger primary story, of which the protagonist is variously called Laurence or Laurent. His conspicuous characteristic is that he is a hermaphrodite. Whether Laurence was part of Howe's earliest conception of this narrative, or whether the two stories arose independently and were later welded, is difficult to determine. One piece of evidence suggests they were conceived simultaneously. On page 30 of her 1843 diary[33] appears this fragment, evidently a piece of a letter to an unidentified person:

> Yet my pen has been unusually busy during the last year—it has brought me some happy inspirations, and though the golden tide is now at its ebb, I live in the hope that it may rise again in time to float off the stranded wreck of a novel, or rather story, in the which I have been deeply engaged for three months past. It is not, understand me, a moral and fashionable work, destined to be published in three volumes, but the history of a strange being, written as truly as I knew how to write it. Whether it will ever be published, I cannot tell, but I should like to have had you read it, and to talk with you about it.

This is almost certainly a reference to the Laurence part of the work, and although the fragment is not dated, its location in the diary adjacent to other fragments (including a copy of the Eva-Rafael poem Howe quoted to her sister in May 1847) argues strongly that the characters of Eva, Rafael, and Laurence all date from this period.[34]

Laurence's origins as a character remain a mystery.[35] The narrative makes clear, however, that "he" is somehow physically both male and female and that he is raised as a male in order to give him freedom "to choose [his] own terms in associating with the world, and secure to [him] an independence of position most desirable for one who could never hope to become the half of another." The tale, which Laurence himself narrates, is of his repudiation by his family; his involvement with an attractive widow; his subsequent wanderings and eventual at-tachment to a sixteen-year-old boy, Ronald, whose tutor and love object he becomes; and his own tutelage at the hand of a Roman nobleman named Berto.

In the story's chronology, the earliest section is the fragment numbered 2–163 (but missing pages 118–32), denoted here as "A."[36] Here we learn how Laurence's parents determined to bring him up, sending him to a boys boarding school "that I might become robust and manly, and haply learn to seem that which I could never be" (A2). He does well academically and socially, but as years pass, he becomes more and more estranged from his family, conscious of the pain he gives them because of his peculiar constitution. On the other hand, he is increasingly perceived as beautiful by everyone else around him. "Women often gave me proofs of a stronger interest than any inspired by mere benevolence, while the eyes of men so scrutinized me that I was fain to hide myself from them with a perturbation for which I could scarce account to myself" (A4). He enjoys friendships with people of both genders, but intimacy, or even the impulse toward it, with neither. Females generally see him as a refuge from their more ardent suitors, seeking him out when they tire of being made love to.

One woman becomes an exception to this pattern—a "handsome and sprightly widow," twenty-eight years old, named Emma von P. Recently arrived from a "gay metropolis," she strikes Laurence and his companions as "a revelation of some thing as yet unseen and unimagined by us"; and perhaps because he is less forthcoming in his attentions to her than his friends are, she soon focuses her own attentions on Laurence. Gradually, coquetry and casual interactions deepen into something more meaningful, yet there is a reserve about Laurence that sparks uneasiness in Emma. As time passes and she fails to see in his eyes the response she hopes for, "she would turn abruptly from me, or push me from her, and close the door upon me with a nervous energy bordering on irritation" (A13). She accuses him of being marblelike, merely a trifler, implying that she both expects and would be receptive to more "manly" behavior.

The episode climaxes on the eve of Laurence's college commencement, when he delivers a poem that seems cryptically to set forth his origins and true nature. Laurence's poem wins the competition, the prize for which is awarded by Emma, but in congratulating him she asks: "Laurence, I hope that you are not one of those unsexed souls." He counters: "Have you never been one?" to which she responds, "Never, since I have learned what it is to be a woman" (A22–23). The phrase "what it is to be a woman" reverberates in Laurence's head all evening, until he happens to overhear two men compare him to the Villa Borghese's "lovely hermaphrodite," at which point he flees distraught to his room. Stripping off his clothes, he throws himself into bed and finally drifts into sleep.

He is awakened by Emma's step. She makes it clear why she has come: she has felt on the verge of death from loneliness and has decided that if she is going to die, it may as well be from shame, instead. She does not expect marriage:

> I am here alone, in your room, in your power, at dead of night—you cannot misinterpret this, it must convince you that I love you better than life, better than honour, better than my own soul and God. Give me but this one night, but this one hour—do you ask where I shall be tomorrow? I can die tomorrow—I shall have been happy. (A27)

Dying the next day (or soon after) is what in fact she does, though not from happiness—rather, from the agony of her discovery that the object of her strenuous passion is no man, but (in her word) a "monster."[37] While she raves and laughs maniacally, muttering over and over the phrase "like the hermaphrodite in the Villa Borghese," Laurence carries her back to her rooms and, after some painful deliberation, decides to return to his father's estate.

Though his father and the whole household are mechanically polite, Laurence finds the environment unbearable until his younger brother Philip, whom he has never seen, appears. A close attachment grows between the two, and Laurence wonders how two such warm beings as he and Philip can have been fathered by a "domestic iceberg." Soon Laurence and his father quarrel over the issue of inheritance (the father wanting to insure that Laurence's rights to the family estate are dissolved); Laurence scorns his father's wealth, relinquishes his entitlement (giving it to Philip), disowns his father, and departs. He passes a funeral procession, discovers that it is Emma's, and spends a night in remorse at the foot of her coffin.

He eventually settles in a woods-enshrouded house, formerly the retreat of a learned nobleman. (The nephew who rents the place to Laurence, unnamed at this point, is later revealed to be Berto, who plays a major role in another section of the narrative.) There is a chapel, and gradually Laurence's purpose becomes a Swedenborgian spiritual quest, a determination to lose earthly passions, and even awareness of a physical self, in contemplation of Truth:

> The curse of my existence, the cruel injustice of nature had for the time quite faded from my remembrance—my body was become a matter of such small consequence to me, that I cared little after what manner it was made; only when by chance one day I saw my face in the mirror, I was glad to observe in it a diaphanous, mortified look which seemed to assure me that the spirit was now lord absolute, and that the flesh had at last learned its place, and would keep it. (A73)

His spiritual exercises take him more and more out of his body, until finally one day he loses consciousness. When he wakes, he finds his head cradled by "one whose sex disclosed itself in a form of perfect beauty" (A79). The person thus ambiguously characterized is Ronald, sixteen years old, whose white forehead, dark hair, innocent mouth, and deep blue eyes make a profound impression on Laurence. Ronald at first believes Laurence to be a woman because of his long hair, but Laurence makes it clear that he is not female. He wants to cut off his hair to prevent further confusion, but Ronald pleads with him to leave it. The boy restores the hermit's life-energy enough to enable them to set out toward the estate of Ronald's father; Laurence, however, too weak to travel the whole way, must first spend several weeks recovering strength in the nearby humble cottage of a huntsman. (Ronald first offers the hut of his old nurse Lischen, also nearby, but Laurence shudders at the thought of being cared for by, or even seeing, a woman.)

Ronald eventually brings his new friend to his father's castle, where Laurence is warmly welcomed and invited to stay as Ronald's tutor. The situation delights them both: Ronald, says Laurence, "attached himself to me with almost feminine fondness, and his presence chased the phantoms from my brain, even as a nursling will often draw away the poison from the sick heart of its mother" (A109). The two roam the fields and woods, dissecting plants, classifying stones, plaiting garlands, singing, improvising dramas. "We were," says Laurence, "the gayest of all the children of the Spring" (A112). Laurence is still made deeply uneasy by the presence of women, and Ronald willingly complies with his friend's determination to avoid them. The two grow continually closer in the pursuit of knowledge, but Laurence, in a cryptic flash-forward, reveals that the relationship is not entirely healthy:

I learned at a later day that I had not understood all that was passing at this period in the mind of my pupil. Some seeds were ripening there which I had never desired to sow, and Nature was slowly arousing in his breast some impulses with which I could not sympathize. (A114)

A preview of these "impulses" comes soon in the midst of a philosophical conversation between the two. Laurence asserts the importance of knowing how and for what we live, to which Ronald responds, "I understand that full well. I know that I live because I love you, and I live to love you" (A115). Disconcerted, Laurence changes the subject.

Fourteen pages of the manuscript (118–32) are missing at this point. Following the hiatus, we find Ronald's father proposing a toast on the occasion of his son and Laurence setting out for the university. In their new environment, Ronald's strong attachment to Laurence becomes more and more obsessive. He ignores other students his age, protesting that all he really needs is his friend's guidance. For his part, Laurence begins to devise strategies to wean his devotee, but with a certain ambivalence of his own: he cannot keep himself from being pleased to retain his sway over Ronald's education and affection. One night, having determined to leave the university for a while so that Ronald will be forced into friendships with others, Laurence inadvertently wakens Ronald during a dream: the younger man throws himself into his tutor's arms, having dreamed him a woman. Laurence roughly rejects his effusions, then, embarrassed at his own agitation, tries to calm Ronald by taking down the guitar and singing with him. Later, Laurence asks to see Ronald's thesis, which turns out to be a version of the Pygmalion story and a barely encoded crypto-erotic rendition of their own relationship. Laurence, perhaps willfully obtuse, stares long into his friend's eyes, wondering, "Hast thou thyself dreamed of passionate desire? hast thou too implored heaven to work the miracle of love in some cold heart that should respond to thine?" (A139). As he takes his leave (Ronald now once again seemingly asleep), Laurence lightly kisses his forehead, at which the boy's "red lips" part to murmur, "Laurence!" Thinks the tutor: "oh soft bloom of adolescence, oh gentle type of nascent manhood! your remembrance will never die out from my heart" (A141).

Laurence stays away a long time, longer than originally planned, sending letters regularly until he receives a terse note from Ronald telling him to stop writing of his love and instead to prove it by returning.

This brings him back, but he finds Ronald subtly altered—sometimes as affectionate as always, but often rough and moody, exhibiting more of the coarseness of the friends he has indeed made in Laurence's absence:

> There were days in which Ronald was content to lay down his arms at my feet, in which he seemed compelled to seek from me the sympathy which none other had ever given him. There were moments in which he essayed, with tears in his eyes, to break the seal that estrangement had set upon his heart, and to unfold to me all the unwonted thoughts that were imprisoned there—but even in these moments, the cold wind of distrust swept over his soul, and he shrank back into himself, the tears unshed, the tale untold. I sometimes asked myself whether some devil's seed had been dropped into Ronald's mind, and was ripening there into dark and unholy life, but no, I could find no evil in him. (A144)

One night a theater troupe performs *Romeo and Juliet,* and for various reasons Laurence is at the last minute pressed into playing the role of Juliet. He rises startlingly well to the occasion, feeling "a nameless pleasure in being something other than myself . . . giving a fervent expression to the glowing words of the Italian woman-child" (A149). During the balcony scene, Ronald, who has been drinking all evening, leaps to the stage in a jealous rage and attacks the actor playing Romeo. Laurence calms him and gets him back to their rooms, where he falls asleep, but before Laurence also drifts into sleep he reflects on a prayer he has heard: "All powerful One, keep me from that I am" (A152).

Ronald is gone the next morning and cannot be found all day. At length Laurence tracks him to a tavern where he has again been drinking heavily. Late that night, Ronald returns, dishevelled and wounded; he says he has defended Laurence's "manhood" against the insinuation of the actor playing Romeo that Laurence is really a woman. Ronald makes it clear that he believes he has defended a "lie" but demands that Laurence "cancel the wrong . . . change my torment to raptures of heaven" by returning his love: "You shall be a man to all the world, if you will, but a woman, a sweet, warm, living woman to me—you must love me, Laurence" (A157). In a speech that verges on the pornographic, Ronald pleads with Laurence to undress:

> [D]o off, do off these hated garments, which wrong your heavenly grace and beauty—float before me, man-like, in loose, light robes—throw off the narrow bondage of that vest—let your heart beat freely, let your

bosom heave high, heave wildly, till the very remembrance of my sorrow be buried beneath its white waves. (A158)

Panicked, Laurence pushes him away and lunges for his pistols—not to defend himself, rather to turn them on his own "blasted bosom"—but Ronald has unloaded them, and now proceeds, crazed, to wrestle with Laurence, determined to seduce him. "Do not struggle," he says, "it is all in vain."

> I fear no curse but that of losing you—God himself, if there be a God, will not come between me and my right. I bear in my bosom a wondrous fire, a strange alchemy, that can turn marble itself to molten flame. You are mine by fate, mine by the power of my will, and my first crime is also yours, for it is born of the union of your soul and of mine. (A159)

There comes a moment when Laurence feels Ronald, at the "hour of volcanic might and ruin," pause for a moment. He seizes the instant to persuade him to let him, too, drink some wine, and when Ronald releases him, he manages to drug Ronald's wine before handing it to him. This is his salvation: Ronald passes out just as he is about to send his "dagger" into Laurence's flesh. (This is presumably an actual dagger, the action expressive of Ronald's fury at discovering the wine to have been drugged, but its symbolic properties are presumably also intended to be evident.) Laurence bolts, tormented by his sense of the devastation Ronald will feel tomorrow but also by his own obscure responsibility for this horror. The section ends with Laurence's dejected conviction that the whole human race is "full of evil and danger—the purest heart among them contains a criminal thought, a wish unblest" (A163).

THE OTHER LONG numbered section (50–171, called "B" here) offers few clear links to the chronology of the "A" section. Its main focus is Laurence's unconventional education, and thus we might expect it to have a place, somehow, in the course of events already narrated. One indirect reference to Ronald makes it clear that this section follows what is narrated in the "A" section, but aside from Laurence himself, the only characters actually reappearing from "A" are Laurence's father and brother Philip. In general, there is less continuity in this section, the two central characters existing, it sometimes seems, only to provide occasions for lengthy tangential narratives and reflections. Yet certain events make it clear that the overarching subject is still Laurence's ambiguous sexual nature.

On page 50—obviously not the beginning of this portion of the narrative—Laurence has been working for a month toward mastering Hebrew with the help of his ebullient Roman tutor Berto. Beyond a vague reference to how such study has helped Laurence forget the "nonsense" that had been working in his brain before, it is not clear why he is doing this or how he has come to be associated with Berto. Now, unexpectedly, Berto wants him to put these studies aside and plunge into the life around them in Rome. Things get off to a fast start with a few bottles of wine and a wee-hours stumble through the streets until sunrise surprises them in the Colosseum.

The real object of scrutiny, though, is to be Roman society—a focus Berto will allow for Laurence (whom he evidently believes to be male), but which he would feel loath to recommend to women of his acquaintance. In society, says Berto, women are educated not to strength or virtue, but rather "to triviality and routine. . . . They are taught to appeal to our indulgence, not to command our esteem" (B59). Berto then tells Laurence the story of his only love, Eleanora, a Swiss girl bred from an early age to a religious vocation. Not long before, he has brought her to Rome, hoping to awaken her to the spectacle of secular life, but despite his strenuous efforts, she is happy only in the convent. Now he has received word that she is about to enter the order as a novitiate. Laurence and Berto attend this service, during which Laurence reflects morosely on the sour underside of lives lived in sequestered devotion to the church. The chapter ends as Eleanora swoons in the arms of the mother abbess.

An abrupt scene change, and we find Laurence and Berto waiting for the curtain to rise on the debut of a young ballerina in a work called *The Hermit of the Alps*. As the piece progresses, Laurence realizes that it is set in his own native canton and that the dancer is his (heretofore-unmentioned) old flame Rösli. The moment the curtain falls, he makes his way to her dressing room, where, interrupting unwelcome advances to Rösli from a dissolute young abbé, he gives her news of her family. Laurence returns night after night, his thoughts always on the danger Rösli faces from the wicked world. One evening he overhears her receive a proposal of marriage—not from one of her many unscrupulous admirers, but from someone pure and evidently honorable: his beloved brother Philip. Although it tears his heart to do so, he leaves quickly without revealing himself, wanting not to reawaken old sorrows.

Back in the theater, Berto scoffs at the notion that this was indeed Laurence's brother, and in succeeding days he continues to weaken Laurence's conviction that his brother is somewhere in the city. Meanwhile, the carnival season arrives. As part of the celebration, the two attend a horse race, where among the spectators they spot the fashionably dressed Rösli. She bears flowers for one of the riders, whom Laurence immediately recognizes as Philip. (Berto confirms that it is he by asking a bystander.) Laurence wants to make himself known, but Berto persuades him to wait until the end of the race. Philip wins but is thrown from his horse and dies; over his lifeless body, Laurence once again confronts their father and, though grief-stricken, points gleefully at this wreckage of his father's hopes for perpetuating his name.

Soon after, Laurence receives a request from his father to visit him; he scornfully refuses. But the two meet accidentally one day in the Protestant cemetery, where Laurence has gone to mourn his brother. The father tries to reinvest Laurence with title and fortune, but Laurence insists coldly that he will not accept them: his father's early rejection of him cannot be revoked. The father departs in grief, and Laurence bows his head at the altar of his brother's grave.

Another abrupt scene- and mood-shift, and we find Laurence dressed as a woman, living with Berto's sisters in the family palazzo. A flashback lets us know that Laurence has consented to masquerade as "Cecilia" in order to hide from his father, who, if he can locate Laurence, plans to have him declared insane. (A secondary reason, though it does not seem to carry much weight with Laurence, is that Berto wants him to experience life as a woman, looking at both men and women through female eyes.) Two of the sisters, Berto has told him, are "too proud to present themselves as candidates for selection in the great woman market of society" (B126); the third, Nina, has had a lover, Gaetano, but unfortunately he had been forced into self-exile to avoid political persecution. Berto fears that Nina's sense is slipping away as she tracks Gaetano's imagined travels and waits for his return.

The general tone of this portion is light, featuring banter among Berto and the two older sisters Briseida and Gigia. However, as Berto takes his leave for Naples, he reveals that he is the nephew of the hermit-count whose forest retreat Laurence occupied between his involvements with Emma von P. and Ronald. This news comes as a complete surprise to Laurence. Just before he leaves, Berto suggests that "Cecilia" read a manuscript given to him by his uncle. After Berto's departure, Laurence escapes to his chamber, where he bemusedly confronts the challenge of liberating himself from the complicated women's clothing Berto has provided and then falls asleep dreaming of "one who had once almost made a woman of me"—that is, Ronald.

Although the ostensible purpose of this interlude is to give "Cecilia" a chance to observe society through differently gendered lenses, not much attention is paid to "her" perceptions. Laurence proves himself an astute observer of behavior and custom, but does not seem to achieve insight as a result of his female disguise. The only significant reference to Laurence's unusual physical nature occurs one night when he sings at a soiree; one of the guests likens his voice to that of Umberto, famous *contraltiste* (read castrato) in the pope's choir. Several weeks proceed in conventional social activity. Briseida's lover, Pepino, is introduced; the irresolute son of a noble family, he has been betrothed since birth to a Polish princess and so can never marry Briseida. Gigia, too, has an amour, the Count Flavio. But the chief interest of Laurence's stay in the house is Nina, "dream-rapt, isolated from the actual world, half corpse, half angel, intently watching and protecting the fortunes of a mortal beloved" (B168).

This section of manuscript breaks off in the middle of a scene describing Laurence's interactions with Nina. There are six other narrative fragments, all much shorter, comprising essentially two sequences—one a continuation of the "B" sequence above (although unnumbered and incomplete), and the other containing more material having to do with Ronald. The first of these describes the reading of the uncle's manuscript—the Eva-Rafael romance mentioned by Julia in her May 1847 letter to Louisa—its startling effect on Nina, and Berto's return. I have designated these sections "C" (lead-up), "D" (Eva and Rafael), "E1," "E2" (a revision of "E1," recounting Nina's rapture), and "F" (aftermath). The piece of additional Ronald material is designated "G."

Laurence remembers the manuscript on a moonlit evening when the sisters are occupied with their lovers; he is feeling lonely, "unloving and unloved" (C1). Briseida requests that he read it to her and Pepino, but Gigia declines to be part of the audience, professing scorn for its central message of constancy even beyond death. The sisters mention the work's profound impact on Nina, suggesting that it may have provoked her mental deterioration.

The work is (here) entitled "Ashes of an Angel's Heart" (C6). It opens on Eva standing vigil at the tomb of Rafael, listening to his words from beyond the grave. The diction and scenic description recall the conventions of medieval romance or folktale. Rafael thanks her for her continuing devotion and urges her to receive the angel of consolation, but she is inconsolable. An angel soon appears, offering however not respite from her grief, but rather a poetic intensification of it; he is the angel of despair. Excerpts from his message:

> Drink deeply to sorrow
> To glorious sorrow,
> The truest thing thy heart can know.
> Joy is a seeming
> Love is but a dream,
>
> . . .
>
> Thou as a mortal
> Lovedst a mortal,
> God chose him for thee,
> Gave thee none other.
> He has left thee forever.
> Where wilt thou seek him
> Or one like unto him?
> There is no resurrection for thy love,
> And the blessing of the past is the doom of the future.
>
> . . .
>
> The arms of thy cross
> Reach wherever thou turnest,
> Northward and southward,
> Eastward and westward;
> Thou'rt bound on it, nailed to it,
> Born to it, wedded to it.
> Persuade the wood to tenderness,
> Caress the iron to softness,
> Then only shall fate take pity on thee,
> And the grave give thee back the dead thou mournest. (D3–6)

Next comes the angel of the living world, who tries unsuccessfully to interest Eva in earth's beauties. To the angel's assurances that beauty and love are to be found in other forms, Eva counterposes her conviction that God will somehow restore Rafael and rescue her from her "hell of loneliness." A third spirit follows, who accuses Eva of idolatry and presses her to go forth and do good works; she brushes him off. Finally the angel of consolation arrives with a message from Rafael: in his breast is planted a golden seed that Eva must nurture until it becomes a flowering plant. She must be there to pick the first bloom, for if someone else plucks it, Eva will not join Rafael in heaven.

Already the plant has begun to grow, and Eva consecrates her life to watching its development. A dove watches while she sleeps and brings her honeycombs for sustenance. One day the vigil is disturbed by the sounds of hunters, and soon Eva's dell is discovered by the king's son, who falls reverently in love with her. Though she is scarcely aware of his presence, he listens day after day to her songs of mourning for Rafael, until eventually the king, exasperated at his son's absorption, determines to separate them somehow. He rides to the dell with a troop of men and moves to seize Eva, but at that moment the plant bursts through Rafael's crystal coffin and blooms. Eva touches the blossom and is "transfigured . . . in light" (D21); her lifeless form sinks while she is taken up into heaven. From there, she and Rafael minister to the king's son (who becomes a pilgrim, impressed by the faithfulness of the heavenly pair) and discuss their union.

Rafael explains a scar on his forehead as the visible sign of a deadly sin of which he was once guilty, but he assures Eva that God and the angels now regard him with compassion. She then wonders why it was necessary for her to abandon all other earthly interests in fidelity to Rafael. In explaining, Rafael shows her two emblematic pictures. The first is of a woman

> of a prudent and industrious character who went to many people with her wares. And she bought and sold, and received in return cumbrous coin which was a weight upon her steps, and which would not pass current in heaven. Her face was also careworn and troubled. (D24)

Opposed to this is another woman who sits at the feet of her "master," into whose lap this "noble and beautiful" man pours "wages, which were of pure gold, and of the coinage of heaven." These are in payment for her entire devotion: "her eyes waited upon his look, her ear upon his bidding, her heart upon his love." Rafael remarks: "One love only is possible, and in that I was that love to thee, thou couldst only, in seeking other things, have lost it. Thank God, therefore, that thine eye was *single*" (D25). The narrative ends with a final revelation (that Eva's constancy has been made possible by God's sustaining anchor) and with her understanding that ultimate devotion, therefore, must be to God. At hearing this, Rafael, overjoyed, exclaims, "now, truly, are we wedded and inseparable, for those who are in him are one forever." Their voices blend "in one harmonious strain" and they vanish from sight.

As the reading ends, Laurence and the others are held for a moment in the spell of the work. Then their lamp flickers out and they hear unearthly music from across the hall. Pepino believes it is the spirit of Eva, but Nina is there, as if ready to receive guests, wildly playing her harp and singing Eva's song: "Release thou, the prisoner of hope" (E1–2). When she finishes, she rises, lifts a glass of wine, and exclaims, "Evviva! evviva!" She drinks half of the wine, commands Briseida to preserve the rest for an unnamed someone who will come to finish it, and then—her state of nervous exaltation suddenly ending—collapses in her sister's arms. Laurence goes off to bed dreaming of the ecstatic voice he has heard.

IN THE REMAINING manuscript fragments, Berto returns from his sojourn in Naples; while Laurence has lived as a woman, Berto has lived as a beggar. This reunion scene is truncated, followed by an account of Laurence shedding his female disguise. He and Berto take great delight in burning the confining, deceptive garments in which he has been imprisoned, and Berto delights in revealing to his sisters the ruse he has perpetrated. He asks Nina if Cecilia is a woman, to which Nina responds ambiguously, explaining, "no man can feel as she feels, no woman can reason as she reasons" (F6). This scene ends with Berto telling Laurence that Laurence's brother Philip has been killed in a fall from a horse and that their father now wants Laurence to reattach himself to the family—evidently a remnant from a relatively early moment in the compositional process.

In the last piece, which begins midscene and apparently while Laurence is living with Berto and his sisters, Ronald has sought out his former tutor to obtain a farewell embrace and blessing. Laurence assures the boy of his good will toward him, but Ronald wants more, wants him to return "that holy love which your heart gave me, and of which your will defrauded me" (G1). He describes his wanderings in search of

Laurence and the eventual death of his hopes (although the passion of the telling seems to revivify them, and both are characterized as in a frenzied state). But, Ronald reports, he at length relinquished his passion by assuming the responsibilities that devolved on him as his father's heir; he has become a dutiful, if melancholy, member of the landed gentry. Laurence wonders if they must now part again forever, to which Ronald says (with obvious grief and regret) yes. Shame and agony vie for control of Laurence, and at last he leaps to his friend's side and clasps him:

> One long gaze of tearless anguish, one mute appeal to heaven, and Ronald was gone, and the beautiful monster sat as before on the heap of stones, in the ancient forum, himself as mute and dead as any thing there. (G7)

Laurence (or Laurent, as he is named in this fragment), beset by misery over Ronald, falls ill and is nursed by Berto and Briseida. Berto and a doctor discuss Laurence's nature; Berto says he is "the poetic dream of the ancient sculptor, more beautiful, though less human, than either man or woman" (G9). To Berto it appears that the masculine element dominates:

> [H]e is sometimes poetical and rhapsodical, but he reasons severely and logically, even as a man—he has moreover stern notions of duty which bend and fashion his life, instead of living fashioned by it, as is the case with women. (G10)

To Briseida, however, Laurence is more woman than man:

> The blood of a man does not so rush so instantaneously to his cheek at the bold glance of another—the eye of a man does not flash so quickly and proudly at the slightest breath of aught unworthy or impure—the tears of no man flow as hers before the sublimity of nature, or the unhappiness of man. It is true that she can reason better than most women, yet is she most herself when she feels, when she follows that instinctive, undoubting sense of inner truths which is only given to women and to angels. (G11)

Eventually they determine to understand him/her in Swedenborgian terms, as a superhuman mystery, an "undivided, integral soul, needing not to seek on earth its other moiety" (G12). Meanwhile Laurence, in his delirium, experiences confused visions and toward the end is tormented by a sensation of being fought over by two beings, one male and one female, both of whom claim him as their rightful love object. He feels his bowels torn asunder by his love for both, a pain that finds expression in an image of crucifixion. A voice whose imagery recalls Eva's angel of despair tells him, "a cross is not formed otherwise than of two loves or two desires which cross each other or conflict" (G14). Gradually Laurence slips toward death; the fragment ends with his consciousness that, in the last moments, Ronald returns to be with him.

IN THIS NARRATIVE, saturated with remarkable issues, certainly the most striking is its featuring of a hermaphrodite as protagonist. Although there is a notable tradition of hermaphroditic and androgynous figures in Renaissance and Romantic European literature,[38] it is nonetheless startling to discover one prominently inhabiting a mid-nineteenth-century manuscript by a young married woman in, of all places, Boston, Massachusetts. The phenomenon of the hermaphrodite, to the degree that it was discussed at all in Victorian America, was a medical and legal issue. It is possible, for example, that Howe read about Levi Suydam, a resident of Connecticut who came to the attention of Dr. William James Barry in 1843; his story appeared in an article in the *New York Journal of Medicine* in January 1847 and was reprinted later in the year in the *American Journal of Medical Sciences*. Suydam's gender became an issue during a closely contested election in Salisbury, Connecticut; his vote was valid only if he was male. Two doctors examined him and found that he possessed a penis and one testicle; thus his vote was counted, "and the whig ticket carried by one majority!" Subsequent investigation discovered that he also had "a beardless chin, . . . narrow shoulders, and broad hips," as well as "[w]ell developed mammae, with nipples and areola." It was revealed, too, that "he" had menstruated regularly for many years. His amorous inclinations were for males, and he had a "fondness for gay colors, for pieces of calico, comparing and placing them together, and an aversion for bodily labor."[39] Other similar recherché information from the byways of medical studies may have reached Howe through her husband's professional library.[40]

The greater likelihood, though, is that Laurence's aesthetic progenitors—to the degree that it is useful to trace them—are Ovid and Lamartine. Emma von P.'s reference to the "hermaphrodite of the Villa Borghese" suggests an immediate source for the concept. During her sojourn in Rome, Howe would certainly have visited the Villa's Galleria and its Sala dell' Ermafrodito, featuring a copy of a Greek statue, *The Sleeping Hermaphrodite,* and paintings by Buonvicini illustrating Ovid's story of Hermaphroditus and Salmacis. The sculpture portrays a nude figure stretched full length on a bed, lying facedown, although the left leg and buttock are slightly lifted so that, if the viewer were appropriately positioned, the region of the groin would be visible. (However, the work is placed in the room so that the figure's left side is to the wall, thus preventing precisely the view that the observer presumably most wants.) The swell of the buttocks and the hint of a right breast pressed against the bed, as well as the refined facial features and carefully coiffed hair, suggest a woman; it is only the work's title and context that instruct us otherwise and give rise to the desire to see what is concealed.

Ovid's Hermaphroditus is not originally an amalgam of two sexes; he is the handsome son of Hermes and Aphrodite who, at age fifteen, encounters the naiad Salmacis while he is bathing. She is instantly enamored and makes her desire known, but his shyness and innocence cause him to draw back and beseech her to leave the pool to him. This moment is depicted in the Sala's large ceiling painting. Cupid has let fly an arrow in Salmacis's direction, while behind the manly Hermaphroditus are his parents, amorously involved and indifferent to their son's discomfort; two satyrs watch salaciously from behind bushes. In Ovid's account, Salmacis agrees to relinquish the pool, but hides nearby to watch him bathe (depicted in a smaller oval painting). When he plunges in, she follows and entwines herself around him. He continues to resist, refusing to yield to her, whereupon she asks the gods to merge them into one body. Her plea is granted: Ovid says, "They two were two no more, nor man, nor woman—/ One body then that neither seemed and both." Hermaphroditus asks his parents that any man who thereafter enters the pool will "Emerge half woman, weakened instantly." They concur, "[d]rugg[ing] the bright water with that power impure."[41] Another small oval painting in the Sala depicts Hermaphroditus, now with breasts, watching his parents' departure, Aphrodite looking sadly back over her shoulder at her altered offspring.[42]

Also part of the backdrop to Howe's Laurence drama, surely, is Lamartine's *Jocelyn,* which had been the subject of her earliest published work, her review for the *Literary and Theological Review.* Lamartine's eponymous hero is a young man studying for the priesthood at the time of the French Revolution who is forced, at the outbreak of the Terror, to take refuge in a cave high in the Alps. Two other refugees, father and son, find their way to Jocelyn's hideout, but the father has been wounded and soon dies, leaving his child—a beautiful boy whose name happens to be Laurence—in Jocelyn's care. Love grows between the two, described at first in asexual quasi-Platonic terms as the attraction of soul for its lost other half,[43] but as intimacy grows, Jocelyn's fascination seems increasingly the product of Laurence's physical appeal. He notes the beauty of his forehead, eyes, hair, voice, way of dressing, and so forth and ultimately is forced to ask himself whether such powerful feelings are not somehow tainted:

> I condemn oft in me those sympathies which melt
> Much too sudden in me, much too sensibly felt,
> Those instincts of the first sight, and those first movements,
> Which of my slight impressions soon make sentiments;
> I've said to myself often, perhaps God doth blame
> Those inclinations which may profane the heart's flame,
> But alas! spite of us tow'rds the light our eyes rove,
> Is't a crime O my God! beauty too much to love?[44]

The emotional center of Lamartine's work is the "Fourth Epoque," essentially a collection of rapturous love duets exchanged between Jocelyn and Laurence that continue until one day Laurence injures himself and Jocelyn discovers, in treating him, that Laurence is actually a woman.

Howe's familiarity with Lamartine's cross-dressing, androgynous character is perhaps significant only as indicating a possible source for her own protagonist's name. Yet her review does indirectly address the oddness, the potential indecency, of the relationship between Jocelyn and Laurence. She praises Lamartine for not "guiding us through the diversified regions of fancy to mislead us at last." Lamartine is not Byron, she says; we do not worry that he is

> casting a robe of noble and majestic imagery around that which in itself is base and polluted; nor that his love for the beautiful, his worship of the sublime is but a mask beneath the shelter of which he may scorn and blaspheme the Being whose image is impressed upon all that is beautiful and sublime. Every word carries with it the conviction that it comes from the abundance of a heart purified and refined by the influences of religion.[45]

Yet these "diversified regions of fancy" did evidently remain in her mind as a possible site for the kind of exploration her own narrative is. Lamartine may have chosen not to be Byron, but the twenty-eight-year-old Julia Howe, secretly writing not a "moral and fashionable work" but rather the "history of a strange being . . . as truly as I knew how to write it," felt herself under no obligation to look only obliquely at the homo-erotic subtext of *Jocelyn*. Its real-life analogue had erupted in her own life and had somehow to be objectified, distanced, so as to be understood.

Howe exulted to her sister at the end of January 1847 that for the first time since her marriage she had "*waked up*," escaped the somnambulistic state in which her concerns were limited to digestion, sleep, and babies. "God only knows what I have suffered from this stupor—it has been like blindness, like death, like exile from all things beautiful and good," she wrote, adding that she was ready to suffer, even die, to avoid a relapse into "that brutal state of indifference."[46] This letter includes the passage quoted near the beginning of this chapter, in which she calls childbirth "materializing and degrading to a woman whose spiritual nature has any strength." Though she acknowledged that the causes of her dullness were in part physical, the burdens arising from childbirth and its aftermath, she also wanted Louisa to understand her husband's role in having produced this lethargy:

> It is partly, sweet child, the result of an utter want of sympathy in those around me, which has, like a winter's frost, benumbed my whole nature. Do not chide me, my blessing, for thus faintly explaining to you what has so long been cold and heavy at my heart. You cannot, cannot know the history, the *inner* history of the last four years.

A sense of secrecy or indirection surfaces several times during the spring in Howe's letters to her sisters—a request to Annie that she send back a rolled-up sheaf of papers ("only very safe, & with other things, that no one may see them"); an ebullient acknowledgment of high spirits (to which she adds the hope that God forgive her for following the "strongest instincts" of her nature, but "I have been doing wrong all my life, in some way or other"); a wish that Annie were with her so she could relay anecdotes "over our tapestry, and under the rose"; and most intriguingly, a reference to a "dear beau" who often appeared at the parties Howe attended and whose "beautiful face" she wished she could exhibit to her sister.[47] Despite the fact that she was ill with a light case of scarlet fever in March, the period was full of energy and confidence, seeming to climax in the May 15 letter to Louisa that included the Eva-Rafael poem. She was "thin & languid," she reported, but clearer of mind than since before her marriage: "I am able to think, to study, and to pray, things wh[ich] I cannot accomplish when my brain is oppressed." Ironic remarks about her husband's generosity are interspersed with rueful confessions of what an indifferent wife she is and her consciousness of being "still a pilgrim in pursuit of something that is neither house, nor lands, nor children, nor health." Many things, she says, were becoming clearer to her as she grew older, and she was feeling both the difficulty and the necessity of holding fast to her soul against the world's efforts to strip her of it.

The Laurence manuscript, I believe, became the ground on which this effort to grasp her soul was played out and the repository for the insights the struggle yielded. Chiefly, it became a means for trying to conceptualize her husband's nature, for understanding his indifference to her (and responsiveness to Sumner) as somehow corporeal, a principle of his very constitution rather than the result of shortcomings on her part. It is not coincidental that Emma von P., the vivacious, richly sexual woman who offers herself to Laurence and is rejected, is precisely Julia Howe's age. Discovering the "truth" about Laurence drives Emma into mental instability and early death, a melodramatic but still recognizeable version of the state of mind Howe describes as hers beginning just weeks after her marriage. Howe's circumstances are also reflected in the plight of Eva and Nina, deserted by their lovers but remaining faithful to their commitment, though it means life destitute of pleasure.

A passage embedded in the second long numbered section speaks to the need for disguise in articulating such matters as these. Berto observes that people during the carnival season relish the opportunity to wear masks that, in fact, express the truth—hiding their faces in order to show their hearts. The man in the mask is "far less disguised than the man one meets every day face to face." Laurence sees this truth in "a wider and a sadder sense":

> So intolerant, so incomprehensive is society become, that fervent hearts must borrow the disguise of art, if they would win the right to express, in any outward form, the internal fire that consumes them. There is scarcely one great passion of the soul which would not, if revealed, offend the narrow sense and breeding of the respectable world, and the few who are

capable of these powerful emotions, and who *must* express them, must speak as with the voices of others. (B99–100)

Howe's version of Dickinson's "Tell all the Truth, but tell it Slant," this principle is at work everywhere in the Laurence materials. But not there only, in this work probably never intended for publication: It is also the chief aesthetic premise driving the work she eventually *did* determine to publish, as close reading of the *Passion-Flowers* poems illustrates. I return to this issue in chapter 5.

Read as encoded autobiography, Howe's treatment of Laurence might be considered remarkably empathetic. Where Emma sees him as monstrous, a reader sees instead the torment Laurence lives with and his readiness to sacrifice his own prospect of happiness in order not to inflict his blasted self on another person. Yet following the debacle with Emma, as Laurence is committing himself to a life of asceticism and spirituality in the count's hermitage, a poem called "Like and Unlike" appears. It seems to be intended as Laurence's reflections on his blighted relationship with Emma:

LIKE AND UNLIKE

I am to thee as one that's dead,
And thou art as the dead to me;
Yet twixt thy sometime love and mine
Methinks, strange difference must there be.

For thine is dust to dust returned,
Corruption, buried out of sight;
A *mortal* feeling, born to die,
And dead, to be forgotten quite.

But mine's the disembodied soul
To heav'n, that gave it life, returned;
It gleams for me a star on high,
That once, on earth, a torch light burned.

And in my bosom garnered up,
Its gentle ashes gently rest,
While its pure essence dwells with God,
And waits for death to make me blest. (A66)

If he is the speaker and Emma is the person addressed, his suggestion is that the sort of love she offered him—passionate, physical—is of an inferior sort, easily forgotten. His, on the other hand—abstract, essential, eternal—will be his eventual salvation. Since Emma is literally dead from grief (not just "*as* the dead") over her discovery that Laurence could never love her as she wished to be loved, the poem, while it might ease Laurence's pain, may strike us as somewhat callous, a self-justifying appropriation of heavenliness as a wrap for his tepid response to Emma. Was this how Samuel Howe led his wife to think about his indifference toward her? Was this her way of understanding the husband whose distaste for kissing was a frequently repeated joke between them?[48]

The character of Ronald, and Laurence's ambivalent response to him, became another means by which Howe understood the "inner history" of her marriage. The younger man, whose beautiful face draws Laurence back from the abyss of a religious trance, replaces Emma in his emotional life; she vanishes from the narrative. Although at first Ronald believes that Laurence is a woman (because his hair has grown long), Laurence, through several gestures, firmly validates his maleness; Howe seems to want it unambiguously established that the affection that grows on both sides is between two men. Ronald's adoration of Laurence is clear from his first appearance, but Laurence's reciprocal emotion is presented as something of which he is imperfectly conscious or inclined to deny to himself. Although he calls Ronald "my pretty young Baron" (A97), and although he cannot decide whether it is the setting sun or "a pair of starry eyes" that warms his soul, Laurence professes to be uneasy when Ronald wants to kiss him or to declare his love. The seeds Laurence says he never intended to sow, the impulses with which he says he cannot sympathize, seem to have a home in his breast as well as in Ronald's.

To posit similarities between the Ronald/Laurence and Sumner/ Samuel Howe relationships may seem overstatement, and a crude one at that, given the equivocal quality of the "evidence." It may even strike some as perverse, in light of the fact that Julia Howe's husband (unlike the Whitman self-described in his infamous letter to John Addington Symonds) *did* indeed father six children. Yet the eroticism in the attachment between Laurence and Ronald seems somehow a function of Julia's feeling that Sumner ought to have been a woman, and Chev to have married "her."[49] Laurence's efforts to deflect Ronald's advances, both verbal and physical, bear analogy to Chev's frenetic exertions toward getting Sumner to abandon his single state (to "forswear what you are," to "bring your affections to the right focus"). Likewise, Laurence's illness after the loss of his beautiful boy plausibly reflects Howe's reading of her husband's physical and emotional state during the time when married life in Boston (represented, perhaps, as the experience of living in women's clothes?) became his permanent reality. But the credibility of particularized associations is insignificant, really, when the central phenomenon of the manuscript, its ambiguously gendered protagonist, seems so patently an embodiment of the "beautiful monster" Howe discovered she had married.[50]

If the Laurence manuscript fully names the grief Howe faced, it also proposes an accommodation to it. As Berto prepares to lose his own aristocratic identity for a month by masquerading as a Neapolitan beggar, so he contrives for Laurence to submerge his masculine nature by passing as a woman. The two reasons given for this plan are, first, that men can learn much by seeing through women's eyes, and second, that Laurence needs to disappear for awhile in order to elude his father. But neither issue really arises again (Laurence, after all, presumably already sees partly through women's eyes), and so the explanations eventually seem like a novelistic device to get Laurence plausibly into the company of Berto's sisters, three women with pronounced ideas about marriage. In this section Laurence is an oddly marginalized character: the many rich possibilities for exploring divergences between male and female perceptions are set aside in favor of foregrounding the sisters' differing provisions for the men in their lives.

Women, says Laurence as he dons female clothes, are "the adored of all, but trusted of none, . . . the golden treasures, too easily lost or stolen, and therefore to be kept under lock and key"; they "cannot stay at home without surveillance" and also "cannot walk about without being interrogated at every turn by the sentinel of public opinion" (B116). Beings so delimited relish the chance to reverse the metamorphosis he is now undertaking and, George Sand–like,[51] to throw off chains along with petticoats and move freely in the world. Laurence lists the keen pleasures women (disguised as men) discover, from being privy to gaming-table talk to delight in the exercise of rights not usually theirs to philosophical satisfaction in discussions free of the "dangerous attraction and repulsion of sex" (B117). And yet, he says, though this "masculine mania" may last long and take her far, it will not last forever:

However strong, or depraved, or metaphysical the emancipated woman may be, she will in the end feel the want of some one to bully and protect her, the necessity of being cherished and admired, or kicked and cuffed. And so some day she will ignominiously strike her flag of defiance, and creep back to her woman's trappings, and to her woman's life as best she may, happy after all her wanderings if she can [find] some kind brute to play the Beast to her Beauty, some one who though he may outrage her best feelings, laugh at her convictions, and offend her taste, will yet praise her eyebrows, and pay her bills. (B117–18)

We can dismiss these as the words of the sardonic male (although it is far out of character for Laurence to be the utterer), yet the general observation foreshadows the ideological drift of this part of the narrative. It also intimates the resolution Howe took in determining, repeatedly, not to cut herself loose from what often seemed an intolerable situation.

Briseida is a writer, her gentleman friend Pepino is many years younger, and their relationship is partly that of mentor-student. He is gentle, sensitive, eager to please, but also passive, willing to let things he loves slip through his fingers—"a creature of sentiment and affection, not of will and passion" (B154). Briseida loves him and fears his foreordained departure to marry the Polish countess, but nevertheless speaks clear-sightedly about the distinctions between love and marriage. Hers is in some sense a cynical view: marriage is "completely an affair of reciprocal interests and convenience" (B158). However, she has chosen not to take a husband on such terms; she will not marry just to give herself liberty to betray her husband.

Gigia, the middle sister, is less well developed as a character; Laurence says she interests him less because the attention her paintings have received has made her calculating. Her romantic attachment, the Count Flavio, is a man of the world who has known many women but who finds himself a bit out of his league with Gigia. Their relationship is "a continued effort on the part of each to sound the depth of the other's coquetry" (B165), but with different objectives: Flavio is out for seduction, Gigia (having ascertained that he is rich) for marriage. Worldly security is her entire goal.

Nina represents Laurence's ideal; he believes her not just clairvoyant, but Orphic. Berto describes her as less clever but more womanly than her sisters and truly in love with Gaetano. When he was banished, Nina had implored her brother to allow her to marry Gaetano so as to be able to share his exile. Her plea denied, in his absence she has devoted herself entirely to him, so much so that most of those around her regard her as mad. In interviews with Laurence, however, she speaks what he feels is the wisdom of heaven. She is, in fact, indistinguishable from Eva in the manuscript to which she responds so powerfully, and the vatic quality of that text underscores and extends the significance of her fidelity.

Nina and Eva, in their loneliness and devotion, reflect Julia Howe's state four years into her marriage. Although Briseida and Gigia pose alternative attitudes toward an alliance with men (a stoic acknowledgment of the cultural barriers to romantic fulfillment, an exploitative cynicism), neither attitude is remotely imaginable in a being like Nina or Eva—or Howe at this point, although versions of the stances of both other sisters sometimes surface in her letters. The song sung to Eva by the angel of despair no doubt echoed in Howe's ears often during these years—"Drink deeply to sorrow . . . love is but a dream . . . the blessing of the past is the doom of the future," and so on. The Nina-Eva story may signify her determination to master this angel, to conceive a myth in which constancy is ultimately rewarded, and then, through an act of will, to live it against temptations spiritual and physical.

The two tableaux Eva witnesses in heaven (forerunners of Elizabeth Stuart Phelps's opposed principles in "The Angel Over the Right Shoulder") graphically distinguish between two types of wives and leave no doubt which is preferable in God's (and Rafael's) eyes. Eva is saved because she has given her full emotional self to Rafael, distracted neither by another suitor nor by any inclination toward self-fulfillment. The Eva tale is of course only a myth, a musty manuscript of Germanic mysticism, but its impact on Nina suggests the power such fictions possess for the attentive. Nina's spiritual beauty derives from her resolution to embody Eva's loyalty.[52]

It was Howe's resolution as well. Signs of renewed determination to commit herself to her husband's interests reflect her embrace of the Eva principle in her own life.[53] And in a letter to Louisa the following year, she plainly articulated the ethos that was guiding her behavior. Annie, she reported, after two years of marriage to Adolph Mailliard was, "like all of us," having to sacrifice many illusions. Like her sisters, she had dreamed of a "perfect union of minds" but was gradually learning to fall back upon her own resources and to understand that "the soul has but two possessions, itself & God." More to the point, though, was Howe's response to the recent behavior of a former servant, Clampit. Now in touch with Louisa and evidently unhappy in her marriage, Clampit had expressed her discontent and suggested that, in doing so, she was only emulating her former employer. Howe was shocked. Such a state of rebellion she found wicked, and she was horrified to hear of Clampit's indiscretion in speaking of it. "I do not see," she wrote,

> why one should pretend to be excessively happy when one is not, or why one should try to say to oneself "I love this man," when love is a matter out of the question. But marriage is not an affair simply of happiness, it does not promise us a boundless gratification of any taste or feeling. It is a contract into which people, for the most part, enter voluntarily, knowing that it has certain advantages, and certain disadvantages—it is a relation in which we assume grave obligations to other people, & it is quite as important that we should make them happy as that we should be happy ourselves.

Acknowledging her gratitude for Chev's "many kindnesses" and for "much that embellishes and elevates" her life, she described herself as satisfied that he assumed a certain supremacy and dignity as his husbandly right—"as much for my own sake as for his." She distinguished herself sharply from Clampit:

> I cannot pretend to say that I am perfectly happy, or that there are not vast and painful longings of my soul which, in this life, will never be satisfied, but I am to live forever, and I shall be more likely to attain happiness hereafter, by cultivating in this life, a spirit of humility, of gratitude, and the love of *uses*. . . . Clampit may very honestly believe that I think differently, for she knew me best in the days of a very painful crisis—I was, at one time, bitterly & dreadfully unhappy, but I hope not perversely so. I still bear in my heart the traces of much suffering, but there was good in it for me, and there shall be good for others.[54]

This life is an affair of *duties,* she emphasized; knowledge and love are the promises of another world. If this rhetoric is somewhat less exalted than that she gave Eva and Nina, the position is very near theirs. The writing of the Laurence manuscript enabled her, perhaps, to reach this solid ground. It was where she stood until—she could not stand there any longer.[55]

FOUR

"Between Extremes
Distraught and Rent"

The Second Trip to Rome and
the Seeds of *Passion-Flowers*

THE SECRECY that surrounded the composition of the Laurence manuscript makes it difficult to place in appropriate relation to it other indications of Howe's late-1840s states of mind. We can guess when it was begun; we cannot know exactly when she stopped working on it, or at what point particular sections were written. A November 1848 letter to Annie looks ahead to Annie's visit the following January with the hope that Julia will have "finished the wretched book" and so will have time to enjoy her sister's company.[1] This may be the Laurence manuscript, but the letter includes no specifics. If she did in fact write steadily beginning in spring 1847, the labor no doubt provided respite from a whole battery of difficulties that seemed to accumulate for a frontal assault in the fall of that year. We look here at the increasing complexity of family life and Howe's gathering frustration—heightened rather than alleviated when she began to receive attention as a poet—at the claustrophobic conditions within which she was determined to nurture her literary and intellectual interests.

The Ward siblings received word in September 1847 that brother Marion had died in New Orleans. The loss was grievous in personal terms, but it had financial repercussions as well. Marion had worked for several years as an agent for Prime and Ward, the family banking business, and had been a mainstay of support for Sam Ward. His death coincided with a series of severe reversals in the business (overinvestment in flour speculations and the failure of banks in England to which

Prime and Ward were tied). So extensive was the loss that the company was forced to declare insolvency, able to pay only thirty cents on the dollar to its investors. Sam was blamed for the failures and widely denounced, by his partner-uncle among others. Nor was his domestic life any solace: his second wife, Medora, dismayed at the prospect of poverty, left him and returned to her mother's home. Howe shared her brother's pain at these developments, the more so because Sam—determined not to bring his sister, too, to financial ruin—resigned his trusteeship of her New York holdings. Thus, control of Howe's extensive Manhattan properties fell to her husband, who, with unsettling shortsightedness, immediately sold them in order to invest in Boston real estate.

On top of these griefs, Howe learned in September that she was again pregnant, due early in March. A September letter to Louisa indicates that she had hoped to travel to Rome that winter; the pregnancy, of course, destroyed that plan. But worse, at least initially, was simply the thought of another child. "I cried & raved about it," she confessed, adding that if the baby was female her name would be Dolores, so sad had the pregnancy made her thus far. Later in the fall she reported another twist of the knife: in Chev's opinion, this third child involved the necessity of a fourth, for otherwise it would have no playmate close to its age. Howe was oppressed by memories of the difficulties she had had when Florence was a baby and Julia Romana not yet standing alone. A move into Boston proper for the winter and a long visit in December/January from Annie, though these cheered her somewhat, could not really offset the "stagnation of intellect" she felt overtaking her.[2]

Yet in January, writing to Louisa in a reflective mood just after Annie's departure, Howe acknowledged that the visit had warmed her heart and had "broken in upon a sort of web of melancholy thoughts, which the last year has gathered somewhat too closely around me." Despite its gloom, 1847 had been a year of great importance, for it had thrown her back on "those more earnest conceptions of good which alone can steady our course when the winds and waves have too rudely beaten us."[3] This sentiment may refer to the pieties of the Eva-Rafael story and her resolution to adapt herself to her husband's expectations (including, perhaps, a willingness to continue to enlarge the family). A year or so before, she had written to him from Annie's house that although marriage and its attendant renunciations had made her a new creature—a better and happier one, she thought—she had felt no appreciation from him for her sacrifices. She had therefore concluded that maintaining her mental stability meant keeping a certain emotional distance from him:

> I will not expect too much from you. I will enjoy all the moments of sunshine which we can enjoy together. I will treasure up every word, every look of your's that is kind and genial, to comfort me in those long, cold, wintry days, when I feel that you do not love me.[4]

Now, even facing childbirth and its intrusive aftermath (nursing, sleepless nights, wet sheets), her resolve seems wound up again. And indeed, when she next wrote Louisa in April to describe her accouchement, her spirits were high. The birth itself had been relatively easy,[5] and Harry was so far such a placid baby that his parents called him "the little saint." Chev was elated that the child was a boy, and Julia was determined to pursue her "studies," knowing that she was good for nothing without them: "I will rather give up the world, and cut Beacon St, but an hour or two for the cultivation of my poor little soul, I must & will have."[6]

Across the Atlantic, meanwhile, events were in motion that would, within the next few years, come to absorb Howe's profound attention. Soon after the election in July 1846 of Pope Pius IX, she had expressed delight to Louisa and had asked to be kept informed of his work. "God protect his precious life, for the salvation of Italy," she wrote; "he is one of the brightest spots, in this century."[7] His first act had been to proclaim amnesty for nearly a thousand political prisoners, thereby providing fuel that drove revolution. Liberal Americans like the Howes felt the excitement, seeing "Pio Nono" as the means by which the various small states of Italy might free themselves of foreign rule and influence.[8] The general excitement lasted about a year and a half. As late as December 1847, Margaret Fuller, writing letters to the *New York Tribune* from Rome, could still praise the pope's wisdom, bravery, firmness, and especially his "generous human heart."[9] But less than a month later she had seen clear signs that when his priestly functions collided with his interest in reform, it was the priest who emerged victorious. In late April 1848 Pio Nono backed away from his support for those in northern Italy trying to repulse the invading (Catholic) Austrians. His appointment later in the year of the aristocrat Count Pellegrino Rossi as his minister further signaled his failure of nerve as a spearhead of reform, and when Rossi was assassinated in November, the pope ignominiously fled to

Gaeta, leaving Rome without its spiritual figurehead. The Roman Republic was proclaimed in February 1849, but by April Rome was under attack from French forces summoned by the pope.

Although there is little explicit reference to European politics in Howe's letters from this period, she followed the situation closely. *Reminiscences* preserves her early exhilaration at the thought of a pope—"for centuries the representative and upholder of absolute rule"—embodying instead the Christian spirit that "liberalizes both institutions and ideas" (193), and she notes that her husband, recording in the family Bible Henry's birth in the "terrible and splendid year of 1848," added "*Liberté, Egalité, Fraternité*" in recognition of the general ascendancy all over Europe of the party of progress. In contemplation of the approaching doom of the "tyrannies of the earth," at least, the Howes were united. Her husband, she notes, had fought for Greek freedom and had suffered imprisonment on behalf of Poland; now, with him, she could believe the "final emancipation and unification of the human race" (194) near at hand.

As the tide turned against the revolutionary cause, Howe, like Fuller,[10] was infuriated by American indifference to those who had risked everything defending principles that America, above all other nations, represented. One of the most powerful poems in *Passion-Flowers*, "From Newport to Rome," voices the rage she felt living among people impervious to others' suffering. The poem portrays a speaker growing to womanhood among the wealthy—"decorous, dutiful, and cold" externally, but fiery within:

> Constrained to learn of you the arts
> Which half dishonor, half deceive,
> I've felt my burning soul flash out
> Against the silken web you weave.
>
> No earnest feeling passes you
> Without dilution infinite;
> No word with frank abruptness breathed,
> Must vent itself on ears polite.

Amid the brilliant but mind-numbing atmosphere of sensual and aesthetic pleasure, she feels herself the only person responsive to the "wailing of the world," the "brother's cry that swept, / Unweakened, o'er the Atlantic wave." Do you not hear it? she asks, but the crowd stares "as at a madman": no, they say, "'We hear the sweetest waltz . . . And not a string is out of tune." The speaker then leaps to the conductor's podium and inveighs:

> "I've sat among you long enough,
>   Or followed where your music led,
>   I never marred your pleasure yet,
>   But ye shall listen now," I said.

The passionate diatribe that follows luridly pictures scenes of battle, brave republicans, the fall of a great city, Death hunting his quarry through the streets, prisoners separated from families—and finally an Italian flag hanging in the Invalides in Paris, with the caption "'Ta'en from a Roman whom we slew, / Keeping the threshold of his home.'" How, she wonders, with knowledge of such horrors, can her astonished listeners "delight in idle tunes" when "ev'n the holy Marseillaise / Sounds for the treachery of France?" But her ardor fails to move them; they want to waltz. In a final appeal directed specifically to women, she reminds them of their responsibility to awaken men's consciences:

> "With fuller light, let women's eyes
>   Earnest, beneath the Christ-like brow,
>   Strike this deep question home to men,
>   'Thy brothers perish—idlest thou?'
>
> With warmer breath let mother's lips
>   Whisper the boy whom they caress,—
>   'Learn from those arms that circle thee
>   In love, to succor, shelter, bless.'
>
> For the brave world is given to us
>   For all the brave in heart to keep,
>   Lest wicked hands should sow the thorns
>   That bleeding generations reap."[11]

The poem memorializes Howe's early emotional involvement in the issues, but it is important to note that the speaker's act—the leap to the podium to harangue her companions—does not signify a commitment to public action on her part.[12] Respectable women did not speak in public in 1840s Boston, and women who did were vehemently attacked. A decade before, outraged at antislavery speeches by Abby Kelley, Angelina Grimke, and Lucretia Mott, the Congregational ministers of Massachusetts had issued a "Pastoral Letter" condemning the participation of women in public forums debating political reform. The letter echoes the Puritan theocracy's response more than two centuries earlier to Anne Hutchinson. The appropriate duties and influence of women, they asserted, are stated in the New Testament; they are "unobtrusive and private." When woman "assumes the place and tone of man as a public reformer . . . she yields the power which God has given her for her protection, and her character becomes unnatural." To do so is to destroy "that modesty and delicacy which is the charm of domestic life, and which constitutes the true influence of women in society"; it opens the way for "degeneracy and ruin."[13] Although abolitionist women did continue to address mixed audiences, the ministers' sentiments were shared by virtually everyone in Boston society, including many women interested in matters of reform. Indeed, so strongly internalized was the sanction against public speaking that the women who organized the first women's rights convention in Seneca Falls, New York, in 1848 found themselves temperamentally unable to assume the responsibility of leading discussion on the convention's opening day.[14] It would be more than a dozen years before Howe would muster the courage to speak publicly in any way.[15]

But if 1848 was not yet the hour for the birth of her public-reformer persona, the year did mark the fulfillment, of sorts, of a long-held dream. Thomas Buchanan Read, a Philadelphia publisher, wrote to request her work for inclusion in an anthology of women poets he was preparing. Meanwhile, Rufus Griswold had also decided to include her in the second edition of his *Female Poets of America*. Between these two volumes, Howe was represented by a total of nine poems, seven in the Griswold book and two in Read's anthology. Considered in the context of the powerful poems in her diaries, these are weak, relying on hackneyed images and conventionally "poetic" diction and sentiments. Her work apparently came to Griswold's attention through an elegy she wrote in her teens for her music teacher, Daniel Schlesinger; this piece had been published in several newspapers at the time of Schlesinger's death and had attracted some notice.[16] In addition to this youthful work, Griswold's sampling included a paean to Wordsworth, a poem about the moon's cycles, "To a Beautiful Statue," "Speak, for Thy Servant Heareth," "A Mother's Fears," "Lees from the Cup of Life" (which had also been published in a Putnam gift book called *Lays of the Western World*), and "Woman." The last is perhaps the most interesting: its speaker describes in reverential terms and at some length the mid-nineteenth century's womanly paragon ("A vestal priestess, proudly pure, / But of a meek and quiet spirit," etc.), but in the last stanza confesses her failure to embody the ideal:

> This is the woman I have dreamed,
> And to my childish thought she seemed
> The woman I myself should be:
> Alas! I would that I were she.

The two poems published in Read's collection were "What I Said to the Dying Rose, and What It Said to Me" and "Mortal and Immortal." Howe included both near the end of *Passion-Flowers,* though neither is as strong as many of the volume's other poems. Although these two anthologies in effect conferred public recognition of her literary ambitions, a letter to Annie from this period suggests that Howe regarded them lightly. Meeting Read's request she described as a process of "hunt[ing] up some trash for him in the course of the week," and she expressed regret that she hadn't sent better work for Griswold's book.[17] The attention was no doubt welcome and must have served to confirm her sense of her talent—but it was not yet a book of her own. Too, the advertisement of her connection to the Griswold project caused tension between her and Chev.

It may have been the threat of this new semipublic status, or it may have resulted from anxieties or differences of opinion on other matters, but whatever the case, by October 1848 Howe was convinced that her husband hated her. To Annie she wrote:

> I only feel as if my death were the one thing desirable for his comfort, but live I must, and I can unhappily be nothing but my poor half crazy self. Don[']t let this make you sad; it does not me. I am quite jolly as usual, but I should like to know how it feels to be something better than an object of disgust to one's husband.[18]

The passage suggests her mode of accommodation—simply to define for herself the terms of her life and to get on as well as possible. Having both Julia Romana and Florence in school part of each day provided some relief. Annie visited for six weeks in January and February 1849, and Julia returned the visit in April. She began again to attend parties, something she had not done for two years. She bade farewell to brother Sam, who

had decided to join the gold-seekers in California; she attended Theodore Parker's Sunday services; she read novels, including *Vanity Fair.*
She spent a great deal of time alone—"pretty much every hour in the
day, & every day in the week," she wrote to Louisa.[19] And she looked
forward to a reunion with Louisa and her family, who, with most other
Americans by mid-1849, had decided to decamp from Rome until its
political future was settled.

    Yet the long-awaited visit was not to prove the leaven and diversion
Howe had hoped for. By late summer she was again pregnant and so
languid that she professed not to be able to sit for five minutes without
falling asleep. As the fall dragged on, life seemed increasingly color-
less. Better days might be coming, she wrote Annie, or worse ones may
have been,

> but it seems to me that I was never before so dull, so lethargic, so devoid
> of interest to myself and to others. As to poor Louisa she cannot but be
> wretched with me—nothing occurs to break the monotony of her visit.
> Were she less a wife and mother than she is, these days would be insuffer-
> able to her.

Chev had little to do with the houseguests, retreating to his library when
he was at home, obliging Julia to shuttle between him and the Crawfords—although she felt she had nothing but tediousness to bestow on
anyone. Julia and Louisa quarreled over Julia's housekeeping and other
matters. Julia portrayed herself to Annie as "too, too sick at heart" to do
more than vegetate: "The pressure of endless discontent which weighs
upon me from without is enough to break a stronger spirit than mine."
By December nothing had improved, and she finally resolved just to
endure, "intent mainly upon holding on to the ropes, and upon getting
through the present without too much consciousness of it." Although
she assured Annie that Chev was "better" than when Annie had last seen
him, and declared her earnest affection for him, she also reported her
brother-in-law's perception that she was afraid of him—"and so I am,
inter nos."[20]

    At some point during the winter or early spring, it was resolved that
the Howes would return to Europe in 1850. It is perhaps a measure of the
extremity of their situation that they would make such a decision. Margaret Fuller's last letter to the *Tribune,* published in mid-February,
painted a dispiriting picture of conditions in Italy. Writing from Flor-

ence, she reported that in Rome, "many want both bread, and any kind of shelter this winter, an extremity of physical deprivation that had seemed almost impossible in this richest land." Politically, things were even worse: "At this moment all the worst men are in power, and the best betrayed and exiled. All the falsities, the abuses of the old political forms, the old social compact, seem confirmed."[21] Yet just over a month after their fourth child, Laura, was born at the end of February, the Howes set out for Annie's estate in Bordentown with the prospect of continuing from there to the Continent. Louisa, who had left South Boston in early January, was now with Annie, and while Chev continued on to Washington, D.C., the three sisters planned a return to Rome. In the turmoil following the French occupation, the Crawfords had acquired an old palace, the Villa Negroni; this spacious residence could easily house all three families. Chev was much less enthusiastic about the plan, partly because it necessitated leaving behind the two older girls. But his own recent poor health and the urging of Longfellow and Sumner at length persuaded him to undertake an abbreviated version of the trip: he would accompany his wife and the younger children until September and then return alone. The truncated family embarked for Liverpool on 12 June, Julia determined to exhibit her gratitude by devoting herself "much" to her husband in the hope that she could help him "forget himself a little."[22]

In March 1850 the Howes' political circle had been buzzing with fury at Daniel Webster's compromise position on the Wilmot Proviso, but within a month the talk was of another issue altogether. Longfellow recorded in his diary for 4 April that the evening papers contained news of divorce proceedings brought by the celebrated actor Edwin Forrest against his wife of twelve years. "Either there is Perjury or Wantonness," wrote Longfellow, "and so a new excitement comes to the public mind, to take the place of the Webster one." Forrest had walked in on his wife enjoying the caresses of another gentleman, and his suspicions were shortly thereafter verified by his discovery of an incriminating letter. Numerous efforts to reconcile the couple had failed, and now Forrest had moved to free himself. It would be more than eighteen months before the trial actually began, but meanwhile the press kept an eager public supplied with gossip.[23]

The specter of this public scandal surely accompanied the Howes as they contemplated their own temporary separation, but as the summer unfolded, life was amicable. The voyage, several weeks spent in England and at Boppard on the Rhine (where Chev took the water cure), the reunion with old friends along the way—these sustained Julia. A letter to Sumner in early September presents them both as relaxed and happy. The parting of the ways, which took place in Heidelberg later in the month, brought on a "*crise des nerfs*" for Chev, who felt himself now alone in the world. He wrote to Sumner, "I long much to see you & be with you. I hope (selfishly) you'll not be engaged this coming winter."[24]

Julia Howe's response to the separation was somewhat less somber:

> After the privations entailed by maternity, the weakness and physical discomfort, the inevitable seclusion . . . I found myself free and untrammeled. . . . I was absolutely intoxicated with the joy of freedom and used to dance across the great salon in my sister's apartment, singing 'Liberty, Liberty!'[25]

Although the plan had been to stay with Louisa at Villa Negroni, Howe immediately rented an apartment in Via Capo le Case—close by, but sufficiently distant to afford a sense of independent life. In the apartment above were Edward and Augusta Freeman, he an artist, she a friendly neighbor who became Howe's companion and guide for walks around Rome. With the assistance of a rabbi from the ghetto along the Tiber, Howe resumed her study of Hebrew.

Reminiscences recounts some of the events of this year of freedom, which lasted until early June 1851. She spent time in study, in caring for her children, in usual social diversions such as balls, operas, drives in the Campagna (sharing all these, she notes, with her sisters). She attended Sunday services regularly with Annie at Ara Coeli and witnessed Christmas observances at Santa Maria Maggiore and St. Peter's. She appreciated the company of Sarah and William Clarke, Margaret Fuller's companions on her excursion to the Great Lakes in 1843, now grieved (as was Howe) by the deaths of Fuller and her family the previous July.[26]

Although signs of the harrowing political upheaval of the year before (including the physical devastation it caused) were to be found if one looked, mostly she saw no trace of them in Roman social life. The pope's failure to adhere to his liberal policies was discussed only in circumstances of extreme privacy. Virtually no one in Italian society publicly professed sympathy with the republicans. In English and American circles Howe occasionally felt called on to defend Italy's right to freedom and self-government, but she met with little sympathy, and indeed was herself, as she said, "too much disconcerted by the recent failure to find in my thoughts any promise of better things" (196).

It seems, however, that there was a story beneath the one included in *Reminiscences*. Allusions to it are few, and, as with other private passages in Howe's life, a biographer's instinct is to tread cautiously, to try not to make the imprudent, impudent leap from suggestion to assertion. What we know most clearly is that something happened in Rome that caused an estrangement between Julia and Louisa; Louisa did not write to her for nearly a year after Julia's return to Boston. We know also that at the time of his death Chev asked Julia to burn all the letters she and he had exchanged during her sojourn in Rome, and also his letters to Sumner from this period. This she did, reluctantly, despite the "pain" many passages caused her.[27] Most tellingly, we know that on 29 April 1851 Annie wrote to Chev to beg him not to insist on Julia's staying away from him and her two older children indefinitely.

The phrases of Annie's letter are careful. She was evidently striving to be ameliorative without precisely acknowledging any obloquy:

> Julia is only anxious to do your bidding and I am sure that a little word from you, added to our entreaties, would bring pleasure to you both, dear Chevie—She is living very quietly with Donald [the nursemaid], in some small apartments near us, and has devoted the winter to her children and her studies—But we all feel that it would be difficult for her to face another one so entirely alone and unprotected. . . . Once on the other side of the ocean, I have at least a home to offer her, should you still wish to prolong her absence—But here she must stand alone, and unprotected; save by her own virtue and dignity. Indeed I cannot tell you, dear Chevie, how much it would grieve me to leave her in such a position. I do not write at her request nor shall I even tell her that I have done so— But I know that you will understand the motive which prompts me to trouble you—

Similarly, when Julia wrote to Louisa the following fall to try to rebuild the bridge, there is a vagueness in her references to whatever caused it to collapse in the first place. Professing readiness to own her "faults of temper, want of consideration, etc.," Julia noted too that Louisa may not have made sufficient allowance for her "eccentric habits of life" during that year. Try to remember, she urged Louisa,

how much there had been to unsettle my mind, how utterly I seemed to
have been cast adrift, and given up to the caprices of fate. I felt sometimes
the pleasure of a naughty child in being bad. I had been much tormented. I liked perhaps to torment others.

And the following summer, after Louisa had finally again written, Julia
in response offered another version of this apology: "I was . . . very full
of my own gratification in divers ways." She gratefully remembered
Rome's having "unfolded its maternal arms" to take her in during that
period of "extremest misery."[28]

What happened? Annie's letter suggests it was a crisis sufficiently
serious to cause consideration of an indefinite separation. This prospect
would surely have thrown Julia Howe into a state of despair, even if
she had somehow precipitated it. To be put aside by her husband—
particularly under these circumstances, severed from two of her children
by an ocean's width—would have subjected her to social censure and
nearly insupportable humiliation. Perhaps the crisis simply *was* the possibility of separation. Yet whether it was the precipitating cause or the
resultant effect, *Reminiscences* and her letters offer hints of an intimacy
with another man during her Roman sojourn.

The man was Horace Binney Wallace. Two years older than Julia, he
had graduated from Princeton in 1835 and, after struggling for a while as
a medical student, had joined his father's law firm. Outside this official
life, however, he was a writer. Two novels, *Stanley* and *Henry Pulteney*,
had appeared pseudonymously in 1838, and through the 1840s he had
published numerous articles, reviews, and short tales. Rufus Griswold
had promoted his work by including it in *Prose Writers of America*
(1847). Ungainly and shy, he initially struck people as cold, yet those
who knew him found beneath his reserve a frank, cordial, ardent person.
Emily Chubbuck, whom he had romanced briefly in 1845, praised
his intellectual look, sweet expression, and especially his conversation
("more improving and interesting . . . than any man's I ever met").
Wallace had come to Europe to study art, and he found in Julia an
agreeable, unencumbered associate.[29]

In *Reminiscences* Howe reports meeting him on Christmas at an
evening dance given by Louisa—or, to be precise, remeeting him, since
their paths had crossed once before in Philadelphia, his usual residence.
At that first encounter she had been put off by his uninformed derision

of Boston society. This time, the two struck fire: it was "the beginning of a much-valued friendship" (198). They visited Rome's monuments together and discussed subjects as diverse as Auguste Comte (of whom Wallace was a disciple) and the characteristics of red-haired people. The two shared this physical phenomenon, and they took delight in elaborating a theory that the highest effort of nature is to produce a *rosso*. Most important, as almost no other man had in a sustained way, he took her seriously as a writer. Her account in *Reminiscences* of their friendship closes with a brief description of Wallace's suicide "some years after this time" (in fact, it was not quite two)—the result, she says, of visiting a friend "whose mental powers had been impaired by severe illness" and beginning to fear that he might suffer a similar disaster. He thus "made haste to avoid the dreaded fate by taking his own life" (200). Howe included an abbreviated version of a poem she wrote (reproduced here as it appears in *Reminiscences,* but see note 30) bearing witness to her "tender and grateful remembrance" of him:

Via Felice

'T was in the Via Felice
　　My friend his dwelling made,
The Roman Via Felice,
　　Half sunshine, half in shade.

But I lodged near the convent
　　Whose bells did hallow noon,
And all the lesser hours,
　　With sweet recurrent tune.

They lent their solemn cadence
　　To all the thoughtless day;
The heart, so oft it heard them,
　　Was lifted up to pray.

And where the lamp was lighted
　　At twilight on the wall,
Serenely sat Madonna,
　　And smiled to bless us all.

I see him from the window
　　That ne'er my heart forgets;
He buys from yonder maiden
　　My morning violets.

Not ill he chose these flowers
  With mild reproving eyes,
Emblems of tender chiding,
  And love divinely wise.

For his were generous learning
  And reconciling art;
Oh, not with fleeting presence
  My friend and I could part.

Oh, not where he is lying
  With dear ancestral dust,
Not where his household traces
  Grow sad and dim with rust;

But in the ancient city
  And from the quaint old door,
I'm watching, at my window,
  His coming evermore.

For Death's eternal city
  Has yet some happy street;
'T is in the Via Felice
  My friend and I shall meet.[30]

Their actual time together in Rome cannot have been extensive. They met on Christmas; in January Wallace went south to Naples and from there to Greece. He returned to Rome in March, but by late April he was visiting Comte in Paris. A few sentimental remarks in the *Reminiscences,* a poem to a friend's memory, even the discreet abridgements—these by themselves suggest nothing especially untoward. Yet a long letter Howe wrote to Wallace in January 1853—a letter she never sent, since she learned of his 16 December suicide just after finishing it—as well as a few enigmatic remarks in letters to others suggest the relationship was more intense than the official account implies. A small possibility exists that Wallace returned from England on the same vessel as Julia and Annie. The two did meet at least one other time after their return to the United States at Annie's home in Bordentown, and several letters were exchanged.[31]

The 1853 letter blends deep affection with pique. Julia was disturbed by Horace's abrupt departure for Europe; they were to have met in New York "for endless talks, and happy communion" just at this moment. Thus:

> My dear Horace, I have been made happy by hearing that you are
> miserable in Paris. I could almost say that you cannot be more miserable
> there than I wish you, so anxious am I to have my best friend on the same
> side of the water with me again. . . . It was so unkind of you to go, and I
> miss you so much, and life is so short, and friendship so precious—ah me!
> I sigh to think friendship is not less uncertain than life—

Having lost him in person, she tries to commemorate or reinvigorate
their intimacy through references to herself by the sobriquet he has
given her (Glauko), through their shared *rosso* theory, and through her
diligence in reading material he has recommended. An especially harsh
deprivation is her loss of a sympathetic reader:

> Horace, these poems lose half their worth to me, for want of your crit-
> icism. I depend much upon it—your severity of taste has already helped
> me to write far better than I could have written without it. You are, on
> this point, an irreparable loss to me—how shall I remedy it?

But worse than that (which she terms "selfish and egotistical") is simply
the loss of his company:

> Far greater is my need of you as a friend. I have been leading a very lonely
> and unsympathetic life ever since I came from New Port. I need to be
> practically reminded that Love is the Religion of Life, and who can bring
> us back to its standard, if it be not one who is dear to us.

She has expected letters; they have not arrived, but whether he writes or
not, she is desperate that he not forget her:

> I am too lonely, too helpless, too orphaned to be deserted by you, my
> brother. Whatever amusement or employment Life may give us, it brings
> us too little occupation for the heart—we must prize and make the most
> of any *dear* relation it brings us, for indifference lies widely all around and
> in us.

A few half-hearted attempts at cleverness in describing the social non-
scene finally sag under the pain of cramped fingers—"were it not for
this, I could not tire of writing to you." Her only consolation in not
seeing him, she says, is that she is "thin and ugly" this winter. The letter
is signed with the pet name—short for Glaukopis[32]—and concludes
with her intention to send it to him through his bank, "not liking to
trust my letter to your brother, or to Mrs D."

There is nothing compromising in any of the particulars here, even in her need to be "practically reminded that Love is the Religion of Life," whatever that may mean. Yet in the aggregate, the letter bears testimony to a high level of emotional involvement with Wallace. Even before hearing of his death—or perhaps because she sensed his instability—she wrote as if the loss of his company were permanent. The letter's disconsolate undercurrent is just a shade away from open grief.

Full expression of that grief took an odd shape, the oddness itself further token of her depth of feeling. Although she wrote Louisa that she had not been "exactly very wretched about him" and that she had "shed few tears" (the loss feeling something like "having had a limb amputated while under the influence of Chloroform, and then waking and feeling the loss in the *want*"), just three days before, she had spent nearly all day composing a letter in French to Wallace's intellectual hero, Auguste Comte. Howe had never met Comte and probably never sent the letter; she mentioned its existence only to Annie, and asked her not to tell anyone. The gesture is extraordinary not just for the letter's freely displayed distress, but for its frankness about her personal situation.[33]

The letter does not essentially revise Howe's *Reminiscences* account of her friendship with Wallace, but it adds detail. She portrays him as an adopted brother, someone who recognized her talents and gently chided her for allowing her capacities to run undisciplined by systematic study. She characterizes herself as having an ardent temperament: "*je souffre et [je] suis heureuse à l'excès.*" Prior to meeting him, her poetry had served merely to embellish her happiness and console her suffering. She flung them at the world as a child throws flowers, happy if they met with approval, indifferent if they did not. Horace had made her understand that the life she was leading was incommensurate with her genius, and she had promised him to focus her energies. Her loss is thus huge. She reads and rereads his letters, marveling at their vigor and vitality, unable to embrace the fact that he is gone. The loss is magnified, she points out, by the narrowness of her current existence—unwilling inhabitant of "*une triste petite campagne,*" uninterested in Boston's meager social diversions, intensely missing "*cette jouissance électrique du rapport d'une âme avec d'autres.*" Worse, she says, she is unhappily one of those women unable to find satisfaction in caring for children. Her health is deteriorating; she must fight not to be devoured by melancholy. Gratitude to Comte, she says, is her reason for writing; he cannot be aware what a consolation his writings are to an ardent, misunderstood, ill-placed woman. Studying his work has taken the place of lovers and friends, helped her forget her troubles, and lent a gravity to the poems she has written under his inspiration.

There is no reason to doubt the truth of what Howe says of her involvement in Comte's writings. But it is difficult not to feel, as well, that the letter is a classic instance of transference, the master standing in for the disciple, enabling the outpouring of a woe that can otherwise find no vent. So hungry had Howe been for exactly the kind of attention Wallace paid her—attention that honored her as a sentient being, an artist, a person of substantial intellect—that she was as if powerless to prevent herself from trying to reestablish it any way she could. Her letter to Comte closes with near-abject flattery, a despairing bid to evoke a reply from him, as if interaction with someone so important to Wallace will somehow plug the hole his death has blasted in her heart.

Perhaps the level of intensity reflected in this unsent letter grew over time—was more a product of Howe's state of mind after her return than a full-blown phenomenon during their relationship in Rome. Still, it is clear that Wallace had offered the one final pleasure needed to make her Roman holiday ideal—a sort of gratification that Boston had not been able to provide, which, if she could still have it to look forward to, might make all other deprivations bearable. When Wallace left Rome some-time in April, homeward bound, Howe too began to plan her return. It was on the voyage home that Wallace's insemination implanted itself: "[W]hen others had retired for the night, I often sat alone in the cabin, meditating upon the events and lessons of the last six months. These lucubrations took form in a number of poems, which were written with no thought of publication, but which saw the light a year or two later" (204).

Though the quality of Wallace's attention to Howe's intellectual work was unique, other men had previously recognized and encouraged her talent, or at least had seemed to. One such person was Theodore Parker, whose presence had brightened a previous Roman spring and who had been through the years a steady source of inspiration and lively conversation. Parker, she had written in 1844, "brought back to me my golden youth" through "the voice of sympathy and gentle praise." He had occasionally (through her husband) sought her opinion of work for his *Review* and had often lent her books from his massive library. In the fall preceding he had, in fact, written to her in Europe explicitly to urge her to take her literary aspirations seriously:

> Do you know that your present life is not altogether worthy of you? It is not earnest enough. Let me look at it only in the *literary* way. You have not merely talent for Literature but *genius,* attended with a nice instinct for [lines?], & great skill in constructing both in larger & in lesser [features?] of truth of literary art. And you—do nothing—nothing of much permanent value.

As Wallace would do a few months later, Parker took Howe's study of Hebrew as an instance of her dilettantish approach to intellectual endeavor. Such efforts kept her from "great things in letters which you can do if you will."[34]

But Parker's encouragement was couched in terms that compromised its value to her. His notion of her appropriate labor derived from her *husband*'s sense that Julia ought to have, as he put it, "some regular literary work," something that "need not interfere with housekeeping,— a disagreeable thing, I have no doubt, but rather necessary to the truthful development of 'woman' in America." Samuel Howe was at this time considering becoming editor of *The Commonwealth,* and the sense one gets from Parker's letter is that Chev had enlisted his help in trying to interest Julia in assisting him with this job. Despite Parker's apparent support, his efforts probably seemed too closely aligned with her husband's attempts to set her agenda.

Another man who expressed interest in Howe's writing—"one of the good inspirers of my life,"[35] as she said—was Edward Twisleton. An Englishman, Oxford-educated, son of a baron, Twisleton had met the Howes in December 1849 during a visit to Boston. Chance made him a passenger on the ship that carried the Howes to England in 1850, and their friendship deepened. When on the homeward trip Howe planned a brief stop in London, she wrote ahead to Twisleton, hoping to see him again. This first preserved letter suggests the nature of the friendship and offers a glimpse of her well-honed social dexterity. She is all charm, an accomplished composer of bon mots, her warmth and vivacity marshaled to pique Twisleton's eagerness for the proposed reunion.[36] Although they failed to make connections, she left "verses" for him, apparently a poem later included in *Passion-Flowers,* "Gretchen to Goethe." He wrote on 11 July to urge her to "cultivate [her] sacred gift" and to offer—evidently at her invitation—editorial advice.[37] Interestingly, he also offered what amounts to a suggestion to censor herself, admonishing her to remember "Collins' lines on the festus of Poetry":

> The *dangerous* passions kept aloof
> Far from the sainted growing woof

This is a somewhat unusual reaction to the poem, which is a plea from Gretchen—not to Faust, as one might expect, but rather to her creator—to unhand her. Its thrust is that a defenseless female stands as much risk from her male engenderer as she does from her fictional pursuer:

Gretchen to Goethe

'Nicht küssen, es ist so raub, aber lieben, wo's möglich ist.'

> Nay, unhand me, gentle stranger,
> For my stainless maidenhood
> Bodes me some unproven danger
> From a kiss abrupt and rude.
>
> Well I know thou'rt far above me,
> Genius gives thee rank divine,
> But if thou wilt purely love me.
> All my grateful heart is thine.[38]

Gretchen acknowledges Goethe's gentleness and intellectual superiority and offers herself fully to him *if* he will "purely" love her, rather than simply bestow a kiss. It is a request for full understanding and careful treatment, for a response to her not as a type but as a creature of gentleness and sensitivity herself. She wants to be written *truly*.

Taken at face value, the poem seems innocuous. But as a gift from Julia Howe, it may well have seemed to bear additional significance. Twisleton's suggestion that good poetry keeps "dangerous passions" aloof from the weave of the poem's lines may have arisen from a sense that he himself was being indirectly addressed in Howe's verses. If he *did* read the poem as from Julia to Edward, he might well have felt obliged to advise her against the too-direct communication of illicit emotions. It is an embarrassing spot: to read it in that way is to ignore its status as poem and very possibly to *over*read it, but to overlook the possibility that the gift may have been intended to convey a personal message would be to risk appearing obtuse and rude. It is not inconceivable that the embarrassing spot is precisely where Howe wished to position Twisleton.

His response proves him her equal in coded verbal jousting (if that is what was going on). His suggestions regarding word choice[39] establish that he is reading the poem as poem (and is a capable, astute reader of poems), while his second quotation from Collins—

> All the shadowy tribes of mind,
> In braided dance, their murmurs join'd

—indicates his awareness that even if dangerous passions are made to keep their distance, they may still find themselves reflected as "shadowy tribes of mind," braided adroitly within the poem's lines and thus accessible to careful readers. In other words (he was perhaps saying), "Overt and covert messages both received."

Although they did not see each other in London, Twisleton was back in the United States two months later. Julia reported to Annie in September that she had been made "very happy" by many pleasant evenings they had spent together, and indeed, one of the few consolations of her homecoming seems to have been the chance to pass a little time in his company. Near the end of October, on the verge of his departure, he asked to read her poems; she used his interest as a spur to complete work on those underway. The following April he wrote to announce his engagement to Ellen Dwight. Julia received the news gracefully, writing to congratulate him. She attended their wedding in May and thereafter regarded both as close, supportive friends. When they determined to spend the winter of 1852–53 in Rome, Julia wrote to Louisa to beg her particular attention to them. In the wake of Wallace's death, Twisleton's interest in her work became even more important; she saw him as a surrogate mentor and even hoped that he might help her arrange publication of her poems in England.[40]

"I SEE BY the papers that Julia has returned," Fanny Longfellow wrote to her sister early in September:

> I hear she was much admired in Rome and her soirees much courted. With her resources of language and clever conversation, I can imagine how attractive she must have made them, where people love society for its own sake. How dull she will find it in South Boston—she is not to be satisfied with the society of husband and children and a social nature like hers requires much more, not to consume itself.[41]

A few days later (11 September) Longfellow encountered her and reported to his journal that though she had never looked better, there was
"a great sadness about her mouth." Her return trip was uneventful,
meditative—"all pleasant," she told Louisa, "except the direction."[42] She
reentered her life at home apprehensively, having worked out an understanding with her husband about the mundane aspects of domestic
organization, but also evidently having accepted their emotional distance as unalterable fact. He was "kind" to her. They met mainly for
meals; Julia was relieved of responsibility for the servants, thus deliver-
ing her from the prospect of Chev's "scoldings." She wrote to Annie that
her nerves were steadier, her temper more tranquil. Her plan for the
winter was to avoid society altogether, devoting herself to studies, her
health, and her children.

Julia Romana and Florence greeted her shyly at first. Their mother
hardly recognized them, remarking (to her sister) on their tanned, freck-
led faces, their petulance and coarse manners, their harsh voices, and
determining to "reform all these things, if their father is willing."[43] Her
sense of the profound uneasiness her year-long absence must have created for them is poignantly expressed in a *Passion-Flowers* poem called
"The Heart's Astronomy," which describes her practice of getting exercise by walking around the house:

> This evening, as the twilight fell,
> My younger children watched for me;
> Like cherubs in the window framed,
> I saw the smiling group of three.
>
> While round and round the house I trudged,
> Intent to walk a weary mile,
> Oft as I passed within their range,
> The little things would beck and smile.
>
> They watched me, as Astronomers
> Whose business lies in heaven afar,
> Await, beside the slanting glass,
> The re-appearance of a star.
>
> Not so, not so, my pretty ones,
> Seek stars in yonder cloudless sky;
> But mark no steadfast path for me,
> A comet dire and strange am I.

Now to the inmost spheres of light
Lifted, my wondering soul dilates,
Now dropped in endless depth of night,
My hopes God's slow recall awaits.

Among the shining I have shone,
Among the blessing, have been blest,
Then wearying years have held me bound
Where darkness deadness gives, not rest.

Between extremes distraught and rent,
I question not the way I go;
Who made me, gave it me, I deem,
Thus to aspire, to languish so.

But Comets too have holy laws,
Their fiery sinews to restrain,
And from their outmost wanderings
Are drawn to heaven's dear heart again.

And ye, beloved ones, when ye know
What wild, erratic natures are,
Pray that the laws of heavenly force
Would hold and guide the Mother star.[44]

The astronomical metaphor is apt, first, as a way of characterizing her sense of powerlessness to modify her path. As a comet, she has experience of both the intensest light and the intensest darkness; these are by turns exalting and deadening, but in any case her movement between them is external to the action of her will. She must let herself be propelled, must do as she does, be who she is. Also skillful is the tension the poem generates between images of star and comet, the static and the erratic. Comets as a group may, indeed, be bound by "holy laws," but the evidence of the operation of these laws in any particular case is partial and always subject to revision. And even if there is reasonable certainty of return, the long dimension of the elliptical orbit is typically so extended that absence is the usual state of affairs. Howe's sympathetic understanding of the anxiety such a phenomenon produces in cherubic astronomers is plain, but a good part of the poem's strength—and perhaps a window into her emotional state after her return—lies in her unwillingness to resolve the tension with the sentimental truism of the penultimate stanza. She can only advise her beloved ones to pray that she is held on course, to suggest that they try to envision her as the star she knows she is not. The poem echoes Fanny Longfellow's perception that finding satisfaction with husband and children would be difficult for Julia Howe.

Having mentioned to Annie that she would not go out much during the winter unless she felt stronger, Julia cautioned her not to misunderstand: "[T]here is no reason for my feeling ill, and no possibility of any—"[45] In light of "The Heart's Astronomy," one has to feel relieved that among the new arrangements in place upon her return must have been an agreement that future pregnancies were out of the question.

What do we know of Samuel Howe's state of mind during this year of his wife's absence? Since he insisted on the destruction of his letters to her and Sumner, there is little material to form a basis for speculation. It is obvious that he saw Sumner as his principal source of emotional solace and depended on him heavily after returning to Boston. A mid-November note from Sumner, responding to some kind of plea from his friend, suggests that the younger man's various commitments kept him for a time from fully being the ally and confidant Chev desperately needed. To his "dearly beloved" friend Sumner wrote apologetically:

> Since your return, my mind & time have been so much occupied, as to make it difficult for me to find any satisfaction, except in the pressing duties before me. I have made no calls of friendship or pleasure. . . . You know what it is to be absorbed by tyrannous thoughts, anxious care, & engagements which cannot be postponed. And you know, from your knowledge of human nature, that these things will subordinate to themselves the indulgence of friendship & even of love.

The letter also reflects, in an outpouring of reciprocal affection, Sumner's gratitude at being thus needed: "In the wreck of my past life, with friends leaving me, I lay fast hold upon you. I cannot let you go. I need yr sympathy, counsel & succor."[46] His own craving to be in a mutual comfort-giving relationship presumably brought the two together often.

During this period Samuel Howe's parental impulses probably also helped him compensate for having been, as he felt, abandoned. Two years earlier Florence had nearly died from dysentery, and as her father had held her writhing body in his arms, he had thought that if she slipped out of life, "all the hours and days after that would be so blank & cheerless that nothing could enliven them." The only solace, he had believed then, would be to die with her—"& next to that to live alone, separated from every one & to cherish her memory." Later, when Sumner discovered and "devoured" Tennyson's *In Memoriam,* urging it on his friend, Chev's response was to wonder who would write the memorial for Hallam *père.* He had met Arthur Hallam's father and been moved by his grief. A friend's love for a friend is touching, and Sumner certainly had capacities for such love, but, Chev wrote, "you have no more conception of some of the ways of love than has a blind man of colours;—the love of children, for instance;—a father's love for his son!" Although Howe felt her older daughters had been left to run wild during her absence, it seems likely that her husband was in fact more considerate of them than he might have been had she been in charge. Perhaps there was something of retribution in his attentions, as well—a need to punish his wife by expertly performing her role.[47]

Howe's return nonetheless signified a determination on both sides to maintain their marriage. In a speech many years later called "Marriage and Divorce,"[48] she delivered her understanding—obviously drawn from experience—of the responsibilities marriage partners assume. A man and woman "of very opposite inclinations" must be sure of the strength of mutual affection before committing themselves for life. And even when affection is indubitable, both must be constantly on guard not to let "the tyrannical instinct" rob the other of innocent enjoyments. "Much heroism," she noted, "is often shown in married life by those who endure such a tyranny, but it is difficult to endure it long without a loss of will power which in the end is seriously demoralizing." Marriage poses "the greatest problem to be solved by Human Society"—how to blend fidelity with the exercise of personal freedom. What life had at last taught her, she said, is that duty must guide behavior. "I see a deep and sober joy crowning those households in which the true sacrifice, self-sacrifice, has proved part of the religion of life. I see an arid waste surrounding those in which the selfish principle has been enthroned and worshipped." While the general truths of this perspective directed her decision in 1851 to resume her South Boston life, she had not yet resolved the fidelity/independence dilemma, nor embraced the principle of self-sacrifice as a means to joy. Indeed, the arid waste stretching out before her was the possibility that her reawakened poetic sensibility would shrivel for want of nurture. The arrangement seems to have been struck to afford each partner a sufficiency of freedom.

It proved more or less workable, at least for a time. Samuel Howe's stability was shaken when, in November 1851, Sumner departed for Washington, D.C., to assume his newly won Senate seat. Although the two had not been frequently together in recent months, Chev foresaw that losing the possibility of seeing Sumner would affect him deeply, and he was right. "I miss you, more even than I supposed I should," he wrote on 6 December: "[I]t makes me sad & almost sick at heart to think that you are where I cannot reach you be my need of sympathy ever so great." His recourse was work—a dependable means, as he said, "to chase away thought—regret—sorrow."[49] A blizzard of notes passed back and forth between the friends during the winter, most on matters facing Sumner in Congress, but some on personal matters, too; there are occasional indications that each was consigning some of the other's letters to the fire.[50] Julia, for her part, maintained the momentum of writing and studying that she had established in Rome, taking heart from Twisleton's interest and Wallace's epistolary guidance. But, like her husband, she was often brought low by the strain of living in a state of tension.

Beginning in December, the tour of the United States by the great Hungarian revolutionary Louis Kossuth occupied Samuel Howe's attention, and eventually Julia was caught up in the fervor, too. Back in March 1848, Kossuth, then a member of the Hungarian diet, had been aroused by news of revolution in Paris and had delivered an impassioned speech in defense of liberty. The speech, printed in German and widely disseminated, ignited workers in Vienna to insurrection; they invaded the imperial palace and caused a terrified Metternich to flee to England. From there, revolution swept through Europe. In October Kossuth had led Hungarian soldiers in driving Austrian troops out of Hungary, but by August 1849 the forces of counterrevolution had asserted themselves. Kossuth was himself driven into exile. Arriving in New York in December 1851 in hopes of raising funds and support for the cause of Hungarian freedom, he received a hero's welcome.[51] Longfellow noted that New Yorkers had gone "clean daft" in their eagerness to express enthusiasm: "They are like the Negro preacher who at a camp meeting, having exhausted every word and gesture of intense excitement, stood on his head, and knocked his feet together!"[52]

In April Kossuth and his entourage reached Boston. The Howes hosted a dinner on 2 May, and Julia saw him on several other occasions.

She was enthralled by the "Hungarian whirlwind," proclaiming him "deeper, greater and better" than she had supposed he could possibly be. The doctor, for his part, was overwhelmed by the degree of confidence Kossuth seemed to place in him. He was, he wrote to Sumner, "the only man to whom my intellect bows quite down."[53] But by the time Kossuth left the United States two months later—disappointed in his hopes of support and increasingly the target of insulting attacks—his value as a site of concord between Julia and her husband had faded.

Julia spent most of the summer of 1852 in Bordentown, assisting Annie during the birth of her second child. This visit also provided a convenient occasion for a reunion with Horace. Her children, or some of them, stayed in Boston with their father. In August, with Annie, Julia went to Newport for a month, settling in accommodations arranged by the Longfellows.[54] She had not been to this favorite spot of her childhood since before her marriage, and the return was exhilarating. Also on the scene, among others, were George Curtis, George Bancroft, the Freemans (who had been Julia's upstairs neighbors in Rome), and Sumner's brother Albert. The gathered company amused themselves with parties, excursions, and evenings of charades, and Julia felt something of the pleasure of social life that Rome had offered. They styled their little enclave the Hotel de Rambouillet, and Julia became their Madame de Sevigné—until Chev joined them.

He had passed the early part of the summer trying to help Kossuth raise money and feeling his own solitude sharply. Only his daughters, and the interest he felt in "the development of their characters" (as he wrote Sumner), kept him from sadness. In midsummer eight-year-old Julia Romana fell ill, and though the attending doctor did not believe she was in serious danger, her emotional symptoms alarmed her father. His account is discomfiting for what it suggests about the possible impact of her parents' alienation on their oldest child:

> She hung about me weeping for a day before the bodily illness manifested itself, & kept continually shriving herself for all sorts of real & imaginary sins. She insisted on telling me every little fault she had ever been conscious of: such as being unkind to her sisters, or being impatient with flies & brushing them away rudely perhaps breaking their limbs. This continued after her illness began, & she seemed to be in a continual state of self-reproachment, & at times almost in an agony at the recollection of the merest trifles.[55]

It is perhaps understandable, then, that when he and the children joined the group in Newport, his spirits were something less than ebullient. Julia recorded his grouchiness at her enjoyment of the society and in particular at her performance of the sleeping potion scene from *Romeo and Juliet,* climaxing with her delivery ("with all the emphasis of one who felt it") of the line, "My dismal scene I needs must act *alone."* When the family returned to South Boston, Julia characterized her crossing of the "severe threshold" as "drop[ping] the flowers, gathered without, that could not live within it, and fold[ing] my hands in prayer, without which, and the support it brings, I could not live here."[56]

If she had relied on the prospect of seeing Wallace occasionally, that hope vanished in October, when she learned he had abruptly returned to Europe. "He is a great loss to me, in various ways," she wrote to Annie; "I am quite desolate at the thought of his going away."[57] Occasional visits from Arthur Hugh Clough, a poet from England who came with a letter of introduction from Florence Nightingale, did little to relieve the gloom: he was very shy, and Chev's indifference to him threw all hosting responsibility to Julia. She did avail herself of his expertise in poetic rhythms, appropriating a variation on the distinctive verse form of Clough's *The Bothie of Toper-na-Fuosich* (1848) for a poem she wrote about Kossuth.[58] Chev had determined that they would no longer serve wine at their dinner parties, and after one disastrous experience Julia resolved not to entertain further.[59] Thackeray's lectures and the opera now and then with Longfellow provided her only winter diversions. Otherwise, she studied and wrote. And then in February came the news of Wallace's death.

TEN MONTHS later, as Howe was proofreading the final galleys for *Passion-Flowers,* she dashed off a curious note to Annie—curious in its suggestion that she had only just become aware, at that very late moment in the process, of the work's connection to Wallace. "I seized upon the publication of my Book," she wrote, "as the only help against grief too bitter to bear. . . . [T]his sorrow departs not from me, day or night. I always loved him, but I did not know how much until I lost him." Her letters from the previous spring, when the book began to take shape, clearly show her on the edge of distraction, keeping herself from lunacy only through the most rigorous application to her work. In the letter to Comte, a total stranger, she portrays her health as deteriorating, her melancholic nature threatening to pull her down into blankness unless she can stay mentally active. To Louisa she wrote on 18 February that although it was madness for her to be using her eyes so much, "I should have a worse madness if I did not cram myself with books. The barrenness and emptiness of life were then insupportable, and that distant but terrible vision of insanity which has haunted my life, would become reality." And to Annie, the same day: "I shall sit with my hands crossed, in despair, if I do not cut my throat. . . . Still, if I can work at my poems, I shall not complain."[60] Her determination finally to complete and publish her collection was forged when she learned of Wallace's suicide, and the book, as chapter 5 argues, bears testimony to the depth of her grief and despair.

Five years earlier Howe had crafted a story incarnating her comprehension of her husband's nature and articulating her resolve to cultivate "a spirit of humility, of gratitude, and the love of *uses.*" The Laurence manuscript—despite its melodrama, despite the fact that it names what would seem a nearly insuperable obstacle to marital harmony—may be read as ultimately a narrative of reconciliation. But time and events had not brought her the reward of feeling truly wedded—nor even the peace projected in Eva as she waits patiently for the blooming of a flower from Rafael's moribund breast. And the spirit of resignation had proved extremely difficult to sustain. Thus *Passion-Flowers* is a text born, as the Laurence manuscript was, from an overpowering need to give voice to pain. But this time, anger, not the reconciliative impulse, would be the primary note. And this time, the text would be public.

1. Engraving of Samuel Gridley Howe. Courtesy Massachusetts Historical Society.

2. Portrait of Julia Ward Howe, painted on her wedding trip, winter 1843–1944. Courtesy Betty Wiggins.

3. Charles Sumner at thirty-five, painted in 1846 by Eastman Johnson. The original is at Longfellow House, Cambridge, Mass. Courtesy National Park Service, Longfellow National Historic Site.

4. Henry Wadsworth Longfellow in the 1850s. Original at Longfellow
House, Cambridge, Massachusetts. Courtesy National Park Service,
Longfellow National Historic Site.

5. The Perkins Institution for the Blind, South Boston, c. 1840.
Courtesy Boston Public Library Print Department.

6. The Hermaphrodite Room, Villa Borghese, Rome. *The Sleeping Hermaphrodite*
is against the right wall. Paintings on the ceiling by Buonvicini and a floor
mosaic illustrate scenes from Ovid's account of Hermaphroditus and Salmacis.
Courtesy Fratelli Palombi Editori, Rome.

7. In one of Buonvicini's ceiling paintings Salmacis, about to be struck by Cupid's arrow, accosts a resistant Hermaphroditus while his parents, Hermes and Aphrodite, follow their own amorous impulses in the background to the right. Satyrs leer from the right foreground; Salmacis's attendants watch with apprehension at the left.
Courtesy Fratelli Palombi Editori, Rome.

8. Second-century Roman copy of the Greek statue *The Sleeping Hermaphrodite.*
Courtesy Fratelli Palombi Editori, Rome.

9. Gathering in Newport, Rhode Island (the "Hotel Rambouillet"), 1852.
Left to right: Thomas Gold Appleton, John Gerard Coster, Julia Ward Howe, Fanny
Appleton Longfellow, Henry Wadsworth Longfellow, and Horatia Latilla Freeman.
Original at Longfellow House, Cambridge, Mass. Courtesy National Park Service,
Longfellow National Historic Site.

10. Portrait of Julia Ward Howe, late 1850s. Begun by John Elliott and finished by
William Henry Cotton. Courtesy of the National Portrait Gallery, Smithsonian
Institution, Washington, D.C. Gift of Mrs. John Elliott.

FIVE

"Ye Shall Listen Now"

Passion-Flowers and the Poetics of Defiance

❦

*P*ASSION-FLOWERS as a book grew from Howe's distraction following Horace Binney Wallace's suicide. Its seeds, though, are to be found in the ten years of pain and growth preceding its December 1853 publication. Its intensity and audacity, as well as its emotional and technical range, I have come to believe, qualify it for regard as one of the benchmarks of antebellum literary achievement. It is Howe's declaration of emotional independence and—despite her disclaimer in the opening poem—it is an instrument of revenge.

She did not invent the title. It was bestowed on the book by Emmanuel Vitalis Scherb, with Longfellow's approval, at a very late stage in its production.[1] Yet the fit is perfect, veiling the vehemence of her sentiments in a drapery redolent of Christian imagery. The passion-flower received its name in the late sixteenth century from Catholic priests who saw in its arrangement of petals and sepals a representation of the ten disciples present during Jesus' crucifixion and in its hairlike rays above the petals a suggestion of the crown of thorns.[2] The perception Howe five years earlier gave to Laurence—that "fervent hearts must borrow the disguise of art, if they would win the right to express, in any outward form, the internal fire that consumes them"—is operative in her embrace of this title, which speaks doubly. These "flowers," it suggests, grow from a profoundly religious sensibility whose intensity and sufferings recall Christ's. But they express another kind of passion as well, those "great passion[s] of the soul" which, if too clearly revealed, "offend the narrow sense and breeding of the respectable world."[3]

George Ripley's influential *New York Tribune* review of the volume assisted in emphasizing the first of these meanings:

The flower that symbolizes to the Christian imagination the throes of agony which preceded the redemption of the world, is not an unmeet emblem of the strains through which is breathed an inner sorrow that finding no rest in earthly things seeks with rapt yearnings for the consolations of immortal hope.[4]

Yet he understood, too, what would in the first heady weeks of 1854 make the book a sensation, almost obligatory reading: that the poems arose from "the spontaneous necessity of self-revelation," the product of "a spiritual history too passionate and intense for concealment." Those to whom Howe sent copies of the book responded—directly or indirectly—to this volatile, self-disclosing aspect. Emerson delicately thanked her for satisfying his curiosity about her thoughts with these "private lyrics, whose air & words are all your own." Oliver Wendell Holmes called it "The first true woman's heart!" But it was Hawthorne, writing to William Ticknor from Liverpool to thank him for forwarding the poems, who voiced the question no doubt uppermost in many readers' minds. Observing that "the devil must be in the woman to publish them" since they seemed "to let out a whole history of domestic unhappiness," he wondered, "What does her husband think of it?"[5]

Samuel Howe was kept in the dark, if not about Julia's general intention to publish a book of poems, certainly about their content. His absorption in his own work made the task of concealment uncomplicated. Beginning in 1852, in addition to his labors at the Institution, he had taken on the task of editing *The Commonwealth,* a Free Soil newspaper. He called often on his wife to produce copy and to assist with editorial duties, possibly believing that her work toward this end might satisfy her desire to publish (and in any case, he very much needed her help).[6] He was also involved in his own publishing venture at this time. James T. Fields wrote him in early May 1853 declining a manuscript he had submitted, it being, in Field's opinion, "too wordy and not welded together strong enough to hold with a sturdy grasp the public attention."[7] Word of Fields's positive decision about Julia Howe's collection came to her in mid-October, but through two months of revision and proofreading and consultation with Longfellow and Scherb (among others), she managed to keep news of its imminent publication from her husband. She agonized for several weeks over whether to involve him in the decision about putting her name on the title page. She wrote Annie:

> I have a great mind to keep the whole matter entirely secret from him, and not let him know anything until the morning the volume comes out. Then he can do nothing to prevent its sale in its proper form. Dear Annie, could one do this? he has known all summer that I intended publishing, and has made no objection, and not much comment.[8]

This anxiety was warranted. The revelation, when it came, was deeply disturbing to Chev: Julia reported that he took it "*very* hard." This first reaction, however—though for her a "bitter drop" that "poisoned all"—gave place fairly quickly to relief at the book's strong early sales and at signs that men he respected found much in the book to admire.[9] Sumner maintained silence until mid-January, when his friend forlornly prompted him: "You have not said a word about Julia's book: I wish you would say to me what you think of it—though I know well it is a vain wish,—you would not wound me by saying all you think, I know." Sumner tersely responded: "The book of poems is a work of genius, which reminds me of Elizabeth Barrett. The genius is rare." What Longfellow said in person can only be conjectured; to his diary he reported: "[H]ere is revolt enough, between these blue covers."[10]

It took a while for this fact about the book to sink in with Samuel Howe, and the story of its sinking-in properly belongs at a later point in this narrative. His early negative reaction was evidently merely to the fact of publication, not to the substance of the poems. In the meantime, the initial crisis over, Julia Howe reveled in the attention and esteem she received. The month or two leading up to this moment had been very difficult,[11] and she was primed to relish every sign of its success. Hundreds of copies were sold in the first week, leading Fields to consider a second edition.[12] More to the point, she told Annie, "every one likes it. . . . It has done more for me, in point of consideration here, than a fortune of a hundred thousand dollars." One particularly gratifying signal of its positive reception was Theodore Parker's quotation from seven of the poems in his Christmas sermon—"the greatest of honours," Howe exulted.[13]

In the reviews, too, she had reason to be thrilled. "A product wrung with tears and prayer from the deepest soul of the writer," proclaimed Ripley in the *Tribune,* which devoted three columns to the book and reproduced six of the poems. "The stamp of 'sad sincerity' is impressed on every line—nothing but the profound experience of a rarely endowed nature could give such an air of reality to such impassioned wails of suffering." The reviewer for *Harper's New Monthly Magazine* observed that the book distinguished itself from "the ephemeral productions of our popular versifiers" through, among other characteristics, its "intense earnestness of feeling" and "unmistakable origin in profound personal experiences." *Putnam's Monthly* echoed these views: the poems are "so full of life, so audacious, so evidently the natural product of the author's experience and self-knowledge; . . . so full of a generous human sympathy, such an unblenching heroism and social independence, that it is impossible not to hail them with the heartiest welcome."

The enthusiasm the book evoked was in part a response to what reviewers saw as an indifference to conventional stylistic elements, a preference for the direct over the elegant. For twentieth-century readers raised, as it were, on Whitman's and Dickinson's much more thoroughgoing break with nineteenth-century poetic traditions, Howe's experiments beyond conventions widely adopted by most poets of her day may be somewhat less than obvious. Contemporary reviewers, however, felt them sharply. "The work abounds in no specimens of dainty fancies, highly-wrought artificial embellishments, or even smooth and facile versification. The writer seems too utterly in earnest to waste a thought on fine, elaborate finish," observed Ripley. "Considered as works of art," the reviewer for *Harper's* noted, "these poems are evidently unstudied and spontaneous," exhibiting, in fact, "an audacious defiance of the wholesome precedents of composition." In words that seem almost to foreshadow the reception *Leaves of Grass* would garner the following year, the *Passion-Flowers* poems are said to proceed from "a wonderful command of language—a plastic mastery over its most rugged forms—and a cunning skill in word-weaving, which is a far higher and rarer gift than a bland docility to artificial rules." They are "altogether free from any thing commonplace or conventional." Ripley bestowed his highest accolade in describing the volume's language as marked by "stern vigor, which betokens an intellect of masculine self-concentration and force." In fact, he added, were it not for the many passages that present a woman's perceptions, "we should not have suspected these poems to be the production of a woman. They form an entirely unique class in the whole range of female literature."[14]

In later years Howe would dismiss her first book as "a timid performance upon a slender reed," deliberately intervening in its critical legacy to mask its revolutionary designs. Its focus, she would say, was the events of 1848, "still in fresh remembrance"—the efforts of the Italian patriots and the struggles of Hungary. The wrongs and sufferings of the slave, too, "had their part in the volume" (229–30). Of the book's forty-four poems, only six or seven directly address these issues, and while these derive a certain prominence from their concentration in the early pages of the collection, their significance is subsumed in the way Howe appropriates their focus as a means of addressing matters much closer to home and heart. Her aesthetic challenge in producing *Passion-Flowers* was to discover how to meld the emphatic, candid voice of her private poetry with a mode of discourse mindful of cultural restrictions on the articulations of women.[15] The book's political concerns were sincere and strongly felt, but they were not, I believe, the force driving Howe's creative energies. These poems were intended to be read *through* their conspicuous subjects as metaphors for situations in her personal life. Or to put it another way: they fuse public and domestic politics, though the latter are submerged, evident only to those who knew her (and to those who would, through sympathetic reading of these poems in their suggestive context, perceive their thematic continuity with other parts of the book). Poems about political events enabled personal discourse—provided a safe venue for expression of feelings that might, were they to find direct and public utterance, bring down forces analogous to those that forged the police states of post-1848 Europe.[16]

Julia Ward Howe was not the first American woman to write and publish poetry that might be considered feminist or in other ways transgressive of cultural gender codes. Emily Stipes Watts notes that pleas for feminine equality were a commonplace of eighteenth-century women's verse and, further, that the development of the apparently restrictive category "female poetry" in the nineteenth century in fact provided a "shelter for experimentation" and a "galvanizing element" for certain adventurous women writers. Maria Brooks, Mary E. Hewitt, Elizabeth Oakes Smith, Frances Osgood, and the Cary sisters all had published convention-defying and startlingly intimate work before 1854.[17] Yet it is clear from the reaction to *Passion-Flowers* that Howe's contemporaries regarded both her boldness and her art as things distinctly new in a woman poet. She was "not an echo, nor a shadow, nor a sweet singer of nothings," said one, but the author of a "powerful, pungent, and unripe" book in which—the word leaps out—the "personalism" was "terrible." Howe's decision to publish *unmistakably* autobiographical poems had few precedents, and none among women as prominently situated as she.[18]

THE OPENING POEM, a three-part "Salutatory," acknowledges that Howe's subjects include the personal—indeed, that "friends and foes" are both topic of and impetus for the book.[19] "Too closely are ye linked with me, / Too much in mine your being blends," she tells them, for her to exclude them from her verse. In particular, she wants the foes to recognize themselves, those who,

> rankling in my path,
> Have torn my feet and pierced my side,
> Holding the eager pilgrim back
> To suffer wounded love and pride.

Although she claims that Nature has made her "Vengeful in none of [her] desires"—a claim I consider below—she makes it clear that she has woven into her "harmless chaplet" the "sharp and bitter forms" of the "briars" who obstructed the aspiring poet's way. We can see in "Rome," the second poem and also the longest, the means by which the book incorporates these briars.

"Rome" begins with a description of emotional deliverance,[20] recalling (for anyone familiar with her circumstances) Howe's return to the city in 1850, when she danced around Louisa's apartment singing "Liberty! Liberty!" and expressed surges of emotion associated with Horace Binney Wallace. We know whose "querulous voice" Rome was a respite from and what set those bounding feet moving:

> I knew a day of glad surprise in Rome,
> Free to the childish joy of wandering,
> Without a 'wherefore' or 'to what good end?'
> By querulous voice propounded, or a thought
> Of punctual Duty, waiting at the door
> Of home, with weapon duly poised to slay
> Delight, ere it across the threshold bound.
> I strayed, amassing wild flowers, ivy leaves,
> Relics, and crusted marbles, gathering too
> Thoughts of unending Beauty from the fields,
> The hills, the skies, the ancient heathen shrines
> Transfigured in the light of Christian day.
> Coaxed by soft airs, by gentlest odors flattered,

> Conquered at last by the all-conquering sun,
> My heart its sadly cherished silence brake,
> And its long sealed tides flowed forth in song,
> While bounding feet in gladdest rhythm moved.

The "grace" the speaker feels on this day is (she makes explicit in the next few lines) "more than maternal." She impiously doubts whether even heavenly angels, given leave to play around Rome that day, would happily return home at evening.

The strong suspicion that we are listening to a personal voice in these opening lines, not an imagined speaker, is reinforced as the poem continues. This ebullient woman is intended to be recognized as Julia Howe herself, whose hair and eyes are "fading in the grasp of Time," whom matronly decorum prevents from wearing gold and gems, but who can still go abroad "wearing my native courage on my bosom" and bringing to corrupt courts "the woodland breath of Liberty / From my far home." She contemplates the winter that stretches "in a boundless glittering" before her; if she is "horizon-bounded," it is only in the way that the sea is—"the sweeping line / Limits the known, but not the possible." Other identifying markers include further references to the fact that she is a mother ("from the narrow gates of childbed oft / Have issued, bearing high my perilous prize"); acknowledgment of the "happiest companionship" that enriched the spring; and an account of first hearing the nightingale's song in the aromatic gardens of the Villa Massimo, a moment that will henceforth attach to the memory of her "friend."[21] The "I"—in "Rome," and in most of the book's poems—refers as it will in Whitman's work to its poetically constructed actual author.[22]

"Rome" in some ways seems, in fact, Howe's "Out of the Cradle Endlessly Rocking," for like Whitman's not-yet-written account of his birth as an artist, "Rome" connects the awakening of poetic intuition with the song of a bird and an encounter with death. The removal of a corpse from a dwelling across the street on the evening of her "day of glad surprise" is a memento mori: from that house, "the lengthening shadow fell / Upon the dial of my life." The menacing possibility that she, too, will die is a segue into the passage describing Villa Massimo and the nightingale's "sound of ravishment." Hearing the bird's falling song, she is initially "Astonished, penetrate, too past myself / To know I sinned in speaking, where a breath / less exquisite was sacrilege."[23]

From this rapture emerges a vision of the past, of a young queenly Rome on the verge of conquest, which might be read simultaneously as an account of Julia Ward's own setting-out from New York years earlier. Following in Rome's footsteps through the city gates, Howe contemplates the impulse to fill an "unknown waste" with "splendor":

> How widely overflowed her noble soul,
> Too great and generous to contain itself,
> Gathering glory from the East, and then
> (With kindred instinct of all luminous things)
> Craving an outlet in the Northern night,
> As if its depth alone could give her scope.

Rome's colonizing program is checked, however, in terms reminiscent of Howe's sense of containment in marriage:

> But the dim North had other laws than hers,
> And took not from her will its destiny;
> Its darkness swallowed up the light she gave
> And seemed to quench it. But, as none can tell
> Among the sunbeams which unconscious one
> Comes weaponed with celestial will, to strike
> The strokes of Freedom on the fettered floods,
> Giving the spring his watchword—even so
> Rome knew not she had spoken the word of Fate
> That should, from out its sluggishness, compel
> The frost-bound vastness of barbaric life,
> Till, with an ominous sound, the torrent rose
> And rushed upon her with terrific brow,
> Sweeping her back, through all her haughty ways
> To her own gates, a piteous fugitive—
> A moment chafing at its limits there
> To enter in, resistless, and o'erwhelm
> With heavy tides of death, her struggling breast.

Then follows a series of reflections on the alliance contemporary despots form with the past to help them "engird with bristling thorns / Broad meadow lands of gracious human growth."[24] The Roman Church provides the readiest illustration of this principle (and an occasion to denounce the oppression the Church now represents), but the particulars of this association are only vaguely addressed. To "the spirit of the Past" she says, simply,

> own that thou art dead,
> Nor bind thy hollow brows with flowers of youth
> That wither as they touch thee. Yield to us
> The wealth thy spectral fingers cannot hold;
> Bless us, and so depart.

Drawing the analogy with her own situation more explicitly, Howe imagines the enchained city as Juliet returning to consciousness:

> Perhaps at midnight here
> Wakes the quiescent city of our day,
> A Juliet, drunken with her draught of woe,
> And wildly calls on Love's deliverance
> Writhing in her untimely cerements,
> And stiffens back to silence when she hears:
> "Love has no help, save that which waits on Death."

Such meditations force her awareness of the fact that, dream as she will, this Roman interlude will end. As she tries to gather strength to endure her uprooting, she becomes Juliet, stiffening "back to silence," desiring her own end:

> So clinging, creeping, craving from men's hands
> A gracious culture, loving so to grow
> And bear the fruit God gave it right to bear
> As genial tribute to Love's genial care;
> I felt the sudden, earnest wish for death
> Shoot like a subtle poison through my veins.

The shade of the drowned Margaret Fuller seems to loom, as well:

> if I must await the tedious ebb
> And days decline, I shall be but a wreck
> That whitens, stranded on the shore, and mocks
> The pilot's skill, with bare dismantled ribs,
> While shattered mast and shredded banner point
> To the rich freight surrendered to the deep.

A moment of crisis, though it brings some kind of fortitude—"I wrestled with myself / And wrenched my hands, by loving friends held back / Till they were free, and stretched on high to God / Who took them"— does not bring resolution and renewed determination. Least of all does it afford her the ecstasy that will give rise to Whitman's "thousand songs." Premonition of her own death, which was the impetus for the poem's reveries, now returns as an embraced certainty: " 'Thou shalt die.' " The poem draws to a gloomy close as Howe leaves Rome, straining to keep St. Peter's in view but eventually losing sight of it: "The dome is gone—gone seems the heaven with it. / Night hides my sorrow from me."

Although I emphasize the personal narrative embedded in "Rome," the poem taken whole—especially since it is followed by one berating Pio Nono for having relinquished his early liberal precepts—is also a lament for the failed revolution. The barbarians from the north who overwhelm Rome's "struggling breast" are the armies of Catholic France, summoned by the pope to retrieve the city from revolutionary forces. The anguished final notes echo the distress Howe expresses in "From Newport to Rome," and they certainly reflect the despair felt by other Americans as they watched the defeat of the cause of Italian freedom.[25] If her self-depiction seems to foreground a personal transition from joyous liberation to near-suicidal resignation, the metamorphosis is plausibly the result of *political* sorrow. The republican matron who goes forth wearing native courage that "will not dim for Prelate nor for Prince," who brings "the woodland breath of Liberty" to the tainted atmosphere of courts, confronts the past, sitting on the ruins of the ancient world "like a harlot, to entrap / The manifold human heart." The poem depicts a profane alliance between this magnificently seductive being and the "despot," greedy for power and wealth. The church, too, in league with the past, "cheat[s] the poor with demon fables, / And glittering trash," with the result that beautiful Rome,

> that were as fragrant as God's Eden
> Could Nature only have her freshening way,
> Must still exhale thee, shuddering, to the world,
> Condemned to propagate the germ of death
> Which thy decay holds festering in her heart.

Against these forces, the plucky lady from the New World runs aground: "Oh, my Rome, / As I have loved thee, rest God's love with thee!"

Howe's achievement here is the melding of these two strains of concern, the private narrative enabled by its congruence with the tragedy of failed revolution. Of course, readers unfamiliar with her circumstances will not understand the poem in this way—or rather, they can do no more than sense the presence in certain passages of an inaccessible story tantalizingly limned. (The speaker has "strayed," and in her "wandering" has let herself be "[c]oaxed . . . flattered . . . conquered" until too-long-pent "tides flowed forth.") This mode of writing has the advantage of heightening interest in the poem (and poet) while still maintaining at least a modicum of reserve, and it certainly had the effect of winning Howe readers, as the reviews and other responses testify. But its greater power, obviously, is over those who *do* know the details—who are positioned to recognize the startling degree of revelation Howe indulges in. It is a poem intended, in some sense, primarily for an audience of one. Or at least it is fair to say that the probable effect on her husband had to have been central in her conceptual work on the poem, since its opening lines so unambiguously identify him as the oppressive force from which Rome means escape. The poem derives much of its energy from its *flaunting* aspect. It says, in effect: "See how I can voice my grief in terms unmistakable to you and our friends, but *discreetly,* decorously filtered through the veil of republican sympathies." If punctual Duty will wait at the door of home, weapon poised to slay Delight, Delight will devise the retaliatory missiles appropriate to her status and talents.

Thus, in the book's apparently most straightforward "political" poem, "From Newport to Rome" (discussed in chapter 4), that dramatic moment when the speaker springs to the podium to lambaste the apathetic assembly assumes a second significance in the context created by "Rome." In publishing *Passion-Flowers,* Howe takes the platform with a fury analogous to the speaker's. Her "burning soul" flashes out against the "silken web":

> "I've sat among you long enough,
>   Or followed where your music led,
>   I never marred your pleasure yet,
>   But ye shall listen now," I said.

Ye shall listen now: this is the driving force of the book, which entices its readers—the disingenuous claims of "Salutatory" notwithstanding—with this spectacle of anger unleashed.[26]

OTHER POEMS, viewed through the lens suggested by "Rome," speak with a similar doubleness. "The Dead Christ" for example, narrates the unpacking of a crucifix and seems to arise from a spirit of contrition (or at least the desire for it):[27]

Take the dead Christ to my chamber,
  The Christ I brought from Rome;
Over all the tossing ocean,
  He has reached his Western home;
Bear him as in procession,
  And lay him solemnly
Where, through weary night and morning,
  He shall bear me company.

The name I bear is other
  Than that I bore by birth,
And I've given life to children
  Who'll grow and dwell on earth;
But the time comes swiftly towards me,
  (Nor do I bid it stay,)
When the dead Christ will be more to me
  than all I hold to-day.

Lay the dead Christ beside me,
  Oh press him on my heart,
I would hold him long and painfully
  Till the weary tears should start;
Till the divine contagion
  Heal me of self and sin,
And the cold weight press wholly down
  The pulse that chokes within.

Yet Howe strips the image of most of its religious significance by emphasizing that the Christ is dead and by regarding the crucifix more as a memento of her personal Rome than as a spiritual emblem.

Reproof and frost, they fret me,
  Towards the free, the sunny lands,
From the chaos of existence
  I stretch these feeble hands;
And, penitential, kneeling,
  Pray God would not be wroth,
Who gave not the strength of feeling,
  And strength of labor both.

Thou'rt but a wooden carving,
  Defaced of worms, and old;
Yet more to me thou coulds't not be
  Wert thou all wrapt in gold;
Like the gem-bedizened baby
  Which, at the Twelfth day noon,

> They show from the Ara Coeli's steps,
>   To a merry dancing tune.
>
> I ask of thee no wonders,
>   No changing white or red;
> I dream not thou art living,
>   I love and prize thee dead.
> That salutary deadness
>   I seek, through want and pain,
> From which God's own high power can bid
>   Our virtue rise again.

Because the figure is Christ, Howe is permitted, without violating religious decorum, to welcome the time when it will be more to her than husband or children. Because it is Christ, it can legitimately be a cause of tears and an instrument to reawaken virtue. But it is also very closely associated with her Roman experiences—even, perhaps, in the lines describing its deadness, specifically with Wallace—and its primary function is to provoke a stretching of her hands away from "reproof and frost," the "chaos of existence," toward "the free, the sunny lands." Heaven, perhaps? Nominally, but more to the point, probably, the Via Felice. The expressions of loss outweigh the perfunctorily voiced hope in the last two lines that "virtue" will rise again. The poem commandeers the vocabulary of piety as a way to speak fairly bitterly of the pain of reassuming the yoke of domesticity.

Another such poem is "Thoughts," subtitled "At the Grave of Eloisa and Abelard, in Père la Chaise."[28] Here, the tragic story of sundered lovers provides a scaffold for a personal subnarrative. Howe addresses Eloisa, "saint of passion," describing herself as a "sister heart" but claiming she invokes Eloisa not as "Love's votary" or "the glorious Sybil of despair," rather as

> the Nun, when deeper voices woke thee
> From thy wild fever-dream, to toil and prayer.

What she wants from this meditation is a sense of how Eloisa managed that transformation and what sustained her once she had assumed the "garb of holiness." In their particularity, her questions imply that she herself faces a version of the difficulties Eloisa encountered: Did heaven console you, or did your "plundered heart" feel hell's flames? Was it ennobling or wearisome to be dressed as a nun? Were the saints who watched over you vengeful or compassionate? Did God's love "make expiation sweet?" Most important,

> Say, did that soul of temper so elastic
> Like a bent bow, of its own tension break,
> Or did the Chaos of thy thoughts grow plastic,
> And from the hand divine new moulding take?

Similarly, Eloisa's intensely imagined response recalls Howe's experience with comparable sensations:

> "Often at midnight, on the cold stone lying,
> My passionate sobs have rent the passive air,
> While my crisped fingers clutched the pavement, trying
> To hold him fast, as he had still been there.

> "I called, I shrieked, till my spent breath came faintly,
> I sank, in pain Christ's martyrs could not bear;
> Then dreamed I saw him, beautiful and saintly,
> As his far Convent tolled the hour of prayer.

> "Solemn and deep that vision of reunion—
> He passed in robe, and cowl, and sandall'd feet,
> But our dissever'd lips held no communion,
> Our long divorced glances could not meet."

From this despair, this "rage for happiness, that makes it sin," Eloisa rose to "calmer, wider contemplation" and a knowledge of holiness, and from this position of composure she offers assurance:

> "Oh thou who call'st on me! if that thou bearest
> A wounded heart beneath thy woman's vest,
> If thou my mournful earthly fortune sharest,
> Share the high hopes that calmed my fever'd breast.

> "Not vainly do I boast Religion's power,
> Faith dawned upon the eyes with Sorrow dim;
> I toiled and trusted, till there came an hour
> That saw me sleep in God, and wake with *him.*"

Howe is advised (advises herself) to seek comfort in this way, to use sorrow to "compel . . . merit and reward" and only occasionally to muse on the love Eloisa bore Abelard. Yet the poem ends not with a resolution to follow this advice, but with an image of the poet reaching inside the grate surrounding Eloisa's grave to pick a "ravished rose." This bloom, she tells us, betokens "woman's highest love, and hardest fate"—a cryptic admission that Eloisa's consolations have fallen on deaf ears. Howe's effort to invoke and internalize the nun phase of Eloisa's existence fails in this signal of her determination to preserve only the earlier phases of passion and despair. The poem is thus, in a subtle way, defiant. Howe proclaims her sisterhood with a woman who fell in love and suffered, with lovers who "stole God's treasure from on high" and who, "[w]ithout heaven's virtue . . . had heaven's glory."[29]

THE NOTION OF defiance implies the conscious positing of a figure who will recognize and understand defiant gestures as such. Did Howe construct her husband as such a figure? Certainly she knew he objected to women who published, but did she expect that, once her poems were in print, he would read through her overt texts to the rebellious subtexts and thereby give her rebellion meaning? I am inclined to think that while one part of her may have hoped that the disguised barbs of these poems would pierce her husband's defensive hide, another part took pleasure in her skill at approaching self-revelation without quite stepping out into the open. Numerous letters testify to her conviction that Samuel Howe's preoccupation with the "cold world of actualities" prevented him from understanding the aesthetic, nuanced world she inhabited.[30] And, in fact, the available evidence suggests that he was uncomfortable when obliged to respond to poetry; his congratulatory letters to Longfellow upon the publication of his friend's books, for example, are studies in awkwardness and evasion.[31] Yet, another aspect of Julia Howe's sensibility pulled back from, was ashamed of, the cruelty implicit in a literary project of this kind—an aspect I treat at greater length below and in the next chapter. But in 1853 the predominant self was the angry self, and Howe seems to have determined to go far in an effort to strike back.

It is difficult to believe, for example, that even an inexperienced reader of poetry could miss the implications bodied forth in the metaphors of "Handsome Harry," a poem evidently describing a sailor Howe took note of on one of her Atlantic crossings:[32]

> Why must we look so oft abaft?
> What is the charm we feel
> When handsome Harry guides the craft,
> His hand upon the wheel?

His hand upon the wheel, his eye
The swelling sail doth measure;
Were I the vessel he commands,
I should obey with pleasure.

Whether he tumbles to the top,
Or in the rigging stands,
I must admire his agile feet,
His ready, willing hands.

He would seem taller, were he not
In such proportions made,
He wears as fair and free a brow
As golden curls can shade.

Fresh youth, and joyance, and kind heart
Gleam in his azure eye,
And though I scarcely know his voice,
I think he cannot lie.

More graceful is his shirt of blue,
Than your best Paris coat,
It drapes his manly shoulders well,
Displays his rounded throat.

He seems a glowing Mercury
Just lighted from the sun,
But Harry stands on two trim feet,
And Mercury on one.

From boyhood's days, the ocean wave
Has cradled him to sleep,
He is a true salt water babe,
An orphan of the deep.

And he can win a maiden's ear,
They say, with ready art;
But who would trust to sailors vows?
The pirates of the heart.

Yet, when I see him at the helm
With heaven about his eyes,
I think he's fit to guide our ship
To naught but Paradise.

The narrator's toying with the prospect of being the vessel under Harry's guiding hand, coupled with her confidence that "Paradise" would be their only imaginable destination, is an astonishingly provocative gambit. Howe had read *Typee* and *Omoo* and thus, we can presume, had assimilated Melville's eroticized sailors, but "Handsome Harry," in its particularity and explicitness, and in the fact of its implied female narrator, borders on the proscribed.[33]

Still, however little a husband may have liked being presented with this evidence of his wife's physical attraction to a young seaman, the more painful goads in *Passion-Flowers* must surely have been the poems that seem to recall Horace Binney Wallace. I need to acknowledge immediately that these poems—there are at least seven that I would include in this group[34]—do not name Wallace as their subject. Only one, in fact—"The Fellow Pilgrim"—incorporates material that (we know from other sources) more or less distinctly identifies the "pilgrim." And it may be argued, with good reason, that my relentless impulse to autobiographize carries me too far: the man or men to whom these poems refer, if there is a specific referent at all, may just as plausibly be Theodore Parker, or Longfellow, or her brother Sam, or Edward Twisleton, or Emmanuel Swedenborg, or even Jesus. What they share is the expression of ardent response to *someone,* Wallace being the likeliest candidate. Whoever it was, it clearly was not Samuel Gridley Howe.[35]

Four of these poems appear together in the center of the book and were probably intended, in their sequence, to suggest a narrative. They follow "The Heart's Astronomy," Howe's acknowledgment to her children of her tendency toward waywardness (discussed in chapter 4), and they may be taken as explanation for her discontent at home. The case for their unity as a group is strengthened by the fact that we find them together in manuscript on loose pages at the back of the Laurence file.[36] The first two, "A Child's Excuse" and "The Royal Guest," express deep pleasure in the company of an honored visitor; the other two, "My Last Dance" and "My Sea-ward Window," depict despondency at the loss of youth and friendship.[37]

"A Child's Excuse," in the manuscript version, was initially subtitled "Excuse to ＿＿ ＿＿ for always asking him to come again." This subtitle is crossed out, suggesting an impulse to obscure the poem's immediate connection to her experience or to a specific person. But even without it, the poem is clearly a record of Howe's delight in intense, high-minded exchanges with this unnamed gentleman. The poem's thread of religious language may suggest that the relationship it describes is between a minister and his parishoner—thus the possibility that Theodore Parker is its subject.[38] I would argue, though, that the purpose of this thread is precisely to create this ambiguity, to mask a different kind of intensity with the veil of religious interchange:

> If that I lay my hand upon thine arm
> Detaining thee, be not impatient, friend!
> Tis that thou journeyest, bearing regal gifts,
> And I, a beggar, bid thee stand and lend.
>
> Half for myself, I ask thy thoughts of thee,
> And holy words, that quicken and reprove;
> Half that my grateful soul may render back
> The seed of wisdom in the growth of love.
>
> Why thou canst give, and I receive, a boon
> So blest and blessing, 'tis not mine to tell:
> Thou art a free-born creature—light and air
> From thee, the dungeon-glooms of Life dispel.
>
> That heavenly Art has formed thee thus, I thank
> Goodness and Wisdom endless—that to me
> Thou art a herald of delight and hope,
> I feel deep joy in thanking only thee.
>
> I am but wearing out my feeble hours—
> Linger thou long in Manhood's golden prime!
> I pass, Life's bankrupt, to eternity,
> Stay thou to reap th'inheritance of Time.
>
> But even as now my spirit rises up,
> And bounding brings its welcome to thine heart;
> Thus, when thou too shalt cross the icy stream,
> I shall feel heavenly virtue where thou art.
>
> And if the lowliest tenant I may be
> Of the high precincts of an angel's home,
> My mates, some day, shall mark a sudden joy
> Transfigure one who cries: "My brother's come!"

Certain variants between manuscript and printed versions reinforce the notion that the relationship described, if elevated, nonetheless had a passional element. Instead of "And bounding brings its welcome to thine heart" in the penultimate stanza, for example, Howe first wrote "And bounds to meet thee, nestling to thy heart." The last stanza's "sudden joy" was, in manuscript, "thrill intense." But even in its slightly tamer published version, the poem's rapturous idolatry of this young "friend" or "brother" whose presence heralds "delight and hope" (antipode to "the dungeon-glooms of Life") surely would have signaled to Samuel Howe that he was emphatically not her source for any of the "regal gifts" she mentions.

"The Royal Guest" is a companion piece, reinscribing the relationship set out in the previous poem as one between a king and a peasant. In the presence of this visitor, the poet is tongue-tied, suffused with a sense of the inadequacy and inappropriateness of her usual feminine artifices. His visits are nonetheless very welcome, for this "friend beloved" elevates her to seriousness of purpose and liberates her "prison'd heart." Yet, although the expression of pleasure in these encounters is still intense, the poem taken whole is less exuberant than the earlier one. The heart that springs forth to greet the guest beats with a "faint pulse" even after emancipation, and, rather than the thrilling transfiguration that ends "A Child's Excuse," here the closing image is of inequality and humility:

> Bethink thee, then, whene'er thou com'st to me
> From high emprise and noble toil to rest,
> My thoughts are weak and trivial, matched with thine,
> But the poor mansion offers thee its best.

In its relative sobriety, it prepares the stage for "My Last Dance," a narrative of the last "prodigal o'erflow of life" and a requiem for lost youth. The "one with cheek unfaded" who asks the poet to dance may or may not be Wallace—she says he "brings / My buried brothers to me, in his look"—but the effect of their brief, wild whirl is to evoke a state of mind very close to that of Howe's letter to Auguste Comte, written after Wallace's suicide. We know this despairing condition will be its outcome before the dance even begins, for the two opening stanzas foreshadow a state of existence in which only the fragile outer image is intact, the core burned away:

> The shell of objects inwardly consumed
> Will stand, till some convulsive wind awakes;
> Such sense hath Fire to waste the heart of things,
> Nature, such love to hold the form she makes.
>
> Thus, wasted joys will show their early bloom,
> Yet crumble at the breath of a caress;

> The golden fruitage hides the scathed bough,
> Snatch it, thou scatterest wide its emptiness.

If the dance seems to hold out the promise of regaining her youth, it instead brings home crushingly its loss:

> Sound, measure! but to stir my heart no more—
> For, as I moved to join the dizzy race,
> My youth fell from me; all its blooms were gone,
> And others showed them, smiling, in my face.

The dancer is made conscious of the illusions she has entertained; death-in-life is her true state. The poem ends grimly:

> Faintly I met the shock of circling forms
> Linked to each other, Fashion's galley-slaves,
> Dream-wondering, like an unaccustomed ghost
> That starts, surprised, to stumble over graves.
>
> For graves were 'neath my feet, whose placid masks
> Smiled out upon my folly mournfully,
> While all the host of the departed said,
> 'Tread lightly—thou art ashes, even as we.'

The sequence's final poem, "My Sea-ward Window," invokes again the setting and tensions of "The Heart's Astronomy," only here the poet is inside the house and—as her children were in the earlier poem—anxious about the loss of an emotional polestar:

> The sweet moon rules the east, to-night,
>   To show the sun she too can shine—
> From his forsaken cell of night
>   She builds herself a jewelled shrine.
>
> From my lone window forth I look
>   Where the grim headlands point to sea,
> And think how out between them passed
>   The ship that bore my friend from me.
>
> A track of silvery splendor leads
>   To where my straining sight was staid;
> It might be there our two souls met,
>   And vows of earnest import made.
>
> But then, the Autumn's noontide glow
>   O'er the still sea stretched far and wide,

> While kneeling, watching from the cliffs,
>   "My friend is dear to me!" I cried.
>
> My little children, dancing, cried,
>   "Why do you kneel and gaze so far?"
> "I kneel to bless my parting friend,
>   And even ye forgotten are."
>
> And one might ask, "What boots this song,
>   Sung lonely to yon wintry skies?"
> It leads me, by a holier light,
>   Where Memory's solemn comfort lies.

Why sing such a song of loss? asks the last stanza. The labor helps memorialize the absent friend and thereby brings comfort, but in the opposition of friend with dancing children, the poem also is a map of Howe's emotional terrain. "*Even*" the children (my emphasis) are forgotten in the distraction she feels at Wallace's departure, as if only they and he burn, in this moonscape, with sufficient brightness to be noticed. Where is the children's father? Conspicuous in his absence—or perhaps faintly represented in the sun that has forsaken the "cell of night," thus affording the sweet moon room to build her shrine. The woman is alone in her house, looking out to sea, grieving.

The poem most obviously about Wallace is positioned at a distance from these others, perhaps in order to keep open the range of meaning in the earlier poems. If "The Fellow Pilgrim" were adjacent, it would be much more difficult to suppose that the "royal guest" or "friend" or "brother" were not also straightforward embodiments of the much-prized comrade remembered here:[39]

> When I read o'er the lines I traced
> When thou and I together were,
> My wandering thoughts restrain their haste,
> The power of thy mind is there.
>
> The mind that laid its grasp on me,
> A friendly grasp, but firm and strong,
> First from my errors shook me free,
> Then led me, brotherlike, along.
>
> Mid lovely sights, and holy sounds,
> And landscapes, smiling green and fair,
> To thought and duty's noblest bounds,
> And heart's delights, refined and rare.

Beside thee, in the solemn aisle
The anthem's swelling notes I heard;
There seemed a glory in thy smile,
A lesson in thy lightest word.

The mighty cadence shook my heart,
Like a frail pennon in the gale,
And while I wept and prayed apart,
Thy cheek with strange delight grew pale.

At tombs of poets and of kings
The pilgrim's pious debt I paid;
Oft as my faint soul spread its wings
Thy manlier thought did give it aid.

Thou knew'st not then how sick a heart
Essayed the measure of thine own,
Nor how thy probings made it smart
With sorrow to the world unknown.

Be blest of God, and so farewell!
Southward, the bird of exile flies,
But in her bosom bears a spell
That changes not with changing skies.

The relationship described is an intellectual one, of course. The great value of this man's attentions is said to inhere in his mind's ability to rid her of "errors" and to lead her to "thought and duty's noblest bounds." He offered "lesson[s]" and, as fellow pilgrim, was the wind beneath the wings of her "faint soul." Howe implies nothing improper; overtly, at least, this is not a lament for a departed lover.[40] Yet it is impossible to overlook the tropes of physicality and romantic attachment in this poem. What is essentially a spiritual union is described in startlingly corporeal terms: his mind "laid its grasp . . . firm and strong" on her and "shook [her] free." When they are together in the "solemn aisle" (with its matrimonial allusion), Howe's heart, too, is shaken by a mighty cadence that may be the anthem or, syntactically more likely, the smile and "lightest word" emanating from her friend. The image of her faint soul spreading its wings is eroticized by the assistance his "manlier" thought offers, and the bird of exile flies away bearing in her "bosom" the indelible memories he has given her.

If these suggestions may not have registered with Chev, he certainly could not have missed his wife's explicit reference to her "sick heart" during the period she and Wallace were together. Although the poem as a whole is addressed to Wallace (probably written after his death), the full power of the second-to-last stanza could be understood *only* by her sister Annie or by her husband. This stanza, from his perspective, publicly acknowledges not just his wife's depression (of which he knows himself to be the cause), but also the intimacy suggested in "thy probings" and the efficacy of a man other than himself in bringing her hope. There is also the implication that, while Wallace may not *then* have understood her pain, he did come to understand it later, presumably when the relationship resumed and deepened. Unless we suppose a Julia so entirely blind and distracted (or so repressed) that she was incapable of imagining Chev's probable reaction, or one so suffused with hopelessness and so needy of self-expression that no other considerations could intrude, we are pushed toward supposing a Julia intending to hurt.

Eventually, we know, Samuel Howe did experience the reaction to the book that we would have expected. Julia wrote to Annie in February to explain why she had had to postpone a planned visit:

> Poor changeable Chev has "chopped round" once more, and New York is further off than ever. He was in such a state of mind that it would have been unsafe to leave him. I have been able to calm and soothe him, somewhat, and he now promises that I shall leave on the first of March, for any length of time agreeable to you, Uncle, and myself. I wrote you a letter about this on Saturday, but so sad that it would have pained you much to receive it. Things are better now, but we have been very unhappy. The Book, you see, was a blow to him, and some foolish and impertinent people have hinted to him that the Miller was meant for himself—this has made him almost crazy. He has fancied, moreover, that every one despised and neglected him, and indeed it is true that I have left him too much to himself. I will not expand upon the topic of our miseries—he has been in a very dangerous state, I think, very near insanity, and if I have done best for him and my children by staying here, you, my darling Annie, will neither regret nor complain of it. . . . But be thankful that you have not been here, so far—you *cannot bear* to see people unhappy—it works upon you—we have had the devils' own time of it, and as I tell you, I hardly know myself, after all that I have endured. You must not blame poor Chev, however, he could not help it. I cannot write any more, dear Annie—things pass before me as in a dream.[41]

The reference to the "Miller" pinpoints the poem that evidently sent the doctor over the edge—"Mind versus Mill-Stream." It is perhaps another indication of his inexperience as a reader of poetry that someone else was obliged to tell him that he seemed to be portrayed in the character of the miller, for in this poem not only do Julia Howe's hostility and insouciance glare from behind the most transparent of masks, but a three-stanza "moral" at the end makes her meaning, one would think, virtually impossible to mistake. Her voice in this poem, as well as the poem's central event, recalls Sumner's characterization of her as Undine and echoes her passionate declaration in "From Newport to Rome": *Ye shall listen now.*

"Mind versus Mill-Stream"[42] recounts a battle of wills between a miller who desires a "mild, efficient brook / To help him to his living" and the volatile, unruly rill he decides to tame. Though he wants a placid stream, his "brilliant taste" draws him to one of "brightest play," one that men in the past have tried unsuccessfully to bridle "by artifice, and force." In an obvious reference to Howe's red hair, the stream is said to be "Coiffed with long wreaths of crimson weed." The miller labors through the winter to build his wheel, and when spring arrives and the stream reemerges (like "a frolic maiden come from school"), the miller bids her turn the wheel. The stream's response:

> "Your mill-wheel?" cried the naughty Nymph,
>   "That would indeed be fine!
> You have your business, I suppose,
>   Learn too that I have mine."
>
> "What better business can you have,
>   Than turn this wheel for me?"
> Leaping and laughing, the wild thing cried,
>   "Follow, and you may see."
>
> The Miller trudged with measured pace,
>   As Reason follows Rhyme,
> And saw his mill-stream run to waste,
>   In the very teeth of time.

Angry now, the miller decides to dam his stream—"'For,' thought our friend, 'this water-power / Must not be lightly lost.'"

> "What? will you force me?" said the sprite;
>   "You shall not find it gain;"
> So, with a flash, a dash, a crash,
>   She made her way amain.

> Then, freeing all her pent-up soul,
>   She rushed, in frantic race
> And fragments of the Miller's work
>   Threw in the Miller's face.

He rebuilds the dam "More stoutly than before," but—cagey this time—he refrains from issuing any kind of challenge, imagining that the wild child will yield gracefully in the face of his obvious determination. No such luck:

> For the water-fury bold
> Was still an instant, ere she rose
>   In wrath and power fourfold.

> With roar and rush, and massive sweep
>   She cleared the shameful bound,
> And flung to utterness of waste
>   The Miller, and his mound.

Then—as if both the message and its intended audience were not already absolutely clear—comes the "moral," so called, pugnacious not just in its basic thrust but in its pointed references to the doctor's age and work-focused existence:

> If you would marry happily
>   On the shady side of life
> Choose out some quietly-disposed
>   And placid tempered wife,

> To share the length of sober days,
>   And dimly slumberous nights,
> But well beware those fitful souls
>   Fate wings for wilder flights!

> For men will woo the tempest,
>   And wed it, to their cost,
> Then swear they took it for summer dew,
>   And ah! their peace is lost!

It is illuminating to look closely at Julia's phrases explaining Chev's reaction: "The Book, you see, was a blow to him. . . . some foolish and impertinent people have hinted to him. . . . this has made him almost crazy. . . . fancied, moreover, that every one despised and neglected him." There seems to be an element of surprise in her account, suggesting, perhaps, that his alleged difficulty in reading her accurately was not greater than hers in reading him. Could she truly not have foreseen this development? Wasn't his reaction, in some sense, precisely the one she hoped to evoke?[43] She takes some trouble, too, to display herself as the concerned, obliging caretaker, unwilling to leave him when he might be a danger to himself, ready to sacrifice her plans to help him through this bad time, eager to divert blame away from him (he, after all, "could not help it"). Whence this solicitude, which could strike us as very close to hypocrisy?

In fact, the penitential note heard beneath the letter's disingenuousness does not sound here for the first time. It is also part of the composition of the book, the aspect of it that (I earlier suggested) reflects Howe's reservations about her project. Two of the poems discussed above, "The Dead Christ" and the meditation on Eloisa, introduce the concept of contrition and express some level of desire for "virtue." This note can be felt in her labor to develop modes of telling the truth "slant"—a route made necessary, of course, by proscriptions on women's discourse, but also arguably one that her own ambiguity about the ethics of marital rebellion might have compelled anyway.[44] It is also discernible in a few other poems in which Howe seems to chide herself for the belligerence on display elsewhere. Although penitence is by no means a prevalent attitude, and although the stoicism that is its major form of expression may easily be read as something more like despair than remorse, the book does include material that complicates the notion of an aesthetic of vengeance.

"Wherefore" is such a poem, a work that appropriates the image of Louis Kossuth as a springboard for reflections that have little to do with him—or with revolutionary politics at all, since Kossuth soon gives way to Napoleon as Howe's major focus.[45] The poem's initial question is, why didn't Kossuth fall when Hungary fell?

> Why could the man not die with his day of dominion?
> His work at end, wherefore live to be scantily pensioned
> By hearts that grudge the reward when it follows the labor?

Howe's shift from Kossuth to Napoleon is at first puzzling, since Napoleon would seem to represent everything Kossuth committed himself to overturning.[46] The firebrand Hungarian's potential as an image of revolution, a figure analogous to the upstart water sprite in "Mind versus Mill-Stream," is ignored; instead, Howe seems to come close to idealizing "the imperial crown . . . the full outpouring of power that stops at no frontier." "Common minds," we are told, "stand agape at his mighty ambition," and when you visit the Invalides, where his remains are entombed,

> his dead presence fastens upon you,
> In proportions unearthly, while choking and swelling,
> The heart in your breast with his passionless ashes claims kindred.

Their politics are beside the point; both men here emblemize life lived fervently, every faculty engaged. Why, Howe wonders, is it so often the case that such figures survive beyond their moment of greatness, thus obliged to endure diminishment, imprisonment, and the pain of being forgotten? Why, by extension, must *any* of us exist past the moment of life's greatest intensity? Why (implicitly) must a Roman spring end, a beloved companion die, the walls of domestic incarceration shut one in?

> . . . this new Prometheus, wherefore remains he
> Held by the torturing will of his dreadful enchainer?
> How is he narrowly caged for his captor's diversion,
> While the coarse vulture sits leisurely tearing his vitals . . .

Why are we "reserved . . . to perish by inches?"[47]

The response, long in coming, while Howe feelingly recreates the great emperor's final days, is this:

> Why died not Kossuth? Men die as God pleases;
> Felons and madmen alone anticipate rudely
> The last consummation, and yet from their doom escape not.
> Think'st thou thy work at end, and thy discipline perfect?
> Other pangs still remain, other labors and sorrows;
> Other the crises of Fate than the crises of Being.
> Let me round my words with one brief admonition:
> Take for the bearings of life, thine own or another's,
> This motto, blazoned on cross and on altar: "God's patience."

Her meditation ends by acknowledging the mystery of God's ways and by swallowing the fact that (ruling out suicide as the provenance only of "felons and madmen") one is obliged to wait out the revelation of those ways. The pangs of existence bear no relation to the turnings of Fate; we cannot know what is intended for us ultimately. If this is not exactly an apology, it is a philosophical objectification of her sadness, an acknowledgment that life in constricted circumstances may yet have something to teach her. It is also, possibly, a distancing of herself from Wallace, whose self-destructive impulse is here associated with criminality or insanity.

Distancing is the theme of "Entbehren," the German title of which (meaning "to do without, to dispense with") may be a gesture of homage to Goethe.[48] The poem recalls Faust's investment in the belief that fulfillment of desire is the last thing humans want.

> Oh! happy he who never held
> In trembling arms a form adored,
> Oh! happy he who never yet
> On worshipped lips love's kisses poured!

If Beauty should spread her banquet of delights in your path, offer you wine, fill your head with visions—resist these blandishments, the poem says. They are phantasmal, not "that high ideal of thought / Which forms the bounds of hope and pleasure." Better not to enchain the soul through "bootless vows":

> The Infinite, that sees us thus
> Mould its transcendent form in clay,
> Tramples our idol into dust,
> And we afresh must seek and pray.

The last stanza acknowledges that resisting the impulse to embody the soul's most enticing visions brings pain, but it also offers assurance that the pain of losing such necessarily ephemeral materializations is greater:

> And thou shalt suffer to be free,
> But most shalt suffer to be bound,
> Pour, then, the cup of thy desire
> An offering upon holy ground.

The poem bears no particular personal marks, but is plausibly a reflection on the loss of Wallace or others who seemed to offer realization of Howe's dreams for recognition and sympathy. Its suggestion that desire for such incarnations be sacrificed is like the commitment at the end of "Wherefore" to a more comprehensive view of existence, one that rests on a clearer sense of what is truly important.

Another such poem is "Midnight," a vivid evocation of the various kinds of intensity that surface at that hour.[49] It is the moment when "all the powers of being / To height and crisis crowd": saint, Bacchanalian, gamester, thief, mourners—all experience their passions most power-fully then. The speaker, too, wholeheartedly relishes this sensation:

> I love to walk the darkness
> On the Midnight's folded arm,
> Between Earth's struggling currents
> And Heaven's blue depths of calm . . .

But the poem ends with a backing-away from this kind of intensity, an image of resolution in heavenly calm:

> Upon my brow and bosom
> Let holy lilies lie,
> By the child Jesus gathered
> In radiant infancy;
>
> Then, when the midnight fever
> Rushes through heart and brain,
> I hold them here, I press them there,
> And God is felt again.

Thus the work—though its conclusion may strike us as conventional and perfunctory—argues for the breaking of passion, the relinquishment of such "ghostly terrors." It suggests that comet-Julia had (on occasion, anyway) an impulse toward stability, religious fortitude, the placid sensibility that might render a balky stream willing to run in its culturally ordained bed.[50]

IN THIS EFFORT to read Howe's first collection as arising out of a particular intense domestic situation, I do not mean to suggest that it is reducible to a single narrative. If the book is in its basic impetus an effort to declare independence, to be heard, to accrue power, it succeeds in part by virtue of its broad presentation of Howe's ardent, wide-ranging sensibility. In addition to being a woman frustrated by her husband's indifference and grieved by the loss of a discerning and supportive friend, she is also a woman who vehemently berates her social circle to wake up to the tragic aftermath of 1848. In this gesture, she took a substantial risk, for as Larry Reynolds has shown, the radical stance was not much admired in America in the early 1850s:

During the year 1848, radical and speculative thought acquired more fearful potency in the American consciousness than it had had since the days of Anne Hutchinson, and as a result, the next several years saw opprobrium cast upon radicals of every sort, who were usually charged with red republicanism, communism, or socialism.[51]

Howe may have found the radical political stance less difficult to adopt because it so completely accorded with her reaction to domestic oppression, but to adhere to it publicly still required independence of thought and a willingness to endure the kind of scorn she had watched her husband and Charles Sumner evoke as they had moved more firmly toward an abolitionist position in the late 1840s. One of the strongest pieces in *Passion-Flowers,* "Whit-Sunday in the Church," lends the radical stance authority by seeing it as Jesus' characteristic attitude toward social evil.[52] In understanding Jesus in this way, Howe portrays herself as distinct from the church establishment's official representative.

Whit-Sunday commemorates Pentecost, for Christians the great moment of linguistic brotherhood when the Holy Spirit descended on the apostles in tongues of flame (as recorded in Acts 2:1–13). Those assembled spoke in languages not their own, but all were intelligible to each other. The opening stanzas of the poem imply an analogy between this sacred occasion of unity—giving "the lost ancestral tongue / Akin to each dismembered nation"—and the pan-national aspect of the 1848 uprisings:

> Men, by convulsive Nature, torn
> And held apart, in strange solution,
> A moment saw how Man should come
> Out of the age's evolution.

But the more specific occasion is Howe's attendance at church on this day, looking to shake off "worldly dust and soiling" and to offer contrition. The minister, she expects, will guide "the brave soul's blind desiring," but what he offers severely disappoints her. Pentecost, in his construction, metaphorically describes what happens as a result of sincere prayer. The descent of the spirit is historically distant (the tongues spoken, he says, were Arabian, Cretan, Syrian, and Persian) and emblematic in these latter days of the fruits of *private* devotion. Cultivate prayerful habits, "[c]ontinue earnest on your knees," attend church often with the intent of fostering the "inward flame"—this is his reading of the meaning of the day.

Incensed by this "flimsy foolishness," Howe conjures instead an image of a vibrant, fervent Jesus sweeping through the aisles, shaking the sashes—an Emersonian Christ who has been "by doctrine slain, / By ritual buried," but who now arises to breathe out "urgings passionate and tender." These urgings call the devout not to song and prayer, but to an activist "rule of work and life; / A work of love, a life of uses." Howe's Messiah declares that the words he uttered were only part of his import; his followers need also perceive him as one whose "hands unto my heart bore witness." He is not to be found, now, within "a church that rests / A comfortable, cold abstraction." He does not sit to hear himself lauded; rather, his "less decorous haunts" are where backs are scourged, limbs tied, among the poor, the seamstresses "Who suffer hell to clothe the world," in circles

> where earnest minds assert
> God's law against a creed dogmatic,
> And from dead symbols free the truth
> Of which they once were emblematic.

In particular, he speaks of himself as one of the politically disenfranchised:

> "He is where patriots pine in cells,
>   To felons chained, or faint and gory
> Ascend the scaffold steps, to leave
>   Their children's heritage of glory.

> "He is where men of fire-touched lips
>   Tell, to astonished congregations,
> The infamies that prop a crown,
>   And paint in blood the wrongs of nations.

> "He cries: 'On, brethren, draw the sword,
>   Loose the bold tongue and pen, unfearing,
> The weakness of our human flesh
>   Is ransomed by your persevering!'

And even more pointedly, lest the implicit analogy of the poem's beginning be overlooked:

" 'Twas for the multitude I bled,
  Not for the greatest, richest, whitest;
  My very cheek, thou knout-arm'd Russ
  Takes color from the cheek thou smitest;

"My very heart, most Christian prince,
  Wakes sullen Spielberg with its sighing;
  My very mother, childless, weeps
  Above those brave young Lombards dying.

"My very child, since children mark
  The earthward ripening of our nature,
  Is sold in yonder negro babe,
  That ne'er shall know its father's feature."

The poem climaxes with a diatribe leveled against those who memorialize Jesus with pomp. The imagery here is explicitly Catholic, reinforcing the poem's focus on recent European political history:

"And when I, passing, see inscribed
  My name upon some costly building,
  Whose deep aisles open up to shrines,
  Splendent with purple and with gilding;

"Where pampered priests, with bell and book,
  A simulation make of praying,
  While the poor, ever-cheated, wait
  Heart-sick with hope, on my delaying:

"I think upon those mocking men
  Who called me Monarch, to deride me;
  Think, they who gave me the robe of pride
  Were ever they that crucified me."

The poem's narrative frame—the poet meditating in church—does not return at the end. Thus there is a sense of a melding of voices: Jesus' powerful call to action issues out of Howe's mouth and is her call, too. The proper appropriation of Pentecostal fire, she says, is in battling the disparities—wealth, race, power—that divide humans from one another and deny freedom to many.[53]

This portrait of an activist Jesus reproduces Margaret Fuller's call, in her twelfth dispatch to the *Tribune,* for "some practical application of the precepts of Christ, in lieu of the mummeries of a worn-out ritual."[54]

Another poem early in the volume, "A Protest from Italy," also recalls Fuller, recording Howe's transformation from indifference to indignation regarding slavery.[55] Swathed in the scent of Italian orange groves, settled into calmness and peace, she admits she registered only impatience at the "wrangling tongues" and "untempered babbling" from the West that threatened her rapture. Her words for abolitionists, then, were: " 'You—frantic champions of the slave, / Bethink—God orders all for good.' " If secession offers the quickest resolution of this noise, well, so be it:

> "Northern and Southron, part in peace,
> Each to his own contentment thrive,
> Since each divergent destiny
> May keep a sacred good alive."

Her return home is an awakening, however, and we hear the first hint of sentiments that will find indelible expression a decade hence in "The Battle Hymn":

> Bathed in your icy Northern springs,
> My slumbering eye is roused to sight;
> The sharp steel wind doth sunder all
> My silken armor of delight.
>
> Mine ear, by mass and anthem lulled,
> The trumpet's brazen voice awakes;
> From its slow pulses, keenly stirred,
> My blood its natural current makes.

From this nearer vantage point, that "untempered babbling" is the articulation of "a plague, long held aloof, / That to the social heart hath crept." If "Base Interest" will trample "Godlike Right," one must speak out, strike the lyre, infuse "palsied hand" with "ancient might." The poem concludes with a promise to her country to do just that:

> however dear
> I hold the light of Roman skies;
> However from the canvas clear
> The soul of Raphael blessed mine eyes;
>
> Howe'er intense the joy of flowers,
> And the spring-wedded nightingale,
> Or deep the charm of twilight hours
> Hushed to the Miserere's wail;

> A holier joy to me were given,
> Could I persuade thy heart from wrong;
> As rapturous birds drop down from heaven,
> With heaven's convincement in their song.

In these and in a few other poems in *Passion-Flowers*—"Pio Nono," "My Lecture," "The Death of the Slave Lewis"—the Julia Ward Howe that her country would eventually canonize is first bodied forth. We hear in these passionate calls for social justice the voice of the woman who would become a potent force in the advancement of women's rights and, more generally, a tireless advocate for freedom of all kinds. The publication of this first book—however tightly the project may for her have been wound up in the articulation of a private grief—thrust her into a still quite small circle of women who, by midcentury, had gathered the courage to "speak" publicly against inequitable political structures.

TWO POEMS EPITOMIZE, for me, the contemplative Julia Howe who, in the moments when preoccupation with the "briars" in her life could be set aside for a time, saw in her art a means of coming to equilibrium. The first of these, "Correspondence," addresses a "thee" whose identity remains veiled.[56] The title may allude to a Swedenborgian principle; Howe had by 1853 read a fair amount of Swedenborg, finding him a consolation and a calming influence.[57] Or an argument could be made that Wallace is the addressee. But "thee" may also be an abstraction—a muse, perhaps, or an idea of relation between the aesthetic object and the vision it strives to embody.

> May I turn my musings to thee
> In my wintry loneliness?
> May my straggling measure woo thee,
> May my deeper thought pursue thee,
> Till thy sunlight, striking through me,
> Pause to fertilize and bless?

Under the sway of this invigorating impulse, speech without anxiety would be possible:

> I, methinks, could speak, unfearing
> Fault, or blemish to unfold,
> Blots, the soul's deep beauty blearing,
> Torturous scars, the frail heart searing—

In such wise and gracious hearing,
Life's arcana may be told.

The poem develops the image of the artist laboring to realize her beautiful conception:

Didst thou ever model slightly
Plastic images of clay,
Touched with grace and feeling sprightly
That a moment might delight thee,
Not too good or precious rightly
To unmake, and throw away?

Hast thou ever paused, despairing,
At a block of Parian stone?
Life and form within thee bearing,
Dreams of Godlike beauty sharing,
Dimly hoping, faintly daring
To develope the unknown?

With the powers immortal vying,
Like an infant armed with fate,
Not a blossom, born for dying,
Not a song that ends with sighing,
But a presence, Time-defying,
Thou conceivest, to create.

Not to bear ignoble traces
Hath this mountain crystal grown,
But that all celestial graces,
Shining out through marble faces,
Should make glad Earth's lonely places
With a glory of their own.

Then the poem takes an unexpected turn: carving out a time-defying, Earth-gladdening work becomes a metaphor for what the speaker has on occasion tried to do in constructing a friendship. Sadly, these have so far proved "fragile and diurnal"—they are "Images of loves eternal / Broken in the play of Time." But they need not be so evanescent, she reasons: as artists preserve their visions, so can *we* (the emphasis is hers) "hold to permanence" these "gifts of Nature's lending." The poem closes with a resolution to do so:

Fate's pure marble lies so whitely,
Formlessly, between us cast,

> I have wrought and studied slightly—
> Thou who knowest all things rightly,
> From my heart's love, but not lightly,
> Mold a Friendship that shall last.

If Wallace's specter is hovering in the background of this work, it is imaginably an expression of Howe's determination, despite the fact that he is physically lost to her, to create some enduring memorial of what his companionship signified. This book may be that memorial. However, whether or not the poem supports so specific a reading, it does thoughtfully articulate Howe's vision of the artist's work, and it testifies to her faith in the redemptive energy available through commitment to developing "the unknown." In this she exemplifies Audre Lorde's claim that poetry "forms the quality of the light within which we predicate our hopes and dreams toward survival and change, first made into language, then into idea, then into more tangible action."[58]

The other poem is "Visions,"[59] the last piece in the collection and, taken whole, not one of its best. Like several others toward the end of the book, it deals in fairly conventional religious images and ideas, yet its evocation of Christ about halfway through opens the door to a very personal voice. It is suddenly as if our ear is pressed to Julia's heart.

> "Nay, my Cristo, help me only
>   To a striving after good;
> Faints my heart in love so lonely,
>   Fails the earnest, hopeful mood.
>
> "Hold in check these nerves so frantic,
>   When the current counter runs,
> Give me patience with each antic
>   Of the wild and thoughtless ones.
>
> "If Displeasure, sourly looking
>   From stern eyelids, wounds my pride,
> Let me hear thy mild rebuking,
>   And the pang in silence hide.
>
> "Clearer vision, joys ecstatic
>   I resign for humbler state;
> But let Life be emblematic
>   Of the soul's immortal fate."

Here, although the poem names the by-now-familiar griefs, there is no anger. There is instead a plea for help in combating them—which does not suggest contrition, but rather a recognition that however much liberty she may take in voicing pain, ultimately her job is to discover how to live with it. Christ hears her, she feels, and points the way; "Hopefully the pilgrim learneth / She must walk to meet the day."

Yet in a last turn of emotion, Howe prevents the poem (and book) from coming to resolution on this sentimental note. Here is the final stanza:

> Then Life rises to entomb me,
> Waking am I all alone;
> Half I feel, Christ passes from me,
> Half I deem, he is not gone.

The terminal image again drives home her solitude, a state that is, in the stanza's deeply ironic first line, death in life. Yes, Christ *may* be with her, but only half her sensibility accepts that as likely. The distinction between "feel" and "deem" seems to characterize the belief of the last line as a considered choice, not as an instinctive confidence. This closure may not negate the resolve to "walk to meet the day," but it does insist on her prerogative to speak her mind, one way or another, while doing so. Her art had afforded her that option.

SIX

"Down the Bitter River She Dropped"

Words for the Hour and The World's Own

FROM A late twentieth-century feminist perspective, there is nothing to do but cheer at such milestones as the appearance of a work like *Passion-Flowers*. Like the 1848 Seneca Falls convention, like the publication of Fanny Fern's *Ruth Hall* later in 1854, like Florence Nightingale's deification two years later, like a myriad of other smaller (or larger) instances of the breaching of barricades to freedom, Julia Ward Howe's step into the public eye has lost, for us, any of the equivocal aspect it had for most of her contemporaries, or for herself. We embrace it as an Emersonian grasp of the scepter, and not a momentary one only, but the kind that represents a claiming and settling of territory that permanently alters the map of the world.

From Howe's perspective, the ground she stood on in 1854 was indeed new, and its topography was not at all well defined. One feature she quickly discovered was the number of land mines it concealed. During the next three years she learned to inhabit this landscape, modifying it when possible to reduce its danger, modifying herself when the environment proved intractable. Her second and third published works—another collection of poems, a play—record this process. Thereafter, although strife between husband and wife continued, circumstances and the terms of the contest altered substantially. Sumner's near murder on the floor of the United States Senate, the increasing polarization of North and South, trips to Kansas and Cuba, John Brown's raid on the arsenal at Harper's Ferry, Theodore Parker's death, and finally the coming of the Civil War and Howe's elevation to celebrity status as a result of "The Battle Hymn"—these mark so sharp a boundary between what had been and what was to come that they form the beginning of another story. *Words for the Hour* and *The World's Own* (both 1857) illustrate how Howe determined to manage the "volcanic resources" that had spewed forth in her first book.[1]

Passion-Flowers was a modest commercial success, selling out two printings and most of a third by April. According to her calculations, Howe earned about two hundred dollars, money she used to buy furniture for the family's newly purchased farmhouse in Lawton's Valley near Newport. But, as she reported to Louisa, the income realized from the book or even the regard of literary critics meant little next to the understanding she garnered from sensitive readers: "[M]ore than either praise or money has been the affectionate sympathy it has awakened for me in divers gentle hearts."[2] One such heart was that of Ednah Dow Cheney, the only woman to review the book. Cheney, nearly a contemporary of Howe's (she was five years younger) and an acquaintance from the days of Fuller's Conversations, was just at the beginning of her own long career as a writer and agitator for women's suffrage.[3] Cheney acknowledged that "many critics, of taste most precise and orthodox, may find some fault with nearly every poem." Let them, she suggested: others will readily bring to the book a much less judgmental spirit,

> Forgetting vulgar rules, with spirit free
> To judge each author by his own intent,
> Nor think one standard for all minds is meant.

"Yet it really is a grave thing, and, in this country, a rare thing," Cheney continued,

> to publish such a book as this. Lively description and subtle sentiment have been the highest characteristics of the almost infinite and infinitesimal brood of female songsters which the Rev. Mr. Griswold has harbored under his wings; timidly, yet earnestly, we have demanded something deeper than these, something truer to the idea of American womanhood. Shall we say that now, for the first time, we have been answered? We surely believe that this work stands for such a want in our Literature, and it is one that very many will not willingly let die.

Interestingly, although Cheney mentioned Elizabeth Barrett Browning (to whom Sumner had likened Julia), it was with *Robert* Browning's work that Cheney compared the *Passion-Flowers* poems. Both, she noted, indicate "a certain tingling of the emotion in every fibre of the writer, which always has a galvanic effect on the reader." In this way Cheney paralleled George Ripley, who had also praised the book by seeing in it "an intellect of masculine self-concentration and force" and declaring its uniqueness among the productions of other women writers. Yet it was the *womanliness* of the poems and their quality of having been written in " 'sad perplexed minors' " that rendered them most valuable in Cheney's eyes. The absence of the note of sadness in others' work, she suggested, was a serious omission; this life is, after all, "a grave problem." The book, she hoped, would provide sustenance of a particular necessary sort: "[W]e shall read these verses from time to time with something of that faith with which the devout ascribe power to the pale lock of hair from some fair Renunciant."

These and other like sentiments, privately expressed, no doubt offered Howe herself such sustenance. Certainly she needed it, for although she could take deep pleasure in the impact her poems were making, life at home had never been worse. We have already seen a glimpse of the havoc Chev began to wreak when the extent of his wife's emotional defection registered with him. Julia kept full vision of it for her eyes alone (although she did, in conversation, pour her heart out to Annie). Still, its devastation is evident in her letter to Louisa, already partly quoted above. One sign of the degree is that she could not bring herself to finish this letter, begun in July 1854, until November. After reporting the income from the book, she continues:

> But I don't think much about it now, the little stir it made is nearly past, and I am quite my own little quiet self again. Not that I was at any time much elated by its success, for my domestic troubles at the time were so overwhelming, that I only kept soul and body together by a strong and intense effort. Chev was very angry about the book, and I really thought at one time that he would have driven me to insanity, so horribly did he behave. He has been much less unkind, for some time past, and I try to please him as much as I can, but when he is angry, he has no control over his own feelings, and no consideration for those of others. Indeed, dear Wevie, you may believe all that Annie tells you of my trials on this score— they are sometimes such that I would not endure them for a day, but for my children's sake.

The fits of fury were not constant, she says; there had been periods of peace. And she acknowledges "many errors and short comings" on her part that she has tried to atone for by "endless patience and self-command," and she knows that others bear similar or worse afflictions with better spirits. Yet . . . and here the letter breaks off, to be resumed four months later, at which point she had achieved sufficient command of the grimmest aspect of the whole experience to be able, at last, to describe it to Louisa. This is our most intimate access to the dynamics of the Howe marriage:

> This letter, begun in Lawton's Valley, was interrupted by some days of such sadness, that I have felt, ever since, unable and unwilling to go back to them so much as to take out these pages from the portfolio in which I then placed them. . . . I see from your letter that you have learned a fact of which I could not have written to you, that of my approaching confinement. You ask whether I am glad or sorry. I can scarcely trust myself to speak of it, so bitter and horrible a distress has it been to me. You recommend ether etc—my dear Wevie, my mental suffering during these nine months nearly past has been so great, that I cannot be afraid of any bodily torture, however great. Neither does the future show me a single gleam of light. I shall not drag this weary weight about with me, it is true, but I can not feel that my heart will be any lighter. I dread to see the face of my child, for I know I cannot love it. I must not write further in this strain—it brings tears, and I never give way to these, lest I should lose the little eyesight I have left. I will only tell you one thing, dearest sister, and that one, because I cannot but wish to be understood by the few who really love me. After three years of constantly increasing unkindness & estrangement, no alternative presented itself to me, but that of an attempt at reconciliation, or a final separation. The latter had been all along in ____'s mind, and was so favorite a project with him, that he w[oul]d bring it up even in our quietest hours, when there was nothing whatever to suggest it. His dream was to marry again—some young girl who would love him supremely. Before God, dear Louisa, I thought it my real duty to give up every thing that was dear and sacred to me, rather than be forced to leave two of my children, and those two the dearest, Julia & Harry. In this view, I made the greatest sacrifice I can ever be called upon to make. God must accept it, and the bitter suffering of these subsequent months, as some expiation for the errors of my life. Burn this—I shall never speak of these things again.

Maud, the Howes' fifth child, was born five days later (9 November). Her conception, thus, occurred in February, just at the moment Chev grasped how he had been represented in Julia's poetry. Julia's letter to Annie from that period, discussed in the previous chapter, includes two sentences that, in retrospect, ring poignantly: "He was in such a state of mind that it would have been unsafe to leave him. I have been able to calm and soothe him, somewhat, and he now promises that I shall leave on the first of March." Maud was, starkly, the price Howe was required to pay for having published *Passion-Flowers.*

Nor was that all. Even this capitulation, substantial as it was, seems to have been not quite enough. There is, to be sure, no evidence of intentional cruelty, and in fact Howe's letters occasionally record gestures of kindness or thoughtfulness on her husband's part. But much of his behavior during the months of this pregnancy suggests that his sense of injury lingered. A late March letter from Julia to Annie records that he did little to make life comfortable for her: "Loneliness, desolation, much fault finding, a cold house, no carriage, weary walks in and out of town, these things go far to counterbalance any pleasure that my Book has given me." Worse, though, was his sudden, independent decision to sell Green Peace, the house the Howes had occupied since 1846. Chev informed Julia by letter while she was visiting Annie (the visit she had repeatedly postponed in order to accommodate his needs) of his intention to move the family back into an apartment in the Institution. She replied from Bordentown (after a delay caused, she noted, not by company or interruption but by the "pain and agitation" his plan caused whenever she thought about it) that his "announcement" was "a very bitter thing to me, and a very sad one to my friends." Opposition of will or temper, she recognized, "would be useless. . . . I cannot struggle with so fierce an opponent." In any case, she said, though his letter had brought great sorrow, "my part is to *bear.*"[4]

Chev had his reasons, some of which he explained to Julia's uncle in a June letter.[5] Living in the Institution would save the family two thousand dollars a year, an amount that, accumulating for five years, would keep them from too heavy dependence on Julia's trust fund "in the contingency of real estate going down." He also said that the Institution's trustees wanted him to live there at least part of the year (though it is hard to understand how residence at Green Peace, very close by, would not satisfy this concern). The apartment, he assured John Ward, was "convenient and elegant." Other considerations were the expense of maintaining the recently purchased farmhouse near Newport (although Julia professed little attachment to it, regarding its purchase the year before "simply as an experiment") and her alleged distaste for the South Boston home. This last reason seems more than a little disingenuous:

Julia—like her husband—often expressed a desire to spend at least the winter months in Boston proper, because of the difficulty of travel back and forth from South Boston. But he now chose to understand such wishes as a sign that she despised Green Peace itself. Julia was able to deter the move for some months (partly by enlisting Uncle John's support) and in the summer was even under the impression that Chev had abandoned his plans.[6] But as her pregnancy drew toward its close, the plan became fact, and by the time of Maud's birth the family was resettled in the Institution.

During the spring and summer Howe experienced several fits of hysteria—"a sort of spasmodic hysteric," she called them, or a "*crise de nerfs*"—which frightened her and at least once forced her to call her husband for assistance.[7] His concerned response suggests that relations between the two were not utterly demolished, but since she viewed these spells as brought on by her determined effort to preserve her eyes by not crying, it is difficult not to place responsibility for them on him. Her solace was to "cram [her]self with Philosophic positive" and to immerse herself in study or in writing to friends. A letter to the Twisletons from this period shows this process in operation.[8] The letter begins ebulliently: she is full of gossip and wickedly humorous jibes at the Ticknors for discovering interest in her poems only after Fields has published them. She is also eager to send the Twisletons a copy of *Passion-Flowers* (viewing them as particularly well positioned to understand the book's subtext) and to repeat compliments she had received. But halfway through, the letter breaks off, and when she takes it up again a week later, her mood has changed totally. Acknowledging this change (but masking the cause), she says she hopes to "forget [herself] for an hour, in your kind company."

> I am trying so hard, so hard, not to shed tears, for the sake of my poor corroded eyes—you shall help me. I will stand between you, taking a hand of each, and so we will go off into the pleasant fields of thought, away from the unkind and cruel things with which neither you nor I have any fellowship.

The physic works: by the end of the letter her resilience has returned ("I have written myself quite out of my crying fit, and am at last quite serene").

This letter's self-representation echoes the woman projected in

Passion-Flowers—its Julia Ward Howe is by turns spunky, a little vindictive, self-deprecating, self-promotional, clever, melodramatic, thought-
ful, studious (a long section recounts her reading in Hegel and Comte),
observant, and intent on preserving her equilibrium and vision against
the (unspecified) forces that threaten them. Her elision of the cause
of her unhappiness—she says the circumstances "would be useless to
explain"—suggests either that the Twisletons will understand it without
explanation or that she wishes to shield her husband's disagreeable behavior from too-open display. Either way, as in her poems, her discourse
is double: it both reveals and does not reveal, thereby embodying her
ambivalence. Her desire for empathy generates the image of Dejected
Victimized Julia; her determination to embrace the quality of for-
bearance produces Virtuous Resolute Julia. These were the poles between which she oscillated in this sad year of 1854.

The letter does, however, articulate unambivalent resistance to one
kind of response her book provoked in some readers. Howe reports
hearing that a lady of her acquaintance found the book's tone too
hopeless—that a more appropriate view of life's difficulties would be to
recognize their usefulness as an education in discipline. Howe herself
had delivered a variation on this theme at the end of "Wherefore" by
suggesting that God's ways with us are inscrutable and that patience,
therefore, is advisable—"God's" patience. Now, though, she finds the
advice repellent, asking, "Could you find any comfort in such a theory?"
Such an attitude causes a diminishment in the amount of "Divine-ness"
attached to God, to suppose him the inventor of the tortures of life.
Instead, "Cruel men invent them, and invoke divine authority for laying
them upon us." The drift of her thoughts, as she suffered through
periodic exhibitions of her husband's anger, was not toward resolution
of grief in sentimental piety.

As for Samuel Howe, during this year he threw himself with increasing zeal into political activity against slavery. Congress's deliberation on
the Kansas-Nebraska Act in early 1854 generated an immediate furious
response in the North; the doctor helped organize Boston's protest meeting in mid-February and later gave support to the creation of the Massachusetts Emigrant Aid Society, which funded settlement in Kansas of
antislavery homesteaders. He spent much time soliciting contributions
from sympathetic Bostonians. Privately, he was nearly as full of grief as
his wife. Writing to Sumner after his friend's departure for Washington,

he described his difficulty hiding his tears (and his indulgence in them once alone) at the loss, once again, of Sumner's comforting presence. He ought to have let them flow, he reflected, for "I have swallowed in silence & with an exterior as calm as might be, bitter tears enough to turn my whole system into gall & wormwood."[9] The letter continues:

> Your friendship,—your presence here,—& the consciousness that I *might* be sure of finding in you all the sympathy, & all the comfort, that the most urgent need could ever call for, has been to me like an anchor of the soul—[unsaid?] indeed,—but valued beyond price. May it be that neither time nor separation shall lessen the reliance I have in you. To lose my faith in you, would indeed shiver, for a time, my faith in God. . . . [D]ear Sumner, it has been, & will be, the pride of my life, to merit & to possess the friendship of a man like you.

Aside from his work and causes, he relied on his ten-year-old daughter Julia Romana as an aid in maintaining emotional stability. After one reunion with her, he wrote Sumner:

> I need not attempt to give you an idea of the rapture I felt at meeting the dear child. She loves me tenderly; and her eager caress, & her gentle attention to my every want, hurrying about to see what she could do for me—made amends for all fatigue & discomfort I had gone through. She has all her mother's intensity & earnestness of nature, but expending little of it intellectually she pours it forth in efforts to make others happy;—not to shine & be pleased herself.[10]

Thus, between outpourings to Sumner and attentions to Julia Romana (obviously she was becoming a surrogate for her mother; this letter also incidentally indicates how much Chev despised Julia's self-expressive impulses), he kept himself afloat.[11]

THE RANGE OF Howe's response to the accumulated sorrows of life in the mid-1850s is exhibited in her second collection of poems, *Words for the Hour*.[12] The range is a narrow one, as reviewers noted.[13] The multi-faceted, complex sensibility embodied in *Passion-Flowers* here seems to shrink to a monaural voice, like a "torrent of lava" in intensity but resolved to sing only sad songs. Howe's letters in the months before its publication barely mention work on the book, and once it appeared, she seemed as much interested in the money it would earn as in the critical attention.[14] In her *Reminiscences* she afforded it a mere three sentences, noting that some critics thought it better than her first book but predicted that it would meet with less success—"And so, indeed, it proved" (230).

George Curtis, writing for *Putnam's*, proclaimed every poem in the book "full of the most passionate feeling, strained with intense emotion," expressive of "a longing, restless, imperious, and affectionate nature." Curtis emphasized the work's confessional nature: "It is a purely private and personal book. . . . [O]f all the many volumes of poetry recently published, Mrs. Howe's seems to us by far the most startlingly real. It is a leaf out of life. She sings what she is." As Ripley and Cheney had done with *Passion-Flowers*, Curtis underlined this distinction between Howe's work and that of other women poets: "After the reign of the *myriad Lady Magazine poetesses* (the mongrel word is appropriate here), ladies who have written the most graceful good grammar about emotions they never had, it is truly refreshing to encounter a torrent of lava streaming out of the heart of real experience. . . . This is no 'woman's poetry,' but the thought and the music of a poet." Yet he acknowledged that the "purely private cast" of the verses rendered them difficult and often obscure and suggested that "resolute emancipation" from this mode of personal expressivity was necessary in order for her to master in verse the emotions that had seemed to master her in life.

The *Harper's* reviewer, impressed by the "compact and resolute intellect . . . armed with triple steel" and the absence of the "effeminate, maudlin, or sentimental," nonetheless echoed Curtis's reservation:

> The wail of private sorrow which forms the keynote of these remarkable poems can never harmonize with universal sympathies. They do not celebrate the mystic burden of humanity in tones to which the heart responds spontaneously, but the griefs of individual experience, which can only call forth an echo from souls that recognize in them their own sufferings. With their intense and almost preternatural subjectivity, the common ear will find no melody in the perpetual recurrence of their sad monotone.

The reviewer for the *North American* went a step further, attributing the "degree of obscurity in many of the poems" to the possibility that only "the author's own coterie" was intended to find them intelligible. The volume has the "strength of thought and powerful grasp of the subjects chosen" that *Passion-Flowers* had exhibited, but also, unfortunately, that work's "crude expression and frequent want of musical harmony, which were all the more provoking for the occasional occurrence of verses of exceeding melody and finished beauty."

For twentieth-century readers, one feature of the book sharply distinguishes it from its predecessor: Howe's decision to speak much more directly about matters she had partly veiled in *Passion-Flowers*. Most obviously, there are several poems about Wallace, one of which—"Via Felice"—explicitly names him as its subject.[15] As noted in chapter 4, this poem seems to divulge several aspects of their relationship—that Wallace's apartment in the Via Felice offered her "daily pleasure," that she would watch from "the window / That ne'er my heart forgets" while he bought her "My morning violets," that she relied on him for consolation (thus confirming his knowledge of Howe's woes that spring), and that she keeps her torch burning in the hope of reuniting beyond the grave:

> For Death's Eternal city
>   Has yet some happy street.
> 'T is in the Via Felice
>   My friend and I shall meet.[16]

The poems preceding and following this one, although less specific in their identification, also arise from Howe's intimacy with Wallace. The first, "On Receiving a Volume Published After the Death of the Author," was probably generated by the 1855 publication of Wallace's *Art, Scenery and Philosophy in Europe,* a collection of essays assembled by his brother John.[17] The volume's arrival is a decidedly mixed blessing:

> What for thy bitter loss shall make amends
> In these sad pages? Wert thou yet on earth
> One happy hour should give us thrice their worth,
> So far the living word all else transcends.

In fact, these preserved thoughts only serve to drive home, painfully, how much she has lost:

> I did not ask such notings of thy thought;
> Holding more dear, with Love's own jealousy,
> The vivid doctrine that thou gavedst me,
> When flashing look, and fiery gesture taught.
>
> Thus bring they, gathered from Samaria's well,
> A droplet that avails no thirst to slake,
> Yet men shall deem it blessed, for his sake
> Whose shadowed sunlight on the waters fall.

These, thy recorded musings, wake again
The heart's deep longing for a music gone;
Thy vibrant voice, whose clear attempered tone
Was like the martyr's rapture-cry in pain.

The poem records her desire to visit his grave, viewing it as "a station to mine own." But recognizing that she is "held by ties that let me not depart / On Grief's wild sweeping pinions any whither," she concludes by calling up patience and bidding farewell once more to her "Brother."

Then appears "Via Felice," suggesting that the train of thought renewed by the arrival of Horace's book was not so facilely derailed; she must recreate as much of that life, that companionship, as she can, to stanch the wound his death caused. And the poem following, "Dilexit Multum" (translatable as "she esteemed him much"),[18] is unambiguously a declaration of posthumous love:

Could I portray thy face, illuminate
With the high glory that it had for me,
Or deathless carve, in marble's sainted slate,
The record of thy vanished majesty;

Or could I, like the grief-inspired of old,
Dream out some Minister of divinest form,
Arch within arch, to cherish and enfold
Love's passing holiness from waste or worm;

Or could I rear towards heav'n a life of good,
Whose date were from our meeting, faultless, strong,
With every thought sublimed and prayer-endued,
The annals of my days should praise thee long.

But gifts like these I have not, to embalm,
Enshrine, englorify thy memory;
Only, from stammering lips, the fitful psalm
Whose music wavers, when it speaks of thee.

Yet take my offering—Nature's simple skill
Shall steal for thee the perfect form of Art,
And my love's record, like to Mary's, dwell
Rich in the shattered vase and lavish heart.

Compared to the Wallace-inspired poems in *Passion-Flowers,* these are astonishingly open—so much so, in fact, that they almost suggest an intensification over time of her feelings about him. More likely, though, these poems (at least the latter two) were products of the period immediately following Wallace's death and were deemed too revealing for inclusion in the first volume. Whatever the case, their appearance here announces Howe's determination to remove her mask altogether and to give full expression to the grief she had half concealed before.[19]

And there evidently was a cornucopia of grief to spill forth. In poem after poem, she searched for articulations that would be commensurate with the mass of woe that needed to be voiced. Although several make the half-hearted suggestion that nothing was to be gained by giving in to the impulse toward lamentation, that in fact evil could come of it,[20] Howe did not seem able to resist the theme in these years. "The Nursery" dramatizes a sequence of tears, remorse, and renewed resolve that must have been replayed often, in various forms.[21] In this poem, children cajole their mother to sing for them instead of sitting idle, grieving. She agrees, and begins, but is "pierced with sudden sorrow"; her voice quavers, the song dies, and she breaks down.

> For misty memories covered
> The children from her ken,
> And down the bitter river
> She dropped—no mother then;
> No sister, helpmeet, daughter,
> Linked to historic years;
> An agonizing creature
> That looked to God in tears.

Eventually rousing herself, she sees the bewilderment on her children's faces and feels their "sympathetic silence" as "worse than her distress." She covers over her weeping, incorporating it in the fairy tale she then spins, with the result that they forget her sadness and she forgets her pain. Reflecting on the incident leads her, interestingly, not to outright repudiation of such behavior. It turns out to be acceptable if it brings about the release of love. But there is also a recognition that full resolution of such woe can come only with the passing of time:

> 'Twere well to pour the soul out
> In one convulsive fit,
> And rend the heart with weeping,
> If Love were loosed from it.
> But all the secret sorrow
> That underlies our lives,
> Must wait the true solution
> The great progression gives.

Waiting out this "great progression" is also the subject of "The Beautiful."[22] Apparently in response to her unvarying melancholy, someone has urged her to "heed the Beautiful." Where and when is it to be found? the poem asks. Howe says she has waited since maidenhood, "Fed with high fancies, all unlearn'd of life, / Save its young promise of ideal good," but so far without fulfillment. Signs of its existence there are—she has found its "temple"—but the shrine is bare and the priest has never arrived. Time, much time, has passed while she has woven her garlands and chaplets, time she has improved as well as she knows how—

> But here she sits, still waiting, dreaming on
> Of some contentment, scarce to be conceived,
> Some soul of blessedness, some smile of peace,
> Some utterance, heard but once to be believed.

In the meantime, her soul dwells in "wreck and ruin . . . uncomforted, alone."

Another poem, "The Shadow That is Born with Us," speaks straightforwardly about the connection between her sorrow and her art.[23] It suggests that, try though she will and must, words can never adequately body forth the misery that gives rise to them. Even a friend's kindness is of little use, and previous efforts to speak have failed to achieve what they attempted. Although the poem's structure and diction reflect the conventions of midcentury, its sense forecasts the slips of paper beginning to accumulate out in Amherst in Emily Dickinson's cabinet:

> One said to me: reveal the untold grief
> Thou holdest, treasured in the inmost deep;
> I have experience that may counsel thee,
> A heart to pity—ready eyes to weep—
>
> I see the cruel furrows in thy face,
> The cheek depressed, the wan and cheerless eye;
> I ask thee wherefore—" 'tis that I am sad"—
> But wherefore sad? Sit here and tell me why.
>
> I can but tell thee; I have tried to frame
> The legendary sorrows of my youth;
> Then wondering paused, as at a fiction strange;
> I spoke in fables—deeper lay the truth.
>
> I've made impatient efforts to uplift
> In words, the weight that hung upon my soul;
> Oh! senseless—while I battled with the air,
> Here lay the burthen, undisturbed and whole.

> Mine is no grief that helps itself with tears,
> Or in wild sobbing passes from the breast;
> Constant as Fate, inalienate as life,
> 'Tis my employ of day, my nightly rest.
>
> It is a strife that heeds no set of sun,
> A discord daring and irresolute,
> A weary business without Sabbath pause,
> A problem ever endless to compute.
>
> Nor hand of leech nor surgeon can avail
> To heal the plague-spot, hopeless of relief,
> The suicidal steel could reach it not;
> I sometimes deem, myself is all my grief.
>
> They say, my mother brought me forth in tears,
> And fed me from a melancholy breast;
> Thus while she sleeps, her sorrow lives in me,
> A tie the envious grave has not supprest.
>
> But Heaven that gave such matter to my life,
> Denied not love of art, nor plastic skill;
> I mould an angel from the sombre mass,
> That, deeply bronzine, is an angel still.
>
> Content thee, then, the secret of my life
> Not ev'n to Love's true hearing may belong,
> Only to His who set, to keep my lips,
> His guardians twain, of Silence and of Song.

The poem entertains the possibility that her malaise is congenital, or at least a part of her since birth, and (in the cryptic phrase, "myself is all my grief," recalling in Milton Satan's "Myself am Hell") the possibility that it has no external cause but is simply fated and therefore ineradicable.[24] I think it is important, however, to distinguish this work from those poems Cheryl Walker describes as expressive of a generalized female "secret sorrow."[25] Although in letters to her sisters Howe occasionally characterized her lot as simply the burden of womanhood, more often she saw her circumstances as unusual, the result of having made a spectacularly inappropriate choice in marriage. Here, though there is the suggestion that the woe is transmitted through maternal inheritance, the more immediate causes are "the legendary sorrows of my youth" and the acute frustrations of trying to "frame" them in words. I hear behind the third and fourth stanzas a particularized lament about the formal inadequacies of both *Passion-Flowers* and the Laurence narrative: neither succeeded, finally, in touching the "truth," the "burthen," that propelled her to write in the first place.

The ironically paired guardians "Silence" and "Song" seem both to impede and to encourage further attempts, ensuring that not even Love's sympathetic ear will receive the "secret" but nonetheless authorizing poetic utterance. The imperfect angel molded from "the sombre mass" evidently represents some compromise, perhaps the gambit essayed in *Words for the Hour*. These poems will not serve as masks for the fact of her unhappiness (as those in the first volume attempted to do), but neither will they unequivocally pinpoint its causes. However, one comes close to doing so—"Love in Exile," a poem protesting her severance from beauty.[26] It reads like a letter directed to Samuel Howe:

> Since ye have banished Beauty from my soul,
> I wander in a faint and drear amaze;
> Gone are the ancient, the familiar ways,
> Strained the fine bonds of sufferance and control.
>
> The utterness of sorrow none can know
> Who have one help, assured, tho' distant far;
> One fiery love, concentrated to a star—
> Night should be sombre that such stars may show.
>
> They venture evil that they little guess
> Who hide that shining mercy from our eyes;
> What though it mark a dreamer's paradise?
> It is a world 'twixt us and nothingness.
>
> Since they are gone, the blissful sights and sounds,
> All hideous forms of ill assuage my mind;
> I hear the Demon's subtle speech behind,
> I see the Present's atheistic bounds.
>
> And then, I cast a shuddering, pitying look
> Upon the fall'n—perhaps their virtue strove
> To bridge th'abyss with daring and high love,
> And, failing, perished in the leap they took.
>
> In this divorce from Beauty lies a wrong—
> I must deny her, I who hold her faith
> Deep in my heart, and fervent unto death,
> While she is outlawed from my sight and song.

My mortal frame is welded to her might,
And my soul worships, as a captive does,
Who murmurs holy words 'mid heathen foes,
While cruel hands forbid the happy rite.

A sentry, forced to keep a foreign door,
A soldier to an alien banner sold,
A priest to whom the shrine is void and cold,
Are of the things men mock at, or deplore.

Eager to check, and tireless to reprove,
Pause, ere you scare the meanest from his right,—
God gives to each his measure of delight,
To every nature its appropriate love.

The precise act against which the poem remonstrates is not named, but its devastating effect is projected in the metaphors that convey her feelings: banishment, divorce, religious persecution, captivity, forced bondage to an alien power. The ban he instituted, whatever it was, she characterizes unambiguously as "evil." The denial of access to Beauty exposes her to devilish suggestions, to the threat of atheism, and worse, to the specter of lost virtue. The fifth stanza's consideration of the plight of "the fall'n" raises the possibility that they fell as a result of just such a deprivation as she has suffered. So might she. Even should "the fine bonds of sufferance and control" remain firm, however, the poem's vivid descriptions of sorrow and the clear attribution of its cause to her reproving husband signify her refusal to receive such treatment uncomplainingly.

THE BOOK ALSO contains an intriguing triptych of poems written in response to Florence Nightingale's celebrity.[27] By 1856, home from the Crimea and universally admired, Nightingale had become England's national heroine. Howe, as a friend and correspondent (and despite the fact that her husband's encouragement of Nightingale's aspirations remained a sore spot), could hardly avoid somehow acknowledging her triumphs. Her tribute generously recognizes the achievement and the desert, but then deftly appropriates the occasion to sing the praises of *all* women and to chide men such as her husband who fail to recognize comparable fortitude in the women in their lives. The three poems are successively more spirited and biting as Howe seems to warm to the subject.

The first, "To Florence Nightingale," begins by sounding a slightly defensive note. Howe explains that she has not heretofore added her accolades to the swelling chorus "Because thy weight of crowns is burthensome; / And that which henceforth least can be thy need / Is human praise, the cordial of weak hearts." But she does not want to be thought cold or indifferent, so she offers a parable. She imagines the curtain calls of a triumphant diva, a heroine laden with more bouquets than she can easily carry, trying to leave the stage. One in the audience, slower than the rest to hurl his own tribute of flowers, sees that the star is "adorned beyond her youth's desire" and so scatters his offering instead to the chorus members who form a "willing background."

> Strange joy and wonder seize those weary hearts
> That do their heavy work unrecognized.
> "What, not illustrious, did you think of us,
> Mere stony echoes of your nightingale,
> And Genius, that doth call us for her use?
> You knew us faithful in the prayer, the march,
> The funeral dirge, and crowned us? God reward!"

She concludes by supposing that Nightingale, the woman of the hour, would turn back to throw this belated offerer an approving look, carrying the message: "The flowers thus sent, fall nearest to my heart."

This graceful attribution of selflessness to Nightingale praises her while it also directs attention to the numerous others who approximate her dedication but ordinarily go unnoticed. The next poem, "Florence Nightingale and Her Praisers," keeps the spotlight trained on this unsung multitude:

> If you debase the sex to elevate
> One of like soul and temper with the rest,
> You do but wrong a thousand fervent hearts,
> To pay full tribute to one generous breast.

Acts of mercy, Howe explains, have been women's impulse and responsibility since the earliest days, when "God left the boon of pity to the world, / And left it garnered in a woman's heart." Throughout history, maidens famously have left the comforts of court or hearth to tend their wounded knights and soldiers, and in these latter days woman has "sprung forward, an enfranchised stream / That runs its errand in the face of day." But, she notes, despite this recent authorization, women able to act on this impulse still possess a freedom unknown to most of their sex:

> hearts akin to hers
> Are held as springs shut up, as fountains sealed,
> The weighty masonry of life must part
> Before their hidden virtue be revealed.
>
> Women who weave in hope the daily web,
> Who leave the deadly depths of passion pure,
> Who hold the stormy powers of will attent,
> As Heaven directs, to act, or to endure;
>
> No multitude strews branches in their way,
> Not in their praise the loud arena strives,
> Still as a flameless incense rises up
> The costly patience of their offered lives.

Costly patience: The poem closes by urging recognition of that expense:

> Then count not the heroic heart alone
> In those whom action and result makes great,
> Since the sublime of Nature's excellence
> Lies in enduring, as achieving Fate.

And then—as if, once wakened, Howe's outrage at the applause directed exclusively toward Nightingale could not be repressed—follows a poem called "Furthermore," the most irate of the three. Despite the generalized "we" and "you" of this work, a gesture toward speaking on behalf of all women to all men, its chief intended hearer was very clearly the man of her own house.

> We, that are held of you in narrow chains,
> Sought for our beauty, thro' our folly raised
> One moment to harem eminence,
> To drop in dreary nothingness, amazed;
>
> We, dwarfed to suit the measure of your pride,
> Thwarted in all our pleasures and our powers,
> Have yet a sad, majestic recompense,
> The dignity of suffering, that is ours.
>
> The proudest of you lives not but he wrung
> A woman's unresisting form with pain,
> While the long nurture of your helpless years
> Brought back the bitter childbirth throes again.

We wait upon your fancies, watch your will,
Study your pleasure, oft with trembling heart,—
Of the success and glory of your lives
Ye think it grace to yield the meanest part.

Ev'n Nature, partial mother, reasons thus:
["]To these the duty, and to those the right;"
Our faithful service earns us sufferance,
But we shall love you in your own despite.

To you, the thrilling mead of praise belongs,
To us, the painfuller desert may fall;
We touch the brim, where ye exhaust the bowl,
But where ye pay your due, we yield our all.

Honour all women—weigh with reverend hand
The worth of those unproved, or overtried,
And, when ye praise the perfect work of One,
Say not, ye are shamed in her, but glorified.

To measure the significance of this stance, it is useful to recall Howe's narrative of womanly fidelity ten years earlier in the Laurence manuscript. Eva, loyal to Rafael, waits tirelessly by his tomb nurturing the golden seed in his breast. In reward for this devotion she is translated into heaven, where her single-minded faithfulness is contrasted with the behavior of the woman who sells her "wares" to others. Eva's constancy in this narrative is in some degree justified by Rafael's full and sincere appreciation of it: if the appropriate action for a woman is slavish attention to the germ of glory in her husband's breast, that for the man is to acknowledge the difficulty and selflessness of this act. Rafael deserves the adoration he receives because Eva need not beg him to recognize that she has given it, and Howe at that point was willing to believe that, were she able to emulate Eva's dedication, her gesture would call forth its analogue from her husband. A decade later, such dreams are vapor. Her husband has become the man who must be reminded of the sacrifices she (and most women) continually make—"dwarfed to suit the measure of your pride"—and, ironically, the man enthusiastic about the woman who rejects domesticity in pursuit of her own genius. The anger here is deep, righteous, and loud.

BUT IF THE BOOK may be said to speak truth to power in fully articulating Howe's despair and resentment, it also incorporates certain gestures of accommodation—not so much to the worse-than-ever conditions of her marriage as to the fact that, veiled or not, sustained vituperation was not going to make her feel better. One such gesture may have been the inclusion of three tributes to her husband's best friend. Of course, Sumner's uncompromising defense of a free Kansas and his resultant martyrdom impinged so forcefully on the lives of most Northerners, especially Bostonians,[28] that the subject, one might say, was all but forced on her. And none of the three poems is fired by particularly personal sentiments or emotion beyond what might be expected from any sympathetic observer.[29] Still, at this strained juncture in their lives, Julia's praise for Sumner's heroism must have pleased Chev, and she must have supposed that it would. The longest of these, "The Sermon of Spring," is the volume's lead poem,[30] occupying a position analogous to "Rome" in *Passion-Flowers*. Marred though it is by rhetorical posturing and a relentless dactylic line never quite under control, its effusions seem sincere:

> For they are holy, the wounds that the Southerner dealt thee.
> Count them blessed, and blessed the mother that bore thee.
> Would that the thing I best love, aye, the son of my bosom,
> Suffering beside thee, had shared the high deed and its glory.

And just at the end, Howe implanted a simile that resonates beyond its context, reflecting a potentially tragic domestic amputation as it describes the specter of secession:

> Heaven enlighten their hearts, ere we close for the death-tug,
> Flinging them far from our bounds with their wrath and their rapine,—
> As the man tears from his side the beloved who betrays him,
> Lest her soft vices insensibly ruin his virtue,
> Lest he too fall, undermined by the white tooth of falsehood.

"May Southerners see reason before we're forced to cast them off, as a man would jettison a disloyal wife": The analogy fits, but there is a forced feel to it, almost as if the (supposedly) primary sentiment is in the poem only to provide an occasion for the encoded guilt in the simile. Such a reading may stretch credibility, for elsewhere in the volume, as we have seen, Howe casts herself as the betrayed party, not the betrayer. Yet occasionally, even in *Passion-Flowers,* we hear the note of contrition. Other poems in *Words for the Hour* suggest a determination to acknowledge—as she wrote to Louisa—"errors and short comings" on her own part as well as an effort to mollify her equally unhappy husband.

She included, for example, several poems about the joy, solace, and distraction children often supply. An especially poignant one is "Maud," actually three poems under one title, in which Howe pours out her affection for the daughter born of her woe.[31] The first of the three, in its simple language and its direct address to Maud, suggests an effort to write a poem that Chev might easily apprehend and appreciate. It speaks to Maud's ability to dispel "Shade of discontent or gloom" and states that her arrival "From the depth of darkness, taught / God could bring the light—." Maud also appears as light-bringer in a "Post Scriptum" to a poem called "Where Is the Beautiful?":[32]

> When thus I reasoned of the Beautiful
> My vexed and querulous thought had not outgone
> The comfort of the since instructing years,
> Nor thy fair face, my last and gentlest-born.
>
> Thou dost the Eastern paradox reverse.
> Towards the far mountain-tops I could not flee,
> Whereon the heavenly vision seemed to rest—
> And waiting, Beauty was at home with me.

A chance encounter, probably in Newport, with one of Fanny Kemble's young daughters produced a moving meditation on the pain of being forced to choose between personal ambition and a mother's responsibilities. Although the poem is called "Fanny Kemble's Child," its focus is Kemble herself, and beyond her, Julia Howe. Kemble, daughter of an illustrious British stage family, was her age's premier interpreter of Shakespeare's heroines and, later on, equally famous for single-voice readings of Shakespeare's plays. Ten years older than Howe, she had fallen for the charm and money of a handsome Philadelphian, Pierce Butler, marriage to whom had brought her a load of sorrow at least as heavy as Howe's.[33] The couple finally divorced in 1849, and Kemble's access to her two daughters was severely restricted. The poem records Howe's compassion for both daughter and mother—daughter, because the girl envies Julia's own children's opportunities for maternal cuddles, and mother, for having been born without one crucial gift:

> Oh! many-passioned Woman—fervid soul!
> Thou, rich in all save Meekness—strong in all

> Save that strong Patience which outwearies Fate,
> And makes Gods quail before its constancy.
> Which was forgotten in thy gifts of birth?
> Of all the powers the greatest only—Love.

Although Howe acknowledges the allure of the life Kemble chose—leaving aside nurturing "[t]o follow stormy feeling round the world"—she registers no regret at not having led the equivalent herself. In fact, she suggests that the greater glory comes from *relinquishing* such dreams. The soul that elsewhere mourns its "wreck and ruin" here argues that an indifferent spouse and the task of raising children are among life's chief pleasures, would Kemble only look rightly:

> Thine was the lot of Woman, only thou
> Wert more than Woman in thy haughty will,
> And less than Woman, in humility.
> Battling for higher tasks, and loftier praise,
> Thy matchless office was unknown of thee.
> A helpful partner? whence are mightiest laws
> But of opposing forces, greatly wed?
> A nurse of babies? what is Nature else?
> See, the stars nestle in the down of Night,
> And, from the calm of one wide Mother-breast
> Doth holy sleep reconsecrate the world.

Recognizing that she cannot be Kemble's teacher on these matters, Howe nonetheless registers alarm at the spectacle of a woman much like herself shrugging her shoulders at "the sentence of the world":

> But wonder seizes on my thoughts, and fear,
> When, in the Drama of our destinies,
> A soul like thine is summoned to the front,
> And maddens with the passion of its part.

The fear is not that the world will disapprove; rather, it is that Kemble's self-prioritizing choices (and, by implication, Howe's) will prevent her from learning, among other lessons, "[t]he impotence of Anger" and the redemptive value of patience.

Another gesture of accommodation in *Words for the Hour* is Howe's inclusion of poems representing her respect and affection for her husband. For one, "The Rough Sketch," we have the authority of the Howes' daughter Laura that her father was its subject.[34] While it can-

not precisely be termed a love poem—and may even, in its portrayal of
its restless protagonist, suggest the reasons it is *not* a love poem—it
still arises from admiration and a desire to honor her husband's most
vivid qualities:

> A great grieved heart, an iron will,
> As fearless blood as ever ran;
> A form elate with nervous strength
> And fibrous vigour,—all a man.
>
> A gallant rein, a restless spur,
> The hand to wield a biting scourge;
> Small patience for the tasks of Time,
> Unmeasured power to speed and urge.
>
> He rides the errands of the hour,
> But sends no herald on his ways;
> The world would thank the service done,
> He cannot stay for gold or praise.
>
> Not lavishly he casts abroad
> The glances of an eye intense,
> And, did he smile but once a year,
> It were a Christmas recompense.
>
> I thank a poet for his name,
> The "Down of Darkness," this should be;
> A child, who knows no risk it runs,
> Might stroke its roughness harmlessly.
>
> One helpful gift the Gods forgot,
> Due to the man of lion-mood;
> A woman's soul, to match with his
> In high resolve and hardihood.

The poet Howe thanks is Milton, whose phrase she borrows from
Comus. It is an odd choice, since in Milton's masque the line is part
of Comus's tribute to the lady who has lost her way at night: He notes
that her sweet song "smooth[s] the Raven down / Of darkness till it
smil[es]."[35] Howe's appropriation of it thus seems a bit of self-praise, for
her skill in taming her husband's gloom. Still, the rueful, ironic last
stanza is noteworthy as a sign of her inclination to attribute some of
their difficulties to herself (and yet, of course, this public acknowledgment of her shortcomings is not exactly an expression of *regret,* and it

also reinforces the indications in the rest of the volume of the emotional distance between the two).

Three other poems are meditations on their marriage, and the common note through them all appears to be a desire for peace and reconciliation after debilitating combat. Two of these poems are yoked by their titles—"As It Seems" and "As It Is."[36] In the first, two people who once knew each other well but who have grown apart "snatch silent greeting, with a crowd between." This exchange of glances takes place "as in a dim cathedral," which represents their relationship. The massive structure is contrasted to the hut erected by the peasant and his wife who, "With little scope of sorrow or desire, / Live out their harmless, vegetative life." Fortune spares this humble house,

> But we, who strove to raise a pile on high
> Fit to embrace the organ-tone of Time,
>
> Who gave to weightiest thoughts an upward lift,
> Laying broad reasons, rounding rhyme to rhyme,
>
> Stand thunder-smitten, yet with stern command
> To bear Life's devastations . . .

They *must* bear up, since to fall—which "else were solemnly desired"—would be to bring ruin to their dependents. Beauty thus is obliged to "fling / Her glowing mantle o'er all havoc made" and thereby to soothe decay with service.

But this melancholy picture is only as it *seems.* The companion poem, though its vision is still far from rosy, at bottom signifies Howe's determination to count her blessings and learn to live with moderated expectations. It begins with an expression of disgust at perennial mourning—"My soul is weary of this chant of woe"—and though it takes us once again through the familiar terrain of early dreams thwarted, battles with the "Grief-serpent" lost, existence perceived as torture, it emerges into a kind of Emersonian resolution, recalling the sober joy of the conclusions of "Experience" and "Fate":

> We who aspire to harmonies divine,
> Taxing Creation for its master-tone,
> Soaring to heights untenable and crazed
> Were once the daring inspiration gone;

> Let us be modest—we are rich to win
> One jewel from the treasure-laden deep,
> Or, from the wreck of affluent loves, to hold
> A single faithful breast whereon to weep.

Or *almost* emerges, for there is a final stanza in which the still-unsatisfied soul cannot refrain from a last sob:

> A breast to weep upon? oh! this at least,
> I cried, with outstretched arm, and sudden wail;
> Experience shuts our asking with one hope,
> Trust in thyself, and God, who cannot fail.

But the sob is quickly stifled, in keeping with Howe's intent not to sing woe anymore, and although it may be argued that the small noise this sob makes subverts her expressed goal, the poem does close with a representation of strength and commitment. If it is not, at last, the kind of reassurance that erases all doubt, heals all schism, it is a distinct step away from the anger and rebellion of other of the book's poems.

"From the Lattice," like "The Rough Sketch," is an effort to offer Chev everything Julia was capable of giving, the nearest she could honestly come to an articulation of assurance and affection.[37] Generosity is its driving emotion, and if its context (a volume heavy with contradictory sentiments) may seem somewhat to undercut that generosity, it does not efface it.

> Let it content thee that I call thee dear—
> Thou'rt wise and great, and others name thee so.
> From me, what gentler tribute wouldst thou know
> Than the slight hand, upon thy shoulder laid,
> And the full heart, high throbbing, not afraid.
>
> No, not afraid—of manly stature thou,
> Of power compact, and temper fervor-tried,—
> Yet I, a weakling, in thine armour hide,
> Or, sick beyond the medicine of Art,
> Hang on the healthful pulses of thine heart.
>
> In waking dreams I see thine outstretched arms
> That conquer night and distance for my sake,
> Like the brave swimmer who was wont to break
> The crystals of the deep in shivering light,
> To bless his Ladye with his radiant sight.

> There is a sense in which I call thee mine—
> Not as possession runs in Youth's hot blood;
> But in the helpful, self-renunciant mood
> Of Aspiration, daring, hand in hand,
> Tasks that in mystical conjunction stand.
>
> Have I not been too thoughtlessly surprised
> Into this mood, so near akin to loving?
> I hold myself to vexed and fond reproving;
> Saying, wert thou then so eager to impart,
> Thou couldst not hide one secret in thy heart?
>
> There is a dead, immortal maiden speaks
> Responsive, from the legendary tomb
> That treasures, incorrupt, her bridal bloom:
> "If I could wish back the advantage ta'en,
> 'Twere to be kind, and give it him again."

The fourth stanza's image of the two of them allied in aspiration may recall Chev's earliest dream for this marriage, the hope sketched in his long letter of June 1842 that he might discover in her a helpmeet animated by his spirit, bound on his errand. Her version, to be sure, does not propose a single, husband-dictated errand that both pursue; they are instead each involved in distinct efforts. But these tasks are "mystically" conjoined, and the aspirants pursue them cooperatively, affectionately. So unforeseen and atypical is this gentle mood that she must interrogate it in the next stanza, yet the concluding appropriation of Juliet's declaration of love (*Romeo and Juliet* II.ii.126–31) signals Howe's desire to let her own confession ("so near akin to loving") stand without further qualification.

The use of Juliet in this way may have been intended to recall an earlier occasion in which Howe's presentation of a scene from the play had caused an argument. The moment was during a charades game in Newport, probably in the summer of 1852; Howe reported it in a letter to Annie:

> I recited that most difficult scene, in Romeo and Juliet, where Juliet takes the sleeping potion—read it over, and imagine me going through with it. I made a very great effort, and was, I believe, quite appreciated by the *best* part of the audience, though many of them, no doubt, were more amused with the nonsense we improvised in other parts, than with this grandiose sketch of a young girl's feelings, ahem, on so extraordinary an occasion. You shall hear me recite this, some time. You will not be surprised to hear

that I delivered with all the emphasis of one who felt it, the line: "My dismal scene I needs must act *alone.*" or that, at the thought of my Cousin's ghost, I went into such fits as would naturally be suggested by the sight of Henry H. in that unsubstantial character. . . . These little artistic successes were the brightest touches in the picture—you can imagine that I paid dearly for them—Chev's sourness of disposition becomes so dreadfully aggravated by any success of mine. He was miserably sick every time he came to New Port, and fearfully cross—would not go out any where, and was strangely indignant at my enjoyment of society, wh[ich] was indeed very moderate.[38]

A similar moment of conflict arises, interestingly, in a section of the Laurence manuscript. Laurence is called to fill in for an actor who was to have portrayed Juliet, and the effect on Ronald is startling:

> Utterly indifferent as I was to the approval or censure of those around me, I soon forgot them, and felt for a moment a nameless pleasure in being something other than myself. My heart warmed, my voice became deeper and fuller, and I found myself giving a fervent expression to the glowing words of the Italian woman-child. . . . [A]t this moment, for the first time, I caught a glimpse of Ronald's face, turned full towards me, with a strange expression. It was entirely white and bloodless, and all the vitality that usually animated it seemed concentrated in the eyes, which were intensely dilated and fixed upon me. Another moment, and the colourless countenance became suffused with angry red—the glittering eye flashed forth its imprisoned lightnings. Ronald sprang forward, and attempted to push Romeo from my side, and not succeeding, would have struck him, had I not seized the half-raised arm, and held it back with all my strength. (A149–50)

The allusion here also recalls the identification forged in "Rome" between Juliet and the vanquished city. Since Howe had, before, used the play to speak her woe, her use of it here to speak love carries added significance.

The three concluding poems also seem efforts to put the book's prevailing mood to rest. The first of these, "High Art," is the volume's only effort in the impudent mode of "Mind versus Mill-Stream" or "Handsome Harry."[39] Addressed to her "friends," it is an apologia of sorts for having appropriated various of their characteristics for the sake of fleshing out the characters of her art—"of sorts," because the confession is not really accompanied by any expression of regret at having done so. The reverse, in fact: there is clearly glee in disclosing that, although a particular saint's hair and brow may come from a certain friend, "here the likeness ends":

> Your eyes, you see, were not the spirit sort,
> Your mouth, a pursed conventionality;
> More than one weary morning's work it took
> To help what was forgotten in your making.

The poem may have been crafted after the model of Browning's dramatic monologues—without, however, a sharply defined persona distinct from the author's own sensibility.[40] The opening stanza sounds a good deal like a voice Howe sometimes adopted in writing to her sisters about her domestic griefs, an ironic, self-mocking, comedic voice that, although it emerged from genuine pain, had determined to put pain temporarily at a distance:

> So, friends, you see my picture brought to end
> With labor manifold of eye and hand,
> And that whose slaves they are, the master-brain.
> Great Angelo's Last Judgment I've reversed,
> And Hell on Earth is what I have to show.
> The subject is more homelike than you think,
> The scenes we move in gave the atmosphere,
> The whole is painted from what's next at hand.

The sentiment recalls the opening poem in *Passion-Flowers,* in which Howe assures her foes that their "sharp and bitter forms" are, indeed, embodied in what follows. Here, though, there is no request for forgiveness or any protestation that vengeance was far from her thoughts. Instead, she says—having "quartered in your haunts so long / That I have got your wickedness by heart"—she sees no alternative but to take herself off to a hermitage somewhere,

> Where converse of the calm immortal souls
> Shall help your poison with its antidote,
> Till Art be purged of grief and bitterness.

This purgation appears to be the task of the book's last poems. "Prelude" presents an economically narrated contretemps between a husband and wife: she has chided him just before sleep, which has resulted for him in a sleepless night and a troubled morning, but when she wakes and offers "the sign of peace," he kisses her hand and harmony is restored.[41] This little parable is counterpointed by the repeated question, "Shall she be proud?" for having resolved the antagonism. The answer is no: it is not she, but "Love," that has enabled peace to return, and the poem then becomes an apostrophe praising this large, beneficent abstraction for its healing powers:

> But thou rebuk'st us too,
> For all our wild ado,
> The want, the waste, the weary fault and fretting;
> How mad the turmoil seems,
> When, in our waking dreams,
> Thou sham'st it with the presence past forgetting.

The last poem, "Adé," begins by declaring "A truce, a truce, a gallant truce!"[42] It is a farewell to "turbulent hosts of rhyme, / Whose wrangling wrought such ill-content" and a vision of life beyond discord:

> Oh! yon, where the sunset's heart is warm
> A fair bird singeth, sorrow-free;
> I am his Sister belov'd, he says,
>   And, wistful, he waits for me.
>
> No bird of Juno's nor of Jove's,
> Nor Pallas, blinking thro' day-shut eyes;
> But a mate-dove, loving so faithfully,
>   That Love did make him wise.
>
> And we will sit as on burnished gold,
> The earth-ball rolling at our feet,
> And whisper of things which, had they been,
>   Had been for song too sweet.

True, the poem's ambiguous identification of this companion-bird as both brother *and* "mate-dove" introduces the possibility that this, like "Via Felice," is an expression of hope to reunite with Wallace beyond the grave. Imaginably, it is. But the fact that this reunion is tied to the *abandonment* of poetic effort, to an eternity of whispered exchanges too sweet to be sung, suggests more strongly that it is a vision of reconciliation with her husband and therefore a relinquishment of the anger that had initially provoked the aesthetic impulse. Howe need write no more poems if she can, at last, purge grief and bitterness.

DURING THE SUMMER of 1856, in the wake of Sumner's beating, Samuel Howe traveled to Kansas to carry the funds he had helped raise in support of the Free Soilers. In his absence, happily ensconced at Law-ton's Valley, Julia worked on a play about the deleterious moral effects of revenge. Little about the work's genesis is retrievable: as with the second poetry collection, she scarcely mentions it in letters that survive.[43] *The World's Own* ran for a week in New York at Wallack's Theater, opening 16 March 1857, and was shortly afterward repeated in Boston for a single performance.[44] Howe attended the opening night in New York and was, after the final curtain, afforded "a tempest of applause" from an audi-ence that the *New York Courier* averred had "not been equalled . . . for the intellectual and social distinction of those who composed it since the days of Edmund Kean."[45] But though it called forth praise from the crit-ics for its literary qualities, the play was blasted for its improbable plot, commonplace characters, and especially its "repulsive" tone (*Courier*).

The play—written in a blank verse that, if it seldom rises to Shake-spearean intensity, is consistently smooth and deft—evoked objection in particular for Howe's handling of the central character. A piece appear-ing late in March in the *Courier* (written by the same critic who re-viewed the play initially) took her to task for presenting "from begin-ning to end such a revolting and untruthful picture of human nature." Its heroine Leonora is "an abomination in petticoats" who out-Iagos Iago in villainy. The writer contrasts her to Camille, who, for all her ignominy, at least strives to free herself from pollution; Leonora, on the other hand, "madly plunges" into that pollution. Howe's protagonist is "a woman crushing every good impulse and committing every abomina-tion solely to gratify a revenge with which such a Devil as MILTON's would not soil his fingers."[46] A letter to Howe from George Ripley on 28 March indicates that this view of Leonora's character upset her a good deal; she evidently considered writing a rejoinder (a plan Ripley dis-couraged). I will return to Ripley's letter, but assessing the justice of the charge first requires sketching the plot of the play.

Leonora, in the beginning, is a simple village maiden caught up in the charms of a traveling nobleman, Count Lothair. His carriage breaks down as he passes through Leonora's hamlet, and while he waits for its repair, he dallies. Later in the play we will learn that he is married and has a young son, but at first his character is ambiguous: it even seems possible that his intentions toward Leonora are honorable. The sudden return of Leonora's childhood love, Edward, an artist who has been studying in Rome, triggers doubts about Lothair's honesty: the count decamps abruptly, but Leonora, unwilling to believe in his perfidy, sets out after him. Edward follows.

About midway through the play, Lothair's dastardly nature is made clear to Leonora when she encounters him with wife and child. She faints; he pretends to his wife that he does not know who Leonora is, and when Leonora's servant tries to detain him, he strikes her. The wife, horrified, tries to help the servant, but Lothair drags her off and later works to persuade her that both Leonora and her servant are "shameless women" (86), simulating virtue for vile ends. His ruse is exposed when Leonora appears; he tries to stab her, and at last the scales fall from her eyes. Leonora throws a curse as she departs—"God has justice, Count Lothair; / When it draws nigh your door, remember me!" (93)—and shortly afterward, swearing "By him who is at home in hell, / And in our hearts" (97), devotes the balance of her life to exacting revenge.

In the last two acts, Leonora is mainly an unseen presence, her status now drastically altered through having become the consort of the prince to whom Lothair pays allegiance. We hear that she has absolute sway over the prince and that, although she is lovely, her "seraph's beauty" masks "a demon's heart" (103). Her evil nature is portrayed (unpleasantly, to a twentieth-century sensibility) through her employment of a stereotyped usurer Jew and an amoral gypsy to effect some of her diabolical ends (including forcing Lothair into ruinous debt and stealing his child). Lothair now, oddly, becomes almost a sympathetic character: unaware of Leonora's new identity, he feels in the grip of an implacable machine that he only vaguely senses.

Eventually all her stratagems succeed brilliantly, and Lothair, utterly destroyed in his prince's estimation, is sentenced to execution. Lothair's wife, too, is near death from grief, and Leonora has taken possession of their child. Alone on stage, she gloats in satanic delight:

> 'T was great,—'t was godlike! I have drunk to the full
> The costly wine of vengeance; and I feel
> Its mighty madness coursing through my veins!
> What pang was left forgotten? What disgrace?
> O, man, so gallant and so reckless once,
> Crushing the poor girl's heart in your white hands!
> Where are you now? (134)

At this point, the old boyfriend Edward—who has with grief watched Leonora's transformation and who has witnessed his best friend Lorenzo die trying to defend her honor—appears masked, presenting himself as "Heaven's righteous messenger" (136) to bring Leonora to a view of the degradation she has embraced. Her "wild and arrogant" love ripened into hate, he tells her, and although help was nearby, in the form of loving friends and "the priceless power / To shame misfortune with true nobleness," she has turned away, plunging "from passion into infamy" (137). Comparing her to Lucretia Borgia and Messalina, ruined souls grown fat on wickedness, he suggests he will enact mercy by killing her. But Leonora grabs his dagger and does the deed herself, breathing forgiveness to Lothair just as she dies. Edward mourns her as "The wreck of all that's fair and excellent; / A thing of tears and tenderness forever!" (141).

Ripley, while urging Howe not to be excessively troubled by ephemeral criticism of the work, did nonetheless second the critical perception that Leonora's almost maniacal thirst for vengeance caused an aesthetic problem:

> The defects as a work of art must all be traced to the want of balance & relief to the infernal & repulsive passion on which it pivots. Iago needs the charms & sorrows of Desdemona & the nobleness of Othello to make him tolerable on the stage. You unveil too much of hell, without a glimpse of heaven, to delight the high & holy aspirations of the saints & Pharosees [sic] of New York. The "World's Own," in short, are too damnably ugly specimens of human nature to gain the suffrage of the "World" to whom they belong. In a drama for representation, this is fatal to sympathy, & a certain kind of success.

However, such an emphasis would not, he suggested, impose barriers to appreciation of the work in literary or ethical terms: "[I]t does not impair the power & beauty of the poem, as a natural & logical development of human passions & a pathetic illustration of the 'great doctrine' of our faith, the fall of man." Ripley offered to expand this point in an essay for the *Tribune* that would serve as a review of the published version of the play.[47]

Ripley's sense that the play illustrates the fall of man focuses attention on Leonora's plummet from grace—not so much as a result of sexual transgression as of her dedication of all her energies toward exacting revenge. (In fact, the play offers no conclusive sign that there *was* a sexual transgression. Leonora and Lothair spend their time in Leonora's cottage learning music and reading plays and novels, and the only offenses we can unambiguously impute in the early scenes are Lothair's attempts to persuade Leonora to be satisfied with "nuptials of the heart" instead of the churchly kind, and her satisfaction with this arrangement.) Approaching the play through Howe's earlier texts, contemplating it through the lens created by what we know of her perplexities and resolutions regarding her own vindictive impulses, we can hardly help reading it, at least in part, as an effort to embody—and thereby exorcise—the ugliness of such behavior. Leonora's loss of virtue recalls exactly the danger Howe envisioned in *Words for the Hour*'s "Love in Exile": when there is nothing blissful to contemplate, she warned, "[a]ll hideous forms of ill" assail the mind and tempt the lover of beauty toward the abyss. What Leonora recognizes ultimately is—as Howe phrased her own perception in "Fanny Kemble's Child"—the "impotence of Anger." Leonora's self-immolation is an analogue of Howe's gesture of renunciation at the end of *Words for the Hour:* no more entertaining of those "turbulent hosts of rhyme, / Whose wrangling wrought such ill-content." Howe's decision to dramatize the potentially awful consequences of such conduct as she herself had inclined toward, to objectify both the monstrousness and the purgation through dramatic action rather than through personal poetic expression, interestingly anticipated George Curtis's suggestion, in his review of *Words,* that in order to master the emotions that seemed to be mastering her in life, she would need "resolute emancipation" from the too often "purely private cast" of her verse.

Little wonder, then, that Howe was troubled by the harsh criticism of her principal character. However readily she would have agreed that Leonora's behavior is abhorrent—it is the play's chief point, after all— she might still have found it difficult, privately, not to hear in the severity aimed at Leonora a condemnation of her own conduct. I do not mean to imply that critics who vilified the plot were intentionally attacking Howe for committing a similar "crime," unless the very writing of the play is understood as such an offense; I suggest only that Howe, struggling to free herself from an ethic of revenge, might have had a hard time not taking the criticism personally. Edward's words to Leonora in the climactic scene are stern enough when he reminds her that she might have ruled the prince's love toward good ends. What remains for her instead is "the Ghoul's feast, corruption, horror, blood" (138). To hear this sentiment reproduced in the popular press and to see Leonora's repentance overlooked or satirized ("Long speeches should antedate stabs," observed the *Tribune*) was perhaps a bitter pill to swallow, both as artist and as penitent. Ripley characterized the plot as a version of the "fall of man"; Howe knew this particular version experientially.

In an astute feminist reading of the play, Tracy McCabe has suggested that it reflects Howe's understanding of the degree to which the idea of womanhood is a cultural construct.[48] Leonora recognizes that when she embarks on a course of revenge, she is no longer describable as a woman; she abandons what (Howe sees) is only a role, not a description of essential nature. Similarly, McCabe shows, Leonora's strategy for exacting her vengeance is a manipulation/inversion of the cultural premise of "womanly influence": she carries out the revenge indirectly, through exercising sway over the prince. Leonora also appropriates a mechanism culturally associated with males—the "gaze"—not, however, as a tool of objectification (as with men) but as a means of awakening guilt. McCabe thus emphasizes the play's divergence from the conventions of literary and theatrical depictions of women. This reading, though, leads to a sense of the ending as weak: out of a need to give viewers an acceptably moral finish, Howe "attempts to resuscitate those ideologies that [she] has exposed and manipulated."[49] Leonora returns to seeing through patriarchal eyes, believing herself essentially the innocent victim who has strayed from her true nature in trying to avenge her wrongs. This last bid for the audience's sympathy, McCabe believes, tends to frustrate the play's narrative logic.

Compelling as this reading is, it slights the fact that Leonora's behavior in the play's second half is truly nasty, an instance of evil transplanted and magnified into something worse than the initial offense. If the play exhibits Howe's awareness that her protagonist's conduct need not be determined by "cultural scripts,"[50] it also demonstrates her conviction that repaying ugliness in kind, with interest, makes the perpetrator a devil. The speech in which (in McCabe's reading) Leonora declares that she can set aside her womanhood is also a clear-sighted statement that, gender-connected or not, the course she has charted is toxic:

> Let no one say I've wept. From these seared eyes
> Poisons may drop, but never human tears.
> Some deadly power is in me. Were he here,
> My breath should wither him. One sudden look
> Should bid the life-blood curdle at his heart,

Never to leave it more. Let me not think!
Avenging God! I was a woman once,—
A thing to nourish children at my breast,
And hear their angels whisper through my dreams,
As she [Helen, Lothair's wife] does nightly, pillowed on his breast.
With sorer travail now shall deeds of wrath
And ghastly horror claim their birth from me. (96)

In fact, Leonora ghoulishly *embraces* her identity as life-giver. Howe seems to use the trope of motherhood in the last two lines to intensify the disgust her audience should feel at the spectacle of unholy dedication to "deeds of wrath and ghastly horror." Before this scene is over, we have received our first illustration of the awful effects of Leonora's vow: she turns Edward's love for her to hate by allowing herself to be the cause of his friend Lorenzo's death. This is the end of act 3. By the time Leonora reappears at the end of act 4, musing over how easy it always is to find "some vile human tool" to work her malice, she has become entirely a monster, conflating her retributive schemes with divine justice. Or if she still understands the distinction, she is indifferent to it, disdaining God's favor in preference for the "downward" way.

In the meantime, we have watched Lothair painfully lay out for his wife the extent of his inexplicable troubles. Although his behavior toward both Leonora and Helen has been despicable, this scene encourages sympathy for him by displaying the readiness with which sympathy flows from Helen. She who has most cause for resentment shows herself a paragon of forgiveness—conduct that Lothair honors by declaring it the product of "true woman's heart" (113). Later, when Lothair is arrested, one of Leonora's most outrageous turns of the knife is her spiteful (and completely baseless) implication of Helen as part of the alleged conspiracy against the Prince—Helen, who in her only encounter with Leonora has extended pity and tried to protect her from Lothair's hostility. Leonora's kidnaping of their child, too—since it attacks Helen more than Lothair—deepens revulsion for the satanic fever driving her. It is arguable, in fact, that the play turns on the contrast Howe develops between the actions of the two chief female characters, yet another echo of the distinctions drawn between the women in Eva's climactic vision. That we are to prefer the woman who braves even witches, if need be, to retrieve her stolen son over "the woman with the wicked smile" who steals him is (to put it mildly) clear.

The degree to which this melodramatic plot embodies Howe's personal ethical concerns may be suggested by a second look at Leonora's speech quoted above. Leonora's dedication to revenge begins in reference to behavior we know had particular meaning for Howe, the shedding of tears. Leonora will not, cannot cry, because her eyes are "seared"; they may shed drops of poison, but never tears. More than anything during these years, Howe feared the loss of sight from crying; it is a constantly recurring theme in letters to her sisters and even to less intimate connections such as the Twisletons.[51] References to weeping also often occur in the poems of *Words for the Hour,* most significantly in "The Nursery," "The Shadow That Is Born With Us," and "As It Is." Yet despite her fear, she regularly depicted herself as unable *not* to cry; indeed, the effort to ward off tears led to some of her worst moments, those debilitating episodes of hysteria in the summer of 1854. However dangerous, tears indicated her humanity, as in "The Nursery":

> 'Twere well to pour the soul out
> In one convulsive fit,
> And rend the heart with weeping,
> If Love were loosed from it.

Conversely, the most serious aspect of the grief detailed in "The Shadow That Is Born With Us" is that it cannot be alleviated through tears. Leonora's inability to cry signifies for Howe a loss more severe than blindness and dramatizes a condition she herself felt threatened by.[52] The play's final line—Edward's description of the lost Leonora as a "thing of *tears* and tenderness forever" (141, my emphasis)—attests to Leonora's salvation. It marks Howe's, as well—for acknowledging the deadliness of the course to which Leonora gives herself and repudiating it through this tracing of its horrific consequences.

Ripley proved a true friend in easing Howe through this period of public review. He consoled her that the play's intellectual merits would be appreciated when it could be read, and he urged her not to "take too much to heart the words of foolish people." She had garnered, he noted, "fame, sympathy, admiration, envy, opposition, & obloquy"; not even the hungriest heart could desire more. Not the least of his fine qualities in her eyes, probably, was his reassurance in response to her anxieties about aging. "Do not wish to take away twenty years of your life," he wrote a few weeks later: "[Y]ou are now more beautiful than ever, & will become still more so with each new experience of the divine in the human."[53]

Whether it was assurances like this one from Ripley or simply a sense that she had, for the moment, reached some sort of internal terminus, Howe's literary activity and need for public recognition diminished after the completion of *The World's Own*. A letter to Annie from the end of this memorable year, marked by the appearance of two books, suggests that though her life proceeded much as before, her characteristic attitude underwent a change:

> Then quarreled with Chev, for making Flossy read Bible with sore eyes—then he pummelled me till I was black and blue in the soul. Then we made peace, fastened up the house, set the watch dog, and parted for the night, as usual—I cursing Philanthropy and he, probably, cursing me. But this is all naughty—I'm reforming, Annie dear, only somehow I want to begin with Chev, and not with myself.[54]

Her next published work was an account of an excursion to Cuba in 1859, appearing that year in the *Atlantic Monthly* and the following year expanded into a book.[55] The following decade would see the publication of two other volumes—a third collection of poetry in 1866 and another travel book in 1868—but the appearance in 1862 of "The Battle Hymn" made a different kind of poet of Julia Ward Howe, and a new kind of person. She began to refashion herself as a lecturer on ethics and, beginning in 1868, as an activist for women's rights. The death from diphtheria in 1863 of Sammy, her sixth child, born four years earlier, caused her to regard all her previous life as shallow and superficial; grief over the death also severely affected her husband's health, though he lived until 1876. Perhaps because these events and others so drastically altered the patterns of interaction in their household, Howe in old age saw the years preceding 1857 as a discrete segment of her life, "almost a period of play when compared to the time of trial which was to follow." It was to seem like "the tuning of instruments before some great musical solemnity" (242).

Since "The Battle Hymn of the Republic" is, for most of us, Howe's signature work, it is perhaps appropriate to conclude by taking a fresh look at it. Despite its seeming distance from the events and concerns that fed her earlier poetry, certain elements of the work (and of its much-celebrated genesis) resonate significantly when we examine it as an outgrowth of the years preceding. During the last fifty years of her life and for decades after her death, the poem and the story of its writing were equally well known in American culture; Howe observed in *Reminiscences* that it was "impossible . . . to say how many times [she had] been called upon to rehearse the circumstances" of its composition in the small hours of the morning of 19 November 1861 (273).

Earlier in the year Chev had been appointed to a commission to oversee sanitary conditions among the Union troops, and on this fall trip to Washington to meet with other members of the commission, Julia accompanied him. It was her first visit to the capital city and the first time she had been in a region of combat. Lodged at Willard's Hotel, she had the sense of being at the center of things, present at the unfolding of world-altering events. Meeting Abraham Lincoln in the White House intensified the exhilaration, as did being pressed, for the first time, into speaking in public.[56] On 18 November she rode out of town to witness a troop review, but a surprise Southern attack forced her party to turn back toward Washington. Progress was slow, since troops jammed the road; she and her friends (among them James Freeman Clarke) passed the time by singing army songs, including "John Brown's Body." Clarke urged her to write new words to the popular tune. The suggestion was thus planted:

> I went to bed that night as usual, and slept, according to my wont, quite soundly. I awoke in the gray of the morning twilight; and as I lay waiting for the dawn, the long lines of the desired poem began to twine themselves in my mind. Having thought out all the stanzas, I said to myself, "I must get up and write these verses down, lest I fall asleep again and forget them." So, with a sudden effort, I sprang out of bed, and found in the dimness an old stump of a pen which I remember to have used the day before. I scrawled the verses almost without looking at the paper. I had learned to do this when, on previous occasions, attacks of versification had visited me in the night, and I feared to have recourse to a light lest I should wake the baby, who slept near me. (275)

The poem, infused with intoxicating biblical imagery, underwent little revision before its publication in the *Atlantic Monthly* in February 1862; its vatic, apocalyptic quality, coupled with the mystique of inspiration associated with its writing, quickly became the stuff of legend. By the end of the war, it held a place in the popular imagination equivalent to that afforded *Uncle Tom's Cabin* a decade earlier.[57]

THE BATTLE HYMN OF THE REPUBLIC

Mine eyes have seen the glory of the coming of the Lord;
He is trampling out the vintage where the grapes of wrath are stored;
He hath loosed the fateful lightning of His terrible swift sword;
His truth is marching on.

I have seen Him in the watch fires of a hundred circling camps
They have builded Him an altar in the evening dews and damps;
I can read His righteous sentence by the dim and flaring lamps;
His day is marching on.

I have read a fiery gospel, writ in burnished rows of steel:
'As ye deal with my contemners, so with you my grace shall deal;
Let the Hero, born of woman, crush the serpent with his heel,
Since God is marching on.'

He has sounded forth the trumpet that shall never call retreat;
He is sifting out the hearts of men before His judgment seat;
Oh, be swift, my soul, to answer Him; be jubilant, my feet;
Our God is marching on.

In the beauty of the lilies Christ was born across the sea,
With a glory in His bosom that transfigures you and me;
As He died to make men holy, let us die to make men free;
While God is marching on.

The poem's language flowed so easily because Howe knew the Bible thoroughly, but I think we can look to other influences as well to understand the evident intensity of the inspiration. At the very least, it is interesting that she tied the composition of this work to practices learned during the years when the need to write had to be accommodated around the edges of maternal responsibilities. Like her earlier work, this piece took shape under conditions that underline the particular challenges faced by *women* writers.

More important is the sense of occasion offered by this moment in Washington. In the pages in *Reminiscences* leading up to the anecdote quoted above, Howe makes much of the means by which she stayed abreast of war-related issues. Recently elected governor of Massachusetts, John Andrew was a close family friend; he often used the Howes' Beacon Hill house as a site of respite from State House pressures. The doctor's friendship with Andrew and his willingness to be directed by him in any activity that might advance the North's cause had led to the Sanitary Commission appointment. Julia Howe notes: "I seemed to live in and along with the war, while it was in progress, and to follow all its ups and downs, its good and ill fortune, with these two brave men, Dr. Howe and Governor Andrew"—and further, that though neither man for a moment doubted the final result, "both they and I were often very sad and much discouraged" (265). It is clear from her brief sketch of Andrew's political activity that she held him in very high esteem.[58] Appended to this is an admiring account of her husband's remarkable understanding and predictive accuracy regarding military operations. In these and other ways, the war brought the Howes closer together emotionally than they had been for many years. Julia must have been profoundly happy to be taken along on the excursion with Andrew and Chev to Washington.

These tributes set the stage for Howe's description of wartime scenes (reproduced in miniature in the "watch-fires" and "burnished rows of steel" in the poem)—and more particularly, for a crucial admission regarding her feelings as she observed the frenetic activity everywhere around her:

> I distinctly remember that a feeling of discouragement came over me as I drew near the city of Washington. . . . I thought of the women of my acquaintance whose sons or husbands were fighting our great battle; the women themselves serving in the hospitals, or busying themselves with the work of the Sanitary Commission. My husband, as already said, was beyond the age of military service, my eldest son but a stripling; my youngest was a child of not more than two years. I could not leave my nursery to follow the march of our armies, neither had I the practical deftness which the preparing and packing of sanitary stores demanded. Something seemed to say to me, "You would be glad to serve, but you cannot help any one; you have nothing to give, and there is nothing for you to do." (273–74)

The scenes were painful in their own right, but especially so, I suspect, because they drove home to her again how decisively she was *not* Florence Nightingale or Dorothea Dix (who, by this time, had become Superintendent of Women Nurses for the Union Army).[59] But on the other hand, the situation in which she found herself—though she does not explicitly say so—could not have helped recalling Margaret Fuller's position in Rome in 1848–49. Like Fuller during the siege of Rome, Howe was located nearly at ground zero, or so it seemed to her:

> The main body of the enemy's troops was then stationed in the near neighborhood of Washington, and the capture of the national capital would have been of great strategic advantage to their cause. In order to render this impossible, the great Army of the Potomac was encamped around the city, with General McClelland in command. Within the city limits mounted officers and orderlies galloped to and fro. Ambulances, drawn by four horses, drove through the streets, stopping sometimes before Willard's Hotel, where we had all found quarters. From my window I saw the office of the "New York Herald," and near it the ghastly advertisement of an agency for embalming and forwarding the bodies of those who had fallen in the fight or who had perished by fever. (270)

If she was not exactly under fire, as Fuller had been, she yet had strongly the visual and emotional sense of being a writer in the thick of an event of international importance, at a critical time. The poem is her own dispatch from the front, her effort to galvanize opinion and cement commitment.

It would be surprising if such a highly charged atmosphere had *not* induced a moment of inspiration in one as finely tuned and as mindful of the sources of her creative energy as Howe. The occasion offered not just an opportunity to write a poem commensurate with the passionate commitment exhibited by her husband and Governor Andrew (one that might actually evoke the former's admiration), but one that could somehow be a gesture equivalent to the heroic acts of women the shadow of whose bravery, in a sense, had rested heavily on Julia Howe's shoulders for years. To suggest that "The Battle Hymn" may be considered in these terms is not to imply that its ringing call to action in a righteous cause is in any way hollow or secondary. Thinking of its genesis in this way merely helps us understand it as of a piece with the work and the life out of which it evolved—yet another instance of the complex root system feeding the growth of one of the century's genuinely remarkable minds.

Yet it should be noted, too, that the poem marks a fairly sharp departure from most of Howe's earlier work, a departure emblemized, perhaps unconsciously, in the poem's shift from the first person singular to more inclusive pronouns. Like the verses in her first two books, this work arose from personal experience and reflection. The "I" who sees God in the Union Army's campfires, who reads "His righteous sentence"

and "fiery gospel," is the woman who rode out into Virginia in the late
fall of 1861 and then the following morning, early, awoke to a vision. But
the God whose cause the poem espouses is pointedly the inspirer not
just of Julia Ward Howe: this is "*Our* God," and Christ's bosom-glory
transfigures all of us, not just the one whose eyes saw it in November
1861. Let *us* die to make men free. The poem's ties to the personal are
loosened, its power residing in the ability of its vision to lift Howe (and
readers) into collective humanitarian action.

By foregrounding this characteristic of "The Battle Hymn," I do not
mean to argue its superiority to Howe's earlier work. What I refer to
above as its vatic quality has certainly made it memorable, but its enduring presence in cultural history may be a function more of Howe's canny
publication (and energetic reproduction) of her predawn vision and of
the poem's attachment to a great tune than of the power of the language.
Indeed, as both Edward Snyder and Edmund Wilson suggest, the work's
imagery is somewhat confusing—biblical in resonance but pointing to
no specific scriptural passages. Lilies, Wilson notes, are associated with
Jesus' resurrection, not with his birth. Howe's distinction as a writer, I
believe, exhibits itself more clearly in the audacity of that "terrible . . .
personalism" of her first two collections; in the strength of mind that at
length enabled her to make public the impassioned, despairing voice in
the poems she wrote in her diary six weeks after her marriage; and in her
adroitness in devising tropes that both veiled and proclaimed their
subjects.

"There is something to be said," Annie Dillard observes, "for writing a memoir early, before life in society makes the writer ordinary by
smoothing off character's rough edges and abolishing interior life."[60]
Although Howe's *Reminiscences* preserves a few such edges (and, when
read attentively, hints at others), the volume did its work in, if not
abolishing, at least keeping well hidden the interior life that this book
seeks to retrieve. That was certainly her intention. On her anniversary in
1865, Howe wrote with exasperation (in her diary) of the terminus of any
illusion she may have nurtured that "The Battle Hymn," if nothing else
she had written, would alter her husband's attitude toward her work: "I
have been married twenty two years today. In the course of this time I
have never known my husband to approve any act of mine which I
myself valued. Books—poems—essays—everything has been contempt-

ible or contraband in his eyes, because it was not *his* way of doing things."[61] The circumstances invite sympathy, no doubt. Yet from this opposition was forged a determination splendidly epitomized in this anecdote from her daughters' memorial to their dauntingly energetic mother:

> During the thirty-four years of her own married life the Doctor was captain, beyond dispute; yet sometimes the mate felt that she must take her own way, and took it quietly. She was fond of quoting the words of Thomas Garrett, whose house was for years a station of the underground Railway, and who helped many slaves to freedom. "How did you manage it?" she asked him. His reply sank deep into her mind. "It was borne in upon me at an early period, that if I told no one what I intended to do, I should be enabled to do it."[62]

"Doing it" meant living a hidden life, shared fully only with her sisters and a small group of friends. But out of it, by 1857, had emerged, beyond the writing, a woman of strength, resilience, and capacious heart whose contributions to American cultural life had barely begun.

Notes

Introduction

1. Ripley's review appeared in the *Tribune* for 10 January 1854. Other reviews quoted here appeared in *Harper's New Monthly Magazine* 8 (February 1854): 426; and *Putnam's Monthly* 3 (February 1854): 224. Ripley's feeling that the *Passion-Flowers* poems were unique among the productions of other women of the time is perhaps a result of Howe's apparent lack of interest in other women's poetry. Her letters, journals, and memoirs—except for several expressions of admiration for Elizabeth Barrett Browning's work—are almost completely devoid of any reference to "female literature."

2. JWH to Annie [Annie (Ward) Mailliard], 29 December 1853 (#550). Letters and diaries, unless otherwise indicated, are part of the Samuel Gridley and Julia Ward Howe Papers at Houghton Library, Harvard University. The papers are cataloged in various ways, depending on the date of acquisition. Those designated by a number preceded by a "#" are part of the earliest collection, #44M-314, individually cataloged in a bound index called "Howe Family Papers." This collection includes letters to Julia and Samuel Howe. Citations for materials in other Houghton collections include the collection's shelfmark. Aside from the Howe materials, I cite extensively from two other collections— Charles Sumner's letters and Henry Wadsworth Longfellow's unpublished journals. Particular letters and journal entries are cited by date alone; shelfmarks for these materials are bMS Am 1.61 (Sumner) and MS Am 1340 (Longfellow). Citation of all these collections is by permission of the Houghton Library.

3. The *Post* review was reprinted in *The Commonwealth*, 5 January 1854.

4. Henry Wadsworth Longfellow, Journal, 24 December 1853: "Julia Howe's 'Passion Flowers' published to-day. Poems full of genius; full of beauty; but what a sad tone! Another cry of discontent added to the *slogan* of the *femmes incomprises!* '¿Quien es ella?' say the polite Spaniards, when they hear of any mischief. 'Who is she?' as if there must be some woman at the bottom of it. And here is revolt enough, between these blue covers." Hawthorne to Ticknor, 17 February 1854, *The Centenary Edition of the Works of Nathaniel Hawthorne*, ed. William Charvat, Roy Harvey Pearce, and Claude M. Simpson (Columbus: Ohio State UP, 1962–), 17: 177; related letters, 261–62 and 277–78.

5. JWH to Annie, 7th February 1854 (#554).

6. James D. Wallace, "Hawthorne and the Scribbling Women Reconsidered," *American Literature* 62 (1990): 201–22. Wallace notes that Hawthorne told Ticknor he "esteem[ed] her beyond all comparison the first of American poetesses" and planned to recommend the book to Richard Monckton Milnes, an English friend.

7. Deborah Pickman Clifford, *Mine Eyes Have Seen the Glory: A Biography of Julia Ward Howe* (Boston: Little Brown, 1979); Mary Hetherington Grant, *Private Woman, Public Person: An Account of the Life of Julia Ward Howe from 1819–1868* (Brooklyn, N.Y.: Carlson Publications, 1994); Cheryl Walker, *The Nightingale's Burden: Women Poets and American Culture before 1900* (Bloomington: Indiana UP, 1982). Noteworthy article-length analyses, in addition to Wallace's, are Mary Suzanne Schriber, "Julia Ward Howe and the Travel Book," *New England Quarterly* 62 (1989): 264–79; Leonardo Buonomo, "Julia Ward Howe's 'Italian' Poems in *Passion-Flowers*," *Annali di Ca' Foscari: Rivista della Facolta di Lingue e Letterature Staniere dell'Universita di Venezia* 30 (1991): 27–35; Judith Mattson Bean, "Margaret Fuller on the Early Poetry of Julia Ward Howe: An Uncollected Letter," *American Notes & Queries* 7 (1994): 76–81; and Tracy McCabe, "Avenging Angel: Tragedy and Womanhood in Julia Ward Howe's *The World's Own*," *Legacy* 12 (1995): 98–111.

8. Five recent anthologies are the basis for this generalization. Three are of women's writing only: Cheryl Walker, ed., *American Women Poets of the Nineteenth Century* (New Brunswick: Rutgers UP, 1992); Janet Gray, ed., *She Wields a Pen: American Women Poets of the Nineteenth Century* (Iowa City: U Iowa P, 1997); and Karen L. Kilcup, ed., *Nineteenth-Century American Women Writers: An Anthology* (Oxford: Blackwell, 1997). Walker offers the largest number of Howe poems (thirteen), all but one composed after 1860. Gray includes six— "The Battle Hymn" and five from the 1866 *Lyrics of the Street*. Howe's work does not appear in the Kilcup anthology. Howe fares no better in two other recent collections of poetry by both women and men—Paul Kane's *Poetry of the American Renaissance: A Diverse Anthology from the Romantic Period* (New York: George Braziller, 1995) and John Hollander's *American Poetry: The Nineteenth Century* (New York: Library of America, 1996), although Hollander does include one poem from *Passion-Flowers*, "My Last Dance."

9. Toni Morrison, introduction to *Adventures of Huckleberry Finn*, by Mark Twain (New York: Oxford UP, 1996), xxxvi.

10. JWH, *Reminiscences 1819–1899* (New York: Negro Universities Press, 1969), 228–30.

11. *Julia Ward Howe, 1819–1910* (Boston: Houghton Mifflin, 1915), 2 vols. The title page reads, "By Laura E. Richards and Maud Howe Elliott, assisted by Florence Howe Hall." Laura Richards also published *Two Noble Lives: Samuel Gridley Howe, Julia Ward Howe* (Boston: D. Estes, 1911), as well as a biography of her father in 1935; she edited a selection of her father's letters and journals in 1906.

12. Louise Hall Tharp, *Three Saints and a Sinner: Julia Ward Howe, Louisa, Annie, Sam Ward* (Boston: Little, Brown, 1956).

13. Mary Grant, "Domestic Experience and Feminist Theory: The Case of Julia Ward Howe," in *Woman's Being, Woman's Place: Female Identity and Vocation in American History,* ed. Mary Kelley (Boston: G. K. Hall, 1979), 220–32.

14. Barbara Miller Solomon, *In the Company of Educated Women: A History of Women and Higher Education in America* (New Haven: Yale UP, 1985).

15. Mary Kelley, *Private Woman, Public Stage: Literary Domesticity in Nineteenth-Century America* (New York: Oxford UP, 1984), 57.

16. Joanne Dobson, "The American Renaissance Reenvisioned" in *The (Other) American Traditions: Nineteenth Century Women Writers,* ed. Joyce W. Warren (New Brunswick: Rutgers UP, 1993), 164–82.

17. Judith Fetterley, "Commentary: Nineteenth-Century American Women Writers and the Politics of Recovery," *American Literary History* 6 (1994): 600–611.

18. Dobson, "The American Renaissance Reenvisioned."

19. Phyllis Rose, *Parallel Lives: Five Victorian Marriages* (New York: Random House, 1983), 9.

20. Adrienne Rich, *What Is Found There: Notebooks on Poetry and Politics* (New York: Norton, 1993), 12–13.

21. Ibid., 133.

22. Ibid., 158.

23. JWH to Louisa [Louisa (Ward) Crawford], 16 February 1846 (#450).

1. "The Thought of What I Have Undertaken"

1. JWH, *Reminiscences,* 43. Intertextual page numbers throughout, unless otherwise identified, refer to this work.

2. Joseph Cogswell and George Bancroft operated the Round Hill School from 1823 to 1834. Based on principles Cogswell had observed in German schools, the institution strove to educate the whole person as an individual. Boys took classes in a wide array of subjects and advanced according to personal ambition and ability.

3. Cogswell's influential role in raising interest in the United States in German writers is described in Henry A. Pochman, *German Culture in America* (Madison: U Wisconsin P, 1957), 70–72. First as Harvard's librarian, then through the Round Hill School, and later as owner/editor of the *New York Review* from 1839 to 1842, Cogswell was one of only three or four Americans in this period who could claim extensive knowledge of German literature. Pochman notes only one U.S.-born woman—Margaret Fuller—who in the 1830s learned German well enough to read it easily. Desultory searching has turned up just a few others—Elizabeth Palmer Peabody, Lydia Maria Child, Elizabeth Ellet, and Julia Ward.

4. See Nancy F. Cott, *The Bonds of Womanhood: "Woman's Sphere" in New*

England, 1780–1835 (New Haven: Yale UP, 1977), 110–25; Susan Phinney Conrad, *Perish the Thought: Intellectual Women in Romantic America, 1830–1860* (New York: Oxford UP, 1976), 27–33; Kelley, *Private Woman, Public Stage,* 56–73; Solomon, *In the Company of Educated Women;* Linda K. Kerber, " 'Why Should Girls Be Learn'd and Wise?': Two Centuries of Higher Education for Women as Seen Through the Unfinished Work of Mary Alice Baldwin," in *Women and Higher Education in American History,* ed. John Mack Faragher and Florence Howe (New York: Norton, 1988), 18–42; Nina Baym, *American Women Writers and the Work of History, 1790–1860* (New Brunswick: Rutgers UP, 1995), 11–28; Christine Bolt, *The Women's Movements in the United States and Britain from the 1790s to the 1920s* (Amherst: U Massachusetts P, 1993), 48–52; Patricia Okker, *Our Sister Editors: Sarah J. Hale and the Tradition of Nineteenth-Century American Women Editors* (Athens: U Georgia P, 1995), 38–46. Charles Capper and Joan von Mehren briefly discuss these issues in their accounts of Margaret Fuller's (atypical) education; see Capper, *Margaret Fuller: An American Romantic Life* (New York: Oxford UP, 1992), 39–40, and von Mehren, *Minerva and the Muse: A Life of Margaret Fuller* (Amherst: U Massachusetts P, 1994), 19–22. Generally speaking, ideas about women's education set forth in 1790 by Noah Webster (it should render them "correct in their manners, respectable in their families, and agreeable in society") still obtained in the 1820s. (Webster quoted in Thomas Woody, *A History of Women's Education in the United States* [New York: Science Press, 1929], 1:151.)

5. Although laudatory articles on Goethe had been published in the United States as early as 1817 (by Edward Everett in the *North American Review*), and although Joseph Cogswell, the scholar Samuel Ward had welcomed into his house, was an enthusiastic Goethean, the great writer's genius was far from universally acknowledged. Susan Phinney Conrad notes that, for most Americans, "Goethe was an untouchable, a fiend whose depravity was matched only by Byron's." When Margaret Fuller published her essay on Goethe in *The Dial* in July 1841 (a reply to a scathing attack two years earlier by George Bancroft), says Conrad, "the fact that a woman defended Goethe was so shocking to the public that the critic seemed as immoral as her subject" (*Perish,* 68–69). This attitude was remarkably long-lived, in certain quarters anyway. In a review of an anthology of essays on Goethe published in 1886, Howe's piece, "Goethe's Women," was attacked for the tolerant attitude she voiced regarding Goethe's liaison with Christiane Vulpius. See Maurice F. Egan, "A Chat about New Books," *Catholic World* 43, no. 253 (April 1886):129.

6. Julia nevertheless had superb musical training, a series of piano and voice teachers culminating in several years of lessons with a renowned intimate of the Garcia family, Signor Cardini. Howe later attributed her general stamina and sizable lung power (a tiny woman, she could even in her late years still be heard in the back rows of large lecture halls) to the rigor of her vocal training.

7. In the summer of 1838, for example, when their father had insisted on Julia's remaining in New York with him rather than playing in Newport, Sam wrote to the elder Ward: "You always exact too much of her in desiring not only

that she obey you but be happier in so doing than in following up certain wishes of her own. . . . Julia writes all day and half the night. One morning she wrote in 5 hours 16 pages. She is murdering herself. Yet she is forced to do this. In the tedium and heat of a large solitude her restless mind must needs work." Sam Ward to his father, 16 July 1838 (Samuel Ward Papers, New York Public Library).

8. JW to Louisa and Annie, 6 July 1838 (#361).

9. E.g., Longfellow to Sam Ward, 3 November 1841: "Your sister Julia's 'Imprisoned Angel' is a *very, very* beautiful poem, both in design and execution. Only in the third Stanza the line 'And gently o'er its fetters sweeps' mars the symmetry of the piece. Though the line in itself is beautiful, I should reject it without mercy." *The Letters of Henry Wadsworth Longfellow,* ed. Andrew Hilen (Cambridge: Harvard UP, 1966), 2:343.

10. "We find in this, as in many of his other productions, flat lines, and obscure phrases. The tale is, as it were, too much spun out. . . . De Lamartine should study conciseness, and cultivate more concentration of thought. He is too apt to dwell upon details which should be passed over, as they become tedious, and diminish the dignity of his style. He weakens by elaboration that which would be much more forcible and energetic if simply expressed." JW, "Review of De Lamartine's Jocelyn," *Literary and Theological Review* 3 (December 1836): 559–72.

11. Tharp, *Three Saints,* quotes a letter from Marion to Sam, no date given: "Much does she seem revolving over some plan for literary distinction, but this, I hope, she will lay aside when she grows older and wiser" (55).

12. JW, *New York Review* 4 (1839): 393–400.

13. Longfellow, *Letters,* 2:143.

14. Quoted in Walker, *Nightingale's Burden,* 30.

15. See Okker, *Our Sister Editors,* 6–37, and Baym, *American Women Writers,* 29–45. Both Baym and Okker emphasize the wide variety of writing by women in this period and urge relinquishing the public sphere–private sphere distinction in attempting to understand what possibilities there actually were for literarily inclined women. While it is true that opportunities were wider than we have supposed, in many individual cases ideologies of domesticity, willingly embraced, did delimit women's options. It is important to avoid *any* totalizing paradigm as we write the history of the intellectual achievement of nineteenth-century women.

16. Useful information about the writings of women in context with one another is found in Conrad, *Perish,* 93–133 and 183–235. Baym, *American Women Writers,* provides additional information about Smith, Peabody, and Ellet.

17. Richards and Elliott mention a letter Julia Ward received about this time, addressed to "*Julie, la respectée, la choisie, l'aimée, la chérie*" and evidently returned to its smitten sender by Mr. Ward with a stern note advising him to relinquish his hopes. A number of young men offered her their attentions. Richards and Elliott quote a friend who knew all three Ward sisters in those

days: "Louisa had her admirers, and Annie had hers; but when the men saw your mother, they just *flopped!*" (*Julia Ward Howe*, 1:29).

18. JW to Mary [Ward] Dorr, 17 September 1839 (#52M–301[350]).

19. These poems were lost or destroyed a few years later. In *Reminiscences* Howe notes tersely: "The anguish which I then experienced sought relief in expression, and took form in a small collection of poems, which Margaret Fuller urged me to publish, but which have never seen the light, and never will" (61). Richards and Elliott note that the "loss" of the collection was "always regretted by our mother" (*Julia Ward Howe*, 1:69).

20. Mary to JW, 11 December 1841 (#196a).

21. In a reminiscence commemorating Emerson's centenary, Howe remembered her earliest sense of him as "the originator of an evil philosophy." A "zealous Calvinist in those days," she "had much to say about the power of Satan over the minds of men." Emerson's opinion that "the angel must be stronger than the demon" she found unbelievable, though the idea continued to vex her. The piece appeared in *Unity*, 7 May 1903.

22. JW to Louisa and Annie, #393.

23. Mary to JW, 26 February 1842 (#196b).

24. "[I]f I could judge from the little I saw of the well known Julie she is inferior to E[llen Fuller] in mind and as affected as she can be." *The Letters of Margaret Fuller*, ed. Robert N. Hudspeth (Ithaca: Cornell UP, 1983), 2:72.

25. Judith Mattson Bean's reading of this letter ("Margaret Fuller on the Early Poetry of Julia Ward Howe") accords with the one I offer here, but it should be noted that the letter could sustain a different interpretation. Although Fuller's praise seems sincere, it is embedded among passages that might be accused of undercutting with light irony the compliments she pays (e.g., "It will always be valuable to me to have seen that the church even now can have an influence so real. . . . I had thought only those who had turned their backs upon the church could see in it a text for pure worship"). Fuller's letter may have been the product of a desire not to offend their mutual friend Mary by disparaging Julia Ward's literary efforts. If Fuller actually thought the poems should be published, she was herself in a position to do so, in *The Dial.*

Julia Ward Howe's response to Fuller was complex and far-reaching. The two had little, if any, direct interaction after the occasion when Mary introduced them. Fuller had already moved to New York by the time Howe was settled in South Boston, and in Howe's account of her awakening to a feminist consciousness in 1868 (*Reminiscences*, 373–74), the list of people who influenced this moment does not include Fuller's name. Yet Howe's was the first (after the 1851 Emerson-Clarke-Hedge *Memorial*) full-length biography of Fuller (1883), and it is a compelling text for what it suggests about Fuller's importance to Howe. Howe particularly emphasizes Fuller's decision to delay her intellectual development when family duty called, her commitment to political thought and action, and (most intriguing) Fuller's success in conflating romantic and domestic interests—all issues that Howe herself faced. I suggest later that Fuller's involvement in Italian revolutionary politics was a spur to Howe's interest in the events of 1848 and that Fuller's image lurks just beneath the surface in several key moments in poems in *Passion-Flowers.*

26. The force of Mary's influence is indirectly suggested by another anecdote supplied by Richards and Elliott. After describing the impact of "a great calvinistic revival," which intensified Julia's grief during these years, they note that the emotional religious fervor was heightened by romantic attentions she began to receive from a "young clergyman of brilliant powers and passionate nature" who pressed his suit forcefully. She consented to a "semi-engagement," but then, during a trip to visit Mary in Boston, "[r]elieved from the pressure of a twofold excitement, breathing a calmer and a freer air, she realized that there could be no true union between her and the Rev. Mr. ____" (*Julia Ward Howe,* 1:32).

27. Later in her life, in an undated sermon entitled "Solitude and Religion," Howe acknowledged relief at her escape from the "dreary phraseology, . . . set pattern of conviction, [and] stereotyped way of salvation" of Calvinism (Julia Ward Howe Collection, Library of Congress, Folder 57). In this migration from Calvinist orthodoxy to Unitarianism, Howe's personal theological narrative reflects large-scale literary trends described by Lawrence Buell in *New England Literary Culture: From Revolution through Renaissance* (New York: Cambridge UP, 1986), 38–39.

28. Frederick J. Blue provides a detailed account of the Sumner-Longfellow relationship in "The Poet and the Reformer: Longfellow, Sumner, and the Bonds of Male Friendship, 1837–1874," *Journal of the Early Republic* 13 (1995): 273–97.

29. Sumner to Longfellow, 9 August 1840. As Sumner discovered the following day, the rumor of Julia's engagement to Edward Norris Kirk, a New Yorker, was false. She did, however, consider marrying this gentleman, a plan her family regarded with deep uneasiness; see Henry Ward to JW, 25 July 1840 (#2003).

30. The most recent biography of Samuel Howe is Harold Schwartz's *Samuel Gridley Howe, Social Reformer, 1801–1876* (Cambridge: Harvard UP, 1956). Earlier works providing useful biographical information are *Letters and Journals of Samuel Gridley Howe,* 2 vols., ed. Laura E. Richards (Boston: D. Estes, 1909); Franklin Benjamin Sanborn, *Dr. S. G. Howe, the Philanthropist* (New York: Funk & Wagnalls, 1891); and Julia Ward Howe, *Memoir of Dr. Samuel Gridley Howe* (Boston: A. J. Wright, 1876).

31. Louise Tharp's *Three Saints and a Sinner,* though sometimes untrustworthy in its facts, entertainingly reconstructs life in the Ward household and in the New York of the 1830s generally.

32. Some of this joie de vivre may have devolved on her from two figures who, after her mother's death, had substantial responsibility for raising Julia Ward and her siblings: her aunt, Eliza Cutler and the man Eliza married in 1829, the physician and historian John Wakefield Francis. Both were people of great good cheer. "Auntie Francis" was renowned in the family for her ability to elevate everyone's spirits, and Edgar Allan Poe described John Francis's conver-

sation as "a sort of Roman punch, made up of tragedy, comedy, and the broadest of all possible farce" (quoted in Richards and Elliott, *Julia Ward Howe,* 1:10). Mary Grant emphasizes the somber side of Eliza Cutler's character and suggests she liked the other Ward children more than she did Julia, but this perception runs counter to the weight of testimony, I believe (Grant, *Private Woman,* 24–25).

33. Richards and Elliott, *Julia Ward Howe,* 1:24.

34. JW to her sisters, probably from Dorchester, 11 February 1841[?] (#382). "I met the Chevalier there, for the first time, but did not talk with him, as he does not dance, and went away early—here is my whole story."

35. SGH, *Letters and Journals,* 2:388.

36. Schwartz, *Samuel Gridley Howe,* 10.

37. SGH to William Sampson, 30 January 1830, in SGH, *Letters and Journals,* 2:364. He continues: "But thank God, there *are a few* whose generous spirits reflect no more upon their own selfish plans of life than absolute necessity demands, and who share their hearts, as their goods with others. The world may censure this, and call it thoughtless wastefulness—or give it harder names. Out upon the world! It censures that which it sees excellent in others because it feels this to be a cutting reproof to its own selfishness and meanness. I had rather see that generous spirit which wastes its possessions upon others, though to its own ruin, than the one which prompts man to act and live as though he alone were pursuing happiness in the world."

38. Ibid., 2:388.

39. Schwartz records Elizabeth Peabody's recollection of this relationship in her "Cuba Journal," 29 November 1834 (*Samuel Gridley Howe,* 104).

40. SGH, *Letters and Journals,* 2:386.

41. Mary to JW, 11 December 1841 (#196).

42. Longfellow wrote to her brother Sam: "Julia is enjoying herself much in Boston, and making many friends and admirers. Felton is in love with her; and in speaking of her uses the superlative degree only." Longfellow, *Letters* (30 January 1842), 2:383.

43. Although Dickens had visited the Perkins Institution in January, he had not met Samuel Howe, who was in Louisville, Kentucky, on a fund-raising mission. The two met personally at New York's welcoming party on 6 June 1842.

44. The first is on microfilm: Series 1, Reel 8, MC272 #23 at Schlesinger. The second is #51M-283 (122). See also Tharp's account of this visit, based on these letters (*Three Saints,* 84–89).

45. Sumner to Longfellow, 6–15 June 1842 and 10 July 1842.

46. Longfellow to Sumner, 22 July 1842 (*Letters,* 2:444); Sumner to Longfellow, 10 July 1842. This analysis of heads is a frequently sounded note in letters of this period. Samuel Howe, like many of his contemporaries, was deeply intrigued with phrenology. In his second long letter to Julia Ward that summer, he attempted to explain her inclination to "scatter shot around continually" as a function of overdevelopment of the "organs of the propensities . . . ranged, you

know, by Phrenologists in the base of the head." The doctor's preoccupation with head shape as a predictor of matrimonial suitability perhaps underlines the fact that considerations in addition to "inadvertent captivation" were driving his interest in Julia Ward. For information about Samuel Howe's infatuation with phrenology, see Harold Schwartz, "Samuel Gridley Howe as Phrenologist," *American Historical Review* 57 (1952): 644–51.

47. The letter, undated, is #392. The ambiguity of the relationship is underscored by a letter from George Hillard, another club member, to Longfellow in September 1842: "I don't know whether [Samuel Howe] and the 'Diva Julia' are converging or not. He is much captivated but whether she has had the sweet spell thrown over her or is only indulging her love of mischief and giving her victim a little line before she finally lands him high and dry on the sands of rejection to sigh and gasp his life out, I cannot say." Quoted in Tharp, *Three Saints,* 89.

48. Many studies in the last two decades of the ideologies underlying courtship and marriage in antebellum America provide a useful context for understanding the forces affecting Julia Ward and Samuel Howe in their preengagement interactions. Samuel's ideas about his ideal mate, limned in his summer 1842 letters, bear the stamp of his era's general assumptions about appropriate relations between husband and wife. Okker (*Sister Editors,* chapters 2 and 3) provides a detailed reading of Sarah Josepha Hale's prescriptions for acceptable female behavior as they were articulated over a thirty-year period in *Ladies' Magazine* and *Godey's Lady's Book;* these accord closely with the premises obviously operating not only in Samuel Howe's mind, but within Ward family discussions, too. The degree to which they were more firmly implanted in the doctor than in Julia or her brothers emerges in the conflicts, discussed below, that ensued almost as soon as the two agreed to marry. Beyond Okker and Cott, *The Bonds of Womanhood,* see Glenna Matthews, *"Just a Housewife": The Rise and Fall of Domesticity in America* (New York: Oxford UP, 1987), chapters 1 and 2; John D'Emilio and Estelle B. Freedman, *Intimate Matters: A History of Sexuality in America* (New York: Harper & Row, 1988), especially 75–76; Karen Lystra, *Searching the Heart: Women, Men, and Romantic Love in Nineteenth-Century America* (New York: Oxford UP, 1989), chapter 6; Bolt, *The Women's Movements in the United States and Britain,* 44–47; and E. Anthony Rotundo, *American Manhood: Transformations in Masculinity from the Revolution to the Modern Era* (New York: Basic Books, 1993), chapters 5–8.

49. This letter is the strongest pre-engagement evidence that Julia Ward did, indeed, want to marry Samuel Howe. Her dismay at possibly losing him shows in her effort to persuade Sam that Louisa is ill-suited for the institutional life that marriage to the doctor would mean.

50. SGH to Sam Ward, 21 February 1843 (#870); JW to Sam Ward, 21 February 1843 (#51M-283 [168]); Sam Ward to JW, 22 February 1843 (#1777). Not everyone was surprised. Henry Cleveland, the man whom Samuel Howe had replaced in the Five of Clubs, wrote to Sumner from Havana: "When a hero and a belle—and *such* a hero, and *such* a belle—are thus connected, the sound of

rejoicing should be spread far and wide over the land. I thought something would come of Howe's catching Julia Ward in the game of blindman's buff last autumn, and I exclaimed 'omen accipio' " (7 April 1843, #143).

51. Sam Ward to SGH, 4 March 1843 (#1778).

52. Brother Marion, in a 3 February 1843 letter to Sam Ward, refers to Samuel Howe as "a bit of Boston granite." This characterization is part of a metaphor in which Marion likens the Ward siblings to gems that polish one another, but are threatened with scratches from the granitic doctor. Samuel Ward Papers, New York Public Library.

53. Sam Ward to SGH, 9 March 1843 (#1780).

54. Sam Ward to SGH, 4 April 1843 (#1782).

55. It is difficult to place this letter precisely in the chronology of indecision. Since it suggests that the issue of Samuel Howe's temporary attraction to Louisa was not yet settled, it could have arisen out of a moment prior to the engagement on 21 February. Yet because doubts over that defection may well have lingered in Julia's mind for quite a long time, and quite plausibly have been reawakened by his April letter to her, we cannot be sure of its date.

56. *Reminiscences* is actually silent on these questions. From the account of the first meeting at the Institution, Howe's narrative jumps ahead to the marriage and wedding trip. The space between is filled with a brief history of her husband's accomplishments, as if these will sufficiently explain her decision to marry him. Of course, by the time she constructed this narrative, she had no reason to dramatize either party's uncertainties; the questions we have are those of *our* age, not hers.

57. JW to Major David Bates Douglass, August 1834, quoted in Tharp, *Three Saints,* 56. Tharp notes several other quasi-romantic interludes as well, 56–59 and 75–76.

58. The diary is #51M-283 (321).

59. JW to Louisa and Annie, 1843 (#394).

2. "Sumner Ought to Have Been a Woman"

1. This poem appears in the 1843 diary (#51M-283[321]).

2. SGH to Sumner, 11 September 1844 (#920).

3. See Charley Shively, ed., *Calamus Lovers: Walt Whitman's Working-Class Camerados* (San Francisco: Gay Sunshine Press, 1987); Jeffrey Richards, " 'Passing the love of women': Manly Love and Victorian Society," in *Manliness and Morality: Middle-Class Masculinity in Britain and America, 1800–1940,* ed. J. A. Mangan and James Walvin (New York: St. Martin's, 1987), 92–122; John W. Crowley, "Howells, Stoddard, and Male Homosocial Attachment in Victorian America," in *The Making of Masculinities: The New Men's Studies,* ed. Harry Brod (Boston: Allen & Unwin, 1987), 301–24; D'Emilio and Freedman, *Intimate Matters,* 121–30; Martin Duberman, " 'Writhing Bedfellows' in Antebellum South Carolina: Historical Interpretation and the Politics of Evidence," in *Hidden from History: Reclaiming the Gay and Lesbian Past,* ed.

Duberman, Martha Vicinus, and George Chauncey Jr. (New York: Meridian, 1989), 153–68; Mark C. Carnes and Clyde Griffen, eds., *Meanings for Manhood: Constructions of Masculinity in Victorian America* (Chicago: U Chicago P, 1990); Karen V. Hansen, " 'Helped Put in a Quilt': Men's Work and Male Intimacy in Nineteenth-Century New England," in *The Social Construction of Gender,* ed. Judith Lorber and Susan A. Farrell (Newbury Park, Calif.: Sage, 1991), 83–103, and Hansen, " 'Our Eyes Behold Each Other': Masculinity and Intimate Friendship in Antebellum New England," in *Men's Friendships,* ed. Peter M. Nardi (Newbury Park, Calif.: Sage, 1992), 35–58; Steven Seidman, *Romantic Longings: Love in America, 1830–1890* (New York: Routledge, 1991); Rotundo, *American Manhood,* 75–91; Thomas P. Lowry, *The Story the Soldiers Wouldn't Tell: Sex in the Civil War* (Mechanicsburg, Pa.: Stackpole Books, 1994); David Reynolds, *Walt Whitman's America: A Cultural Biography* (New York: Knopf, 1995); Byrne R. S. Fone, *A Road to Stonewall: Male Homosexuality and Homophobia in English and American Literature, 1750–1969* (New York: Twayne, 1995), especially chapters 3 and 4; D. Michael Quinn, *Same-Sex Dynamics among Nineteenth-Century Americans: A Mormon Example* (Urbana: U Illinois P, 1996); and Vincent J. Bertolini, "Fireside Chastity: The Erotics of Sentimental Bachelorhood in the 1850s," *American Literature* 68 (December 1996): 707–37.

4. But consider John Creech's argument that speculation about such apparently anachronistic concepts as "coming out" or the "closet" in relation to writers working "before the invention of homosexuality" may eventually reveal that "our conceptual arsenal contains instruments still too unrefined to catch the nuances of attitude and behavior in the mid-nineteenth century" (*Closet Writing/Gay Reading: The Case of Melville's "Pierre"* [Chicago: U Chicago P, 1993], 69). Other instances of such readings of nineteenth-century texts are Shively, *Calamus Lovers,* and Bertolini, "Fireside Chastity," 707–37.

5. Donald Yacavone, "Abolitionists and the 'Language of Fraternal Love,' " in Carnes and Griffen, *Meanings,* 85–95. Quinn makes the same point forcefully in the "Introduction" to *Same-Sex Dynamics:* "In nineteenth-century America, same-sex friends of all ages held hands while walking down the streets of cities and towns. Few people regarded it as remarkable when same-sex friends kissed each other 'full on the lips' in public or private. Fewer still saw anything unusual in the common American practice of same-sex friends sleeping in the same bed, sometimes for years at a time. Rather than regarding this sleeping arrangement as a grim necessity of overcrowded houses, American teenagers and married persons of that era indicated that they looked forward to their next opportunity to share a bed with a same-sex friend. Whether in privileged society or working-class culture, letters between same-sex friends in the nineteenth century had emotional intensity and passionate references. . . . To twentieth-century ears, these sound like sexual activities we associate with romantic love. However, the intimate same-sex dynamics of most nineteenth-century Americans did not involve homoeroticism" (1).

6. Quinn, *Same-Sex Dynamics,* 114.

7. The standard biography of Sumner is David Herbert Donald's *Charles*

Sumner and the Coming of the Civil War (New York: Knopf, 1960) and *Charles Sumner and the Rights of Man* (New York: Knopf, 1970). As Donald explains in the introduction to a recent one-volume edition of these works, they were originally conceived as a single biography. Since the text of this new edition is essentially unchanged from its original publication, my citations refer to the initial separately published works as likely to be more readily available to scholars. See Donald, *Charles Sumner* (New York: Da Capo Press, 1996), xix. Of limited usefulness for my purposes (because the selection emphasizes Sumner's public labors) is *The Selected Letters of Charles Sumner,* ed. Beverly Wilson Palmer (Boston: Northeastern UP, 1990).

8. Frederick Blue's reflections on these letters and on the hitherto unemphasized "extremely human and vulnerable" side of Sumner's character (Blue, "The Post and the Reformer") are mostly congruent with the argument I make here regarding the Samuel Howe–Charles Sumner friendship, but Blue does not raise the possibility that the letters may reflect a homoerotic attachment. He is right not to: the friendship between the lawyer and the poet seems to have been a safe haven for Sumner, a respite from the kind of tension I document in Sumner's relationship with Samuel Howe.

9. Sumner to Longfellow, 24 January 1839.

10. SGH to Sumner, December 1841 (#865); 30 January 1842 (#867); 1 February 1842 (#868); Hillard quoted in Donald, *Coming of the Civil War,* 87; Felton to Sam Ward, 17 July 1842. Felton continued: "They tear over the pavements on their quadrupedantic monsters, to the great dismay of all sober citizens, who shake their heads and bode bruises and broken bones. We are thinking of shutting them up in a cage and taming them."

11. Donald, *Coming of the Civil War,* 89.

12. Lieber to Sumner, 15 October 1843; quoted in Donald, *Coming of the Civil War,* 90. Sam Ward to Longfellow, 14 January 1841 (bMS Am 1340.2[5820–136]). Vincent Bertolini provides a useful perspective for understanding Sumner's anxiety about his bachelor state. The currency of what Bertolini names the literature of "bachelor sentimentalism" was provoked by cultural fears of the unmarried male, who represented "one of the worst threats to nineteenth-century bourgeois social and sexual ideology." Bachelorhood was perceived as "a transitional state because the bachelor has left properly constituted boyhood, in which the young man's sexuality is monitored, chastened, and directed towards proper objects by the mother, but not yet entered properly constituted manhood, in which the wife extends the maternal regime within the bounds of a limited, procreative, conjugal sexuality." Bertolini examines the "regulatory work" done by such texts as "The Old Bachelor" (a two-part story that appeared in *Godey's Lady's Book* in 1850) that attempt to propel unmarried men toward the domesticating female. As will become apparent, many of Samuel Howe's letters to Sumner in the year following his marriage deploy the rhetoric of this literary mode (Bertolini, "Fireside Chastity," 707–37).

13. See Conrad, *Perish,* 17–18, 20.

14. Sumner to Longfellow, 6–15 June 1842; Sumner to Lieber, 27 June 1842. For expressions of personal longing, consider his letter to Longfellow, 10 July 1842: "Would that Providence w[ou]ld send me such a wife. Full & overflowing as her woman's love might be, mine should be greater. Oh! with what ardour I would pour my gushing affections into her soul—as the Parthians filled the head of Croesus with the gold he loved too well. Her cravings of sympathy should be more than satisfied. She should lean on my arm, & not a wind of heaven visit her too roughly. But why has my pen fallen into this vein? Because, in writing to you, it utters the unchecked feelings of the heart. When will these visions, Iris-colored, come to pass, & this uneasy spirit be at peace?"

15. Sumner to Longfellow, 29 August 1842; emphasis mine.

16. Longfellow, *Letters*, 2:513–14.

17. Sumner's letter is quoted in Richards and Elliott, *Julia Ward Howe*, 1:38.

18. La Motte-Fouqué, *Undine and Other Stories*, trans. Sir Edmund Gosse (London: Oxford UP, 1896), 42.

19. I find no evidence to suggest that Sumner had the rest of the tale in mind, but it is interesting to note that in its course, Huldbrand's love fades. Undine, though she is ennobled and morally invigorated by her marriage, is gradually replaced in her husband's affections by his old love, Bertalda. Undine sadly accepts this new development, striving self-sacrificingly to make room for Bertalda in their household and to protect the couple from her wrathful water-relatives. The image of a wife uncomplainingly relinquishing emotional exclusivity to accommodate her husband's former love reverberates eerily in the Chev-Julia-Sumner triangle. Cornelius Felton, too, jokingly associated Julia with Undine in his part of one of Samuel Howe's letters to her in the summer of 1842 (#51M-283[122]). Julia's brother Marion, however, responding to her uncertainties regarding the doctor around the time of the engagement, assured her: "Thou art no Undine but a woman who has soul enough to give to an Undine half of it." Francis Marion Ward to JW, n.d. (#1999).

20. SGH to Sumner, 22 February (#873); 29 March (#877); 3 April (#879); 13 May (#884). Sumner to George Sumner, 31 March.

21. Sumner to Longfellow, 12 May and [?] May 1843.

22. SGH to Sumner, 13 May 1843 (#884): "[Y]ou know what I mean, that is as well as you can be expected to know—you who know not the delights of love, & who can form about as good an idea of the glorious light which it throws over our existence as can a mole of [the] center of the solar system."

23. SGH to Sumner, 18 June 1843 (#887).

24. SGH to Sumner, 2 July 1843 (#891).

25. SGH to Sumner, 27 August 1843 (#892); 12 September (#893); 6 October (#894).

26. Julia's brother Marion met them in Paris and noted the doctor's preoccupation with his investigations of educational and reform efforts; so caught up in them was he that he paid little attention to what might interest Julia and Annie. See Marion to Louisa, 29 September 1843 (bMS Am 1869.1[15]).

27. SGH to Sumner, 16 October 1843 (#895); 8 November (#897).

28. SGH to Sumner, 30 January 1844 (#958): "I have but one feeling now dear Sumner—all others are swallowed up in that—even you I think less of than formerly for a father's love fills my soul: Of you *less frequently* only, for less tenderly I cannot[,] the love I bear you growing by that which it feeds not upon."

29. SGH to Sumner, 2 February 1844 (#904); Sumner to Longfellow and his wife, 1844 ("I have had two warm love-letters from ＿＿ Howe. He is as earnest a lover, as philanthropist.").

30. Longfellow's journal, 4 and 10 April 1844; Sumner to SGH, 30 April 1844.

31. Donald, *Coming of the Civil War,* 23, 35–36, 38.

32. Donald, *Rights of Man,* 314, 271.

33. Karen Lystra reminds us that the "most serious problem of studying sex in the Victorian or any other historical period is the temptation to apply contemporary definitions and views to an erotic ethos that changes over time. For example, in contemporary American culture sex is often taken to mean intercourse; but this culturally constricted view of erotic activity must be expanded in order to examine the past sympathetically and critically. . . . Erotic activity has many forms, and the presumption that one dimension of sexual expression defines it or is superior to other forms is naively culture-bound" (*Searching,* 57).

34. Sumner to SGH, 27 August and 8 September 1844; SGH to Sumner, 4 September (#919).

35. The "Sumner ought to have been a woman" letter is #920; the other 11 September letter is #921.

36. All poems quoted here are from Howe's 1843 diary.

37.   I miss a leaf in my note book,
                       The record of my years,
                       A leaf which, if I had it now,
                       Would be all wet with tears.

                       And scarce I dare remember
                       That when we met to part,
                       That tender thought of my inmost soul
                       Lay treasured on thy heart.

                       I miss a chord in my lyre,
                       A chord I dare not touch,
                       To find its thrilling music gone
                       Would grieve me all too much.

                       And sadly I remember
                       That its tones so wild and free
                       Were tones that long had slumbered,
                       Were tones awaked by thee.

I feel a void in my bosom,
A something gone for aye;
It was my music when I sang,
My faith, when I knelt to pray.

It was the quickening current
That made me live and move,
Oh! would I did not remember
It was thy dear, lost love.

3. "The Internal Fire That Consumes"

1. JWH to Louisa, 2 July 1843 (#52M-301[430]).

2. SGH to Sumner, 8 November 1843 (#897); 16 March 1844 (#908).

3. Marion to Louisa, 29 September 1843 (bMS Am 1869.1 [15]); Sam Ward to SGH, 14 October 1843 (#1785).

4. And, of course, her culture vociferously encouraged her to do so. See Barbara Welter, "The Cult of True Womanhood, 1820–1860," *American Quarterly* 18 (1966): 151–74; Cott, *Bonds of Womanhood*, esp. 84–92; and Carl Degler, *At Odds: Women and the Family from the Revolution to the Present* (New York: Oxford UP, 1980).

5. JWH to Louisa, 31 January 1847 (#465).

6. Tension surfaces occasionally in a diary Howe kept during an excursion to northern England and Ireland in July 1843. These notes were probably taken at her husband's request, Howe serving as his amanuensis. Among accounts of model schools, prisons, workhouses, and political rallies they observed are these remarks about a visit to Maria Edgeworth: "She talked long, and with much animation, to my husband—they discussed O'Connel—repeal, Irish politics, her own being moderately conservative—Dickens, his American notes, slavery, and various other subjects, while I conversed with a charming Spanish woman. . . . Miss E. said to me what one says to little women in general, this was all my share, and I took it quietly. I am much accustomed to that non committal sort of conversation, in which one expresses neither thoughts nor feelings. I weary of it in my heart. She spoke of Laura Bridgeman & praised my husband. This gave me pleasure" (1843 diary). Compare the account in *Reminiscences*, 113–14. Note also Howe's parody, reproduced in *Reminiscences* (142–43), of a report Samuel Howe wrote on his visit to a woman who was blind, deaf, and crippled:

Dear Sir, I went south
As far as Portsmouth,
And found a most charming old woman,
Delightfully void
Of all that's enjoyed
By the animal vaguely called human.

She has but one jaw,
Has teeth like a saw,
Her ears and her eyes I delight in:
The one could not hear
Tho' a cannon were near,
The others are holes with no sight in.

Her cinciput lies
Just over her eyes,
Not far from the bone parietal;
The crown of her head
Be it vulgarly said,
Is shaped like the back of a beetle.

Destructiveness great
Combines with conceit
In the form of this wonderful noddle,
But benev'lence, you know,
And a large *philopro*
Give a great inclination to coddle.

Howe notes that her husband was "much pained" when he read it, but she also remarks, with a certain archness, that this unfortunate woman was "one of a number of trebly-afflicted persons . . . whom Dr. Howe found time to visit on this wedding trip."

7. SGH to Sumner, 11 September 1844 (#920); Sam Ward to SGH, 23 September 1844 (#1786); Sumner to SGH, 25 September 1844. Sumner's vehemence on the Crawford matter—his compassion for his friend and his obvious annoyance at the female who was causing that friend such pain and embarrassment—is remarkable. His letter continues:

Teach her, too, that, if she ceases to respond to the love, which has followed her for months, she owes at least in return the greatest tenderness, the most constant friendship. Let her not listen to the suggestions of coldness, & add to the pains of the lover, the mortification of indifference or contempt. . . . here is grievous *wrong*, which ought to trouble the conscience of those, or of her, from whom it proceeds. But beyond this, will be the bitter condemnation of all good people. The artist has already enlisted the sympathies of a wide circle, & his name, in which his country begins to take pride, will give wide circulation to his story. A friend in Wall St said to me to-day that Mr J[ohn] W[ard] was "notoriously a hard man & venal." It is reported that he or somebody about him complained of C[rawford] "because he had no grand-father." I do not believe this; but the world will not be idle in its scandal, nor can L[ouisa] expect to escape the severest judgment.

He adds that although he was "touched" earlier in the month when he had seen Louisa by "her beauty, her grace, her gentleness, & her kindness to me," he feared that he could "never wish to see her again."

8. Marion Ward to SGH, 14 October 1844 (#51M-283[294]); JWH to Louisa, 1 November 1844 (#369). For Samuel Howe's assurances about his wife's affection, see, for example, SGH to Sumner, April 1845 (#939): "You know my regard for you, but you have yet to find out how sincere and warm is Julia's esteem & friendship for you."

9. JWH to Louisa, November 1844 (#410). Howe complained to Annie that their Aunt Francis was no longer among her correspondents because "she takes every possible opportunity of laughing at my husband, and I begin to resent it" (JWH to Annie, 14 February 1845 [#421]). Note also JWH to Annie, spring [1845?], #494: "Sam and Marion speak of Chev in a manner which gives me pain—how little they understand his noble character; I hope they do not criticize him to you."

10. JWH to Annie, March 1845 (#443); April 1845 (bMS Am 1595[1213]).

11. In the fall of 1846, while Howe was visiting Annie in New Jersey, Chev evidently read some of her poetry and wrote to her about it. This letter is lost, but her reply suggests that he was wounded somehow by what he read. She explains the reason for her inclination to secrecy: "if I have not told you every thing, & shown you every thing, it is not because I have not the disposition, but because you have made me feel that in spite of all your kindness, you could not take much interest in my spiritual experience, such as it has been. It has seemed to me therefore both wiser and kinder to sink all these things, and to live only in the present and future, which are all that I possess in common with you" (JWH to SGH, #376).

Consider also this passage in Longfellow's journal for 12 June 1846: "Sumner said at breakfast that Julia Howe was eager to publish a volume of poems; Howe is opposed to it, but does not wish to exhibit his 'inimicitiam [?] in fronte promptam.' Sumner advised strongly against it; and Howe said that Julia has no regard whatever for Sumner's opinion in poetical matters, and quite as little for mine."

12. In 1909 the Howes' daughter Laura Richards published a biography of Florence Nightingale aimed at young people, in which she too attributes Nightingale's life-changing decision to the encouragement Samuel Howe gave her at a crucial moment. She quotes her father as saying: "Go forward, if you have a vocation for that way of life; act up to your aspiration, and you will find that there is never anything unbecoming or unladylike in doing your duty for the good of others. Choose your path, go on with it, wherever it may lead you." See *Florence Nightingale: The Angel of the Crimea* (New York: Appleton, 1909), 34–35. Nightingale's namesake, Florence, also memorialized her father's connection to the heroine of the Crimea by publishing an article in *Harper's* about a 1902 visit to her and by editing ten of Nightingale's letters to her parents. A microfilm of the typescript is at Schlesinger Library.

13. JWH to Louisa, 15 December 1845 (#438): "You must not blame me for Florence's name—it was Chev's choice, not mine. I would much rather have called the child for you, but he was so sadly disappointed about it's [sic] sex, that I thought it most politic to let him have his own way about the name in the hope that it would make him love the little creature."

14. #51M-283 (320), Box 3. Two diary entries from the mid-1860s (#814) suggest that Samuel Howe's admiration for Florence Nightingale was a constantly festering issue for his wife. The entry for 23 April 1865 records a family argument arising out of Howe's plan to deliver a sermon at the Charlestown prison. Her husband, she wrote, "attacked me with the utmost vehemence and temper, called my undertaking a mere display, a mere courting of publicity, would not argue, nor hear me at all." To restore the peace, Howe agreed not to go, but she reflected: "I feel utterly paralyzed and brought to a stand-still—know not how to live and work any further. I have been married twenty two years today. In the course of this time I have never known my husband to approve any act of mine which I myself valued. Books—poems—essays—everything has been contemptible or contraband in his eyes, because it was not *his* way of doing things."

For the next day appears this astonishing entry:

Chev read what I wrote yesterday in my Diary about him, and left a note (he has gone to Newport) coolly desiring me to destroy it all, which I shall not do. I have suffered all day from the nervous agitation and trouble of yesterday, and have done little or no work. . . . Chev said among other things on Sunday that if he had been engaged to Florence Nightingale, and had loved her ever so dearly, he would have given her up as soon as she commenced her career as a public woman. This phrase needs no comment. His sex in general will not endorse it.

15. David Gollaher's recent biography of Dix, *Voice for the Mad: The Life of Dorothea Dix* (New York, Free Press, 1995), does not specify exactly how Samuel Howe became involved in Dix's crusade. He may have met her through Horace Mann, who the previous year had tried to hire Dix for a supervisory teaching post at his newly opened normal school in Lexington. Gollaher's work on Dix is a felicitous addition to the stock of information about the experience of ante-bellum New England women; as he notes, she "fails to fit into the main explanatory frameworks historians have used to interpret women's lives" (viii).

16. Quoted in Dorothy Clarke Wilson, *Stranger and Traveler: The Story of Dorothea Dix, American Reformer* (Boston: Little Brown, 1975), 124.

17. He went on: "I recollect what you were then, I think of your noble career since, & I say, God grant me to look back upon some three years of my life with a part of the self approval you must feel!—I ask no higher fortune. No one need say to you go on, for you have heard a higher than human voice, & you will follow whither it calleth. God give you as much strength as you have courage for your mission" (SGH to Dix, 15 June 1845 [bMS 1838/357]).

18. JWH to Louisa, 23 July 1845 (#418); JWH to Annie, [June] 1846 (#440).

19. The Howes had met Parker in Rome. He had baptized Julia Romana, and once the family settled in South Boston, his church in Roxbury was within range. Howe noted in *Reminiscences:* "One offense against fashion I would commit: I would go hear Theodore Parker preach. My society friends shook their heads" (150). From their earliest acquaintance, Howe felt she had found in him an empathetic soul. A poem from the spring of 1844 called "Parting From a New Friend" (1843 diary) is probably about Parker:

> Thou has brought back to me my golden youth,
> The early days I passed with such as thou;
> I know the look that dwells in thy blue eyes,
> I know the thought that sits upon thy brow.
>
> Again I hear the sounds of other days,
> The laugh, the jest, the pleasant melody,
> The voice of sympathy and gentle praise,
> The breath of kindred souls comes back to me.
>
> Thus, for a little hour, I can look back,
> Can live a moment in the happy past,
> And, in the glowing embers of my heart
> Again trace visions far too bright to last.
>
> They fade, they die, and I pass on once more,
> And yet, my spirit gladly lingers here,
> And, when thou sittest in the twilight dim,
> Perchance its quiet voice may reach thine ear.
>
> Thus will it speak: "mourn not thy lonely state
> Kind spirits hover round where thou dost dwell,
> Unseen, unheard, upon thy steps they wait,
> For true friends part not with their last farewell.["]

20. JWH to Louisa, 14 January 1845 (#415); 1 October 1845 (bMS AM 1869. 1[9]).

21. JWH to Louisa, 1845 (#414).

22. JWH to Louisa (#450).

23. Later in this letter Howe notes, as she frequently did, that "My good Chev has lately been very kind & affectionate to me." But she continues in terms that suggest an accommodation, not a genuine recognition and appreciation of her defining characteristics: "I think he is better satisfied with me than he used to be." And she ends by mentioning a detail of their domestic arrangement noted in several letters to Louisa: they are sleeping apart. Julia Romana's period of nursing came to an end too early, Howe felt, due to the beginning of her second pregnancy; thus she was determined to prolong her nursing of Florence as long as possible as a way of avoiding becoming pregnant again.

Consider also an 1846 letter from JWH to SGH (#376), written probably while she was visiting Annie in Bordentown:

> From you, dear husband, I would have no secrets—if I have not told you every thing, & shown you every thing, it is not because I have not the disposition, but because you have made me feel that in spite of all your kindness, you could not take much interest in my spiritual experience, such as it has been. It has seemed to me therefore both wiser and kinder to sink all these things, and to live only in the present and future, which are all that I possess in common with you. [T]hese three years of married life have wiped out, as with a sponge, all living memory of the past. I have gone with you into a new world, and am become, in many things, a new creature, and, I think, a better & happier one. I firmly resolved, when I married you, to admit no thought, to cultivate no taste in which you could not sympathize. [Y]ou *must know* that my heart has been very loyal. It was long before I learned that you neither desired nor appreciated this renunciation on my part. This last year has destroyed more illusions than either of its predecessors. [Heavily crossed out sentence.] Still, I assure you, I am nearer the attainment of peace of mind than I have been. I will not expect too much from you. I will enjoy all the moments of sunshine which we can enjoy together. I will treasure up every word, every look of your's [sic] that is kind and genial, to comfort me in those long, cold, wintry days, when I feel that you do not love me.

Also to be noted in this context is an undated entry in Howe's 1843 diary, presumably written about this time:

> I live in a place in which I have few social relations, and all too recent to be intimate. I have no family around me, my children are babies, and my husband has scarcely half an hour in twenty four to give me. So, as I think much, in my way, and nobody takes the least interest in what I think, I am freed to make to myself an imaginary public, and to tell it the secrets of my poor little ridiculous brain. While I am employed with fictions, my husband is dealing with facts, but as we both seek truth which lies beyond either, we do not get so very far apart as you would think. At least, I know all that is in *his* mind, if he does not occupy himself much with mine. I have nothing but myself to write about, for four months past I have seen and heard only myself, talked with myself, eaten and drunk myself, made a solemn bow to myself every morning, and condoled with myself that I was about to be left to myself for another day. Oh cursed self, how I hate the very sight of you! do stay away one day and send me somebody else's self to keep me company!

24. JWH to Annie, December 1845[?] (#334).

25. See Schwartz, *Samuel Gridley Howe, Social Reformer,* 84–87, for a brief overview of this controversy.

26. In the context of Samuel Howe's relative insensitivity to his wife's moods, his effort in this note to engage and respond to Sumner's downcast state is remarkable:

> You were sad to day in thinking of some failures in your kind efforts for others,—but would you not make any & all of them over & over again, with the faintest hope of success? You should rejoice that *you have made them;* for when you made them, you gained what never can be lost, the advantage of having acted from a high & noble motive: never mind what consequences it brings on your head,—that advantage is secure. No matter what motives may be ascribed to you,—no matter if your best friends do not duly appreciate them, it were no matter if even God had not given you credit for them,—you have secured what fate cannot take from you,—self-approval. You will think it strange perhaps, but I must say I envy you for what you have been *trying* to do; & would that I had been employed for two weeks as you have been. But a truce to this: I love you Sumner, & am only vexed with you because you will not love yourself a little more. (SGH to Sumner, Monday 9 P.M. April 1845 [#939])

Sumner wrote back on 24 April: "Dear, dear Howe, All that you do or say, I know, is for my good. Your friendship is a chief solace of a melancholy life."

27. Samuel Howe's response to Sumner's speech is 5 July 1845 (#941). SGH to Sumner, January 1846 (#955): "It makes me sad to think that I can throw no sunbeam across the dark path in which you walk. I would I could have imparted to you one half, (I would not assume the whole even to you) of the extasy [*sic*] I felt yesterday when my little Julia, toddling up to my knees, raised her sweet face & said, for the *first time* distinctly, *papa, papa!* Such sounds sweep over strings of the heart of whose existence we were not aware, & make sweet music within us. I have no fonder heartier wish than that you may be a sharer in such joys." See also SGH to Sumner, January 1846 (#956).

28. JWH to Louisa, 30 May 1846 (#452); 24 July 1846 (#453).

29. SGH to Sumner, September 1846 (#976). Writing to her husband in October from Bordentown, where she had gone to visit Annie, Howe sent her love to their housekeeper and added, "I would say to Sumner also, but that I am afraid of making you both laugh" (#457). One hears a similar ironic overtone in Sumner's request, in a note directed to Brattleboro, to give his love to "your gem-wife of purest ray serene" (26 July 1846); Sumner's reference to Gray's "Elegy" can only be intended sardonically. Julia's letter expressing tempered sympathy is #325. Chev reported to Sumner in November that Julia sympathized with him and was "learning" to love him nearly as well as he did (7 November 1846 [#985]). Julia's 1 December 1846 letter to Louisa is #460.

30. The manuscript (#51M-283[320], Box 4) is in a disorderly state, its various sections difficult to date precisely. Bridge passages are missing, and even when it's clear how Howe intended various episodes to fit together, there is still ambiguity about chronology. One section's pages are numbered 2–163, another

section is 50–171, a third is 1–27, and the packet includes several unnumbered sequences as well. The handwriting and paper are consistent throughout all sections, the hand closer to that of letters from the late 1840s than to the larger, less-controlled hand when Howe's eyes began to fail in the 1850s. The account given here is based on my suppositions about Howe's intentions as derived from letters, scraps pasted in her 1843 diary, and the manuscript itself.

Mary Grant in *Private Woman* is the only other scholar to have analyzed this manuscript, calling it *Eva and Raphael*. She argues that the narrative encodes "repressed sexual yearning, the beginnings of feminist thinking, and anxiety about death." She sees it as a direct representation of Howe's "fantasy life" but, incredibly, suggests that it not be too rigorously scrutinized: "The possible interpretations seem both limitless and limited, for although numerous ideas spring to mind, this is still only one piece of evidence rescued from a lifetime of writing and dreaming. Any interpretation, too, must be balanced by the recognition that normal, happy people may have weird fantasies from time to time. Most people simply do not write them down." Grant's analysis, aside from its minimizing of the text's significance, is marred by errors of fact and a misunderstanding of how the disparate pieces of the manuscript are related to one another. See *Private Woman*, 121–25, 227.

31.   Eva to Rafael

>   Do not fear to let me see thee,
>   Soul-enshrined as thou art,
>   God said not that thou shoulds't flee me,
>   But thine over anxious heart.
>
>   Pluck for me a passing flower,
>   Breathe to me a gentle word,
>   I will ask no more, but thank thee
>   For the token seen or heard.
>
>   Many a rose tree stands before thee,
>   Proud to show her conscious charms,
>   Spreads her lucious beauty o'er thee,
>   Clasps thee in her thorny arms.
>
>   I am modest, I am mournful,
>   Thou mayst crush me 'neath thy feet;
>   I'll not even say: "tread lightly,"
>   Death itself from thee were meet!

32. JWH to Louisa, 15 May 1847 (#467).

33. Although this diary is dated 1843, Howe used it as a repository and scrapbook at least through 1853.

34. The various diary notes referring to the Laurence narrative were written originally on other paper and then pasted into the diary. They appear in the diary as follows:

Page 21 [ellipses indicate paper edges]: Oh yes! ye have been steep . . . beauty of his eyes, ye have . . . him, ye can never again . . . but the heavenly. . . . ye have been consec . . . by the kisses of love . . . but Rafael . . . never utter an . . . and true.

Pages 22–23: Most men are afraid of madness—few will defy its dark power, or even attempt a struggle with its advanced guard—at the first look, we behold, something mightier than we, and turning like frightened children scramble back to our strong hold crying to god to fight the demon for us.

Earnestly do I speak of the revelation of God to the solitary soul—it is the knight watching before the altar the arms he has not yet borne, it is the virgin waiting with fear and longing for the bridegroom—it is the heavenly wedding to which all are bidden, but to which men must be compelled to come. But that it does not exhaust the energies and necessities of man's nature is evident from the fact that unto all who have received the first a second one is necessary—the soul that ventures to the utmost [23] bound of those unknown regions is at length scourged back by its own terrors, and warned to come thither alone no more. Having learned the extent of that which can be accomplished by a solitary mind, it remains for him to learn how much more can be effected by the conjunction of two that form one, and to see reflected in that other half of himself the other half of that truth which once his imperfection could but imperfectly receive. Blessed lesson, what cost of blood, of meat, of tears is too great to pay for thee? Learned oftenest in momentary rapture, and lifelong desire and regret, but if learned, the key to the highest, holiest lesson, the lesson of the three-in-one of God, the soul, and the soul's . . .

"member your brother Laurent." one more look, one more benediction, and I was treading my lonely way, through the solid darkness of the night, and knowing only that God would lead me.

let us consume the world ere its earth worms consume us

Page 24: though she loved me not. the creature breathes not, except yourself, who can say that he was happier than I.

Page 25: [a copy of the poem, "Eva to Rafael," which Howe sent to Louisa in May 1847]

Page 26 (untitled poem):

> Yes! I have humbled me before thy wrath,
> And thou canst rail at me, & so rail on.
> But know, thou canst not paint me wholly vile
> My sins may lie deeper than thy virtues.
> So far as love is holier than hate
> As resignation is than every [?]
> Pour Contrition then self-righteousness
> 'So far, found one, my virtues rival thine
> Then plant me as you will, take yr small pleasure
> For narrow souls lack room to bury grudges.

> Shall the world lie between us like a tombstone
> [?] then, nor I have strength to [?] it.

Although it has no obvious connection to the Laurence narrative, the passage quoted above in note 23 ("I live in a place in which I have few social relations . . . ") appears on page 31 of the diary and may help explain why Howe would undertake this project.

35. It is likely that Howe did construct the details about how her character came to have his unusual attributes, but the first page of the work—where we would expect to be told such information—is not among the others that have been preserved.

36. Chronology of composition is difficult to establish. The section I am designating "A" introduces information that other sections refer to and rest on. In the Houghton folder this section includes a sheet bearing the name "Joseph Willard" and a date: "Feb. 51." Joseph Willard (1798–1865) was recording secretary of the Massachusetts Historical Society from 1835 to 1857. In light of his political and religious associations (Whig, Free-Soiler, abolitionist, and Unitarian) and social ties, he was no doubt a familiar of the Howe family, but I can find no other reference to him in connection with either wife or husband. Why this manuscript would have been in his possession in 1851 (if indeed it was) is unclear. In February Howe was in Rome on her own; her husband had returned to Boston three months earlier.

37. Laurence tells her they can never marry: "[T]here are between human beings relations independent of sex, relations of pure spirit, of heavenly sympathy, of immaterial and undying affinities—such are the only relations that can exist between us, dearest Emma.'" Light suddenly dawns on her, and she scrutinizes his body: "she came slowly up to me, and uncovering my arm, held it up to the light—it was round and smooth as her own. With the same deliberation, she surveyed me from head to foot, the disordered habiliments revealing to her every outline of the equivocal form before her. She saw the bearded lip and earnest brow, but she saw also the falling shoulders, slender neck, and rounded bosom—then with a look like that of the Medusa, and a hoarse utterance, she murmured: 'monster!'" (A28).

38. Studies of this tradition include the following: Diane Long Loeveler, *Romantic Androgyny: The Women Within* (University Park: Penn State UP, 1990); Ann Jones and Peter Stallybrass, "Fetishizing Gender: Constructing the Hermaphrodite in Renaissance Europe," in *Body Guards*, ed. Julia Epstein and Kristina Straub (New York: Routledge, 1991), 80–111; and Grace Tiffany, *Erotic Beasts and Social Monsters: Shakespeare, Jonson, and Comic Androgyny* (Newark: U Delaware P, 1995). See also Gilbert Herdt, ed., *Third Sex, Third Gender: Beyond Sexual Dimorphism in Culture and History* (New York: Zone Books, 1994), particularly Gert Hekma's essay, " 'A Female Soul in a Male Body': Sexual Inversion as Gender Inversion in Nineteenth-Century Sexology," 213–39. A useful study of the figure in Greek and Roman culture is Marie Delcourt's

Hermaphrodite: Myths and Rites of the Bisexual Figure in Classical Antiquity, trans. Jennifer Nicholson (London: Studio Books, 1961).

39. William James Barry, M.D., "Case of Doubtful Sex," *New York Journal of Medicine* (January 1847):57–58.

40. The entry on hermaphroditism in Robert Spencer Todd's then standard reference work, *The Cyclopaedia of Anatomy and Physiology* (London: Sherwood, Gilbert, and Piper, 1836–59), 678–738, for example, runs to more than fifty densely printed pages and includes numerous descriptions of instances of the phenomenon in humans, animals, and plants.

41. Ovid, *Metamorphoses,* trans. A. D. Melville (New York: Oxford UP, 1986), 85.

42. In a fourth painting, perhaps representing Buonvicini's compassionate response to the Ovid myth, Hermaphroditus is portrayed sleeping in exactly the posture of the room's statue. The two satyrs from the ceiling painting are standing over him/her, one lifting the drapery from the groin region, the other gesturing obscenely at what is revealed; their action both fulfills and mocks the desire of visitors to the room to gain access to the unapproachable side of the statue. Buonvicini, in seeming to invite scorn for the voyeurs and disgust at their violation of the sleeping figure's privacy, understands that no insignificant part of Hermaphroditus's curse is the loss forever of privacy, the affliction of being eternally the object of prurient interest.

William Vance's exhaustive two-volume study of American responses to Rome records no particular reaction to this room in the Villa's Galleria, although Nathaniel Hawthorne's disgust with the Bernini statues exhibited there is familiar: "One does not enjoy these freaks in marble." See Vance, *America's Rome* (New Haven: Yale UP, 1989), 2:85.

43.
                    each soul is sister to a soul;
God made them man or woman, and left them to stroll;
The world may for a time separate them in vain
Their fate is, sooner or later, to meet again;
And when these heavenly sisters here below meet,
Invincible instinct each to each draws their feet;
Each soul its other half attracts with all its force,
And friendship or love of this attraction's the source,
By a diff'rent name called, union one and the same,
In the sex or the being where God lights the flame,
But 'tis truly the flash which reveals to each one,
The being which completes him, of making two one.

Alphonse de Lamartine, *Jocelyn,* trans. Mme F. H. Jobert (London: Edward Moxon, 1837), 122.

44. Ibid., 137.

45. JW, "Review of De Lamartine's Jocelyn," 561.

46. "Men," she added, "think it glorification enough for a woman to be a

wife and mother in any way, and upon any terms." JWH to Louisa, 31 January 1847 (#465).

47. This "beau," if it was in fact an actual person, remains anonymous; I have found no other reference to him in letters or diaries. See JWH to Annie (#462 and #439) and JWH to Louisa, 31 March 1847 (#466).

48. See, e.g., a letter from 1846, cited above in note 11: Howe writes, "I long for the sound of your voice, for the sight of your face, I would say, for a thousand kisses, were I not afraid of vexing you, & making you say: 'get out, you beast.'" Elsewhere in this same letter she confesses: "When you are affectionate to me, I am too proud, too happy—je serais toujours belle et joyeuse, si tu m'aimirais toujours." See also a May 1846 letter (#463), in which she jokes that when Chev returns from Washington and "humbly claims the slight reward of a kiss," she will turn her back on him and exclaim, "get out, you beast."

49. For Howe, her spouse was himself, in some sense, a "woman" in the intensity of his feelings for Sumner. Since he was married, however, and therefore by cultural definition male, the female element in the conjunction would have to be supplied by Sumner, though it resided in both.

50. Although Emma's plight plausibly reflects Julia Howe's grief in marriage, Howe may also have found the character of Laurence useful as a screen on which to project certain aspects of her situation. Laurence might be understood as Howe's guilty sense of herself, a being fusing culturally ascribed impulses of both genders and thereby consigned to a loveless and sexless existence. Ronald, in this reading, becomes the fantasy-lover whose adoration arises precisely *because* Laurence evades definitive assignment as either a man or a woman, and Laurence is the more admirable because he acknowledges, yet denies himself the ultimate pleasures of, Ronald's love. This view (suggested by Kenny Marotta in correspondence with me) gains credence in association with biographical material regarding Howe's relationship with Horace Binney Wallace, presented in the next chapter. Beyond its autobiographical implications, the Laurence manuscript offers rich ground for speculation about the nineteenth century's understanding of the construction of gendered identity.

51. The *Foreign Quarterly Review* in the spring of 1846 published a review—which Longfellow mentioned in his journal—of several of Sand's recent novels; soon after, he began to read Sand appreciatively. Howe, however, had been reading Sand since the mid-1830s, when her brother returned from Europe with several of her books in his newly acquired library. In *Reminiscences* Howe contrasts Sand and Balzac:

> Of the two writers, George Sand appeared to me by far the superior, though I then knew of her works only "Les Sept Cordes de la Lyre" [1839], "Spiridion" [1839], "Jacques" [1834], and "André" [1835]. It was at least ten years after this time that "Consuelo" [1843] revealed to the world the real George Sand, and thereby made her peace with the society which she defied and scandalized. (58–59)

Margaret Fuller, too, had read Sand before most other Americans and had urged her on her friends, despite certain reservations about Sand expressed in *Woman in the Nineteenth Century* (1845). Patricia Thomson's *George Sand and the Victorians* (New York: Columbia UP, 1977) offers much useful information about Sand's impact on British writers, but the detailed account of her reception in the United States has yet to be written.

52. When Nina, infused with Eva's spirit, sings, Laurence says, "we were borne with it to unseen realms, to unexplored depths of feeling and of foreboding. I was astonished at the power, richness, and variety of her voice. She seemed inclined to task its powers to the utmost, for her song, or rather the various snatches of song which succeeded each other in her strain, varied with strange caprice from the highest to the lowest notes, from light and gay to slow and solemn measures. It was difficult to determine whether of the two feelings predominated in her heart, their light and shade were so strangely mingled—there was a rapture in her anguish, and an anguish in her rapture. Perhaps the two are ever thus indistinguishably blent, in the intense moods of intense minds" (E1–4).

53. In May and June 1847 Samuel Howe and Sumner were passionately debating the prison issue, advocating the Pennsylvania (solitary confinement) system over the Auburn system. Julia Howe attended seven of the eight debates, eager to exhibit her willingness to enter into the matters that occupied him and his best friend. On 30 June she gave a dinner for the Five of Clubs, an event she enjoyed but which nonetheless had the aspect of an obligation: "[W]e had a pleasant time upon the whole, that is, they had—for myself, it is easy for me to find companions more congenial than the Club," she wrote to Louisa on 1 July (#470).

54. JWH to Louisa, 13 June 1848 (#486).

55. For a sound discussion of the tensions leading to Howe's stance as a domestic feminist, see Grant, "Domestic Experience and Feminist Theory," 220–32.

4. "Between Extremes Distraught and Rent"

1. JWH to Annie, 17 November 1848 (#489).

2. JWH to Louisa, 20 September 1847 (#52M-301 [383]); 1 November 1847 (#474).

3. JWH to Louisa, 23 January 1848 (#52M-301[383]).

4. JWH to SGH, no date (#376).

5. The degree of ease was a function of who was telling the story. Chev's version, in a letter to Louisa on 5 April (#998), called it "a very pleasant accouchement, absolutely an *enjoyable* affair," lasting about twenty minutes and involving a "laugh," a "growl," and "one short yell" on the part of the mother. He portrayed himself as taking charge—sending the visiting Sumner for the doctor and the maid for the midwife—and handling all the tasks of

parturition before anyone returned. The speed of Henry's arrival reminded him of a woman he knew when young, who delivered while gathering firewood and went right on gathering. She was a lesson in how "wrong" and "wicked" it is for women to make themselves delicate creatures: "[T]he pains & perils of child birth," he intoned, "are meant by a beneficent Creator to be the means of leading them back to lives of temperance, exercise, & reason."

In Julia's account to Louisa two weeks later (18 April, #485), it is *she* who sends Sumner and the servants on their errands, and although she concurs that the birth was quick, the words "pleasant" and "enjoyable" are replaced in her description by the term "ridiculous." As for the yell, Julia said it happened thus: "I suffered very little for the head, but as Chev did not know how to assist me, I had to make a tremendous effort for the shoulders, & gave one horrid scream, the only one of wh[ich] I was guilty." She also reported significant postpartum pain, a detail missing from Chev's rendition, but one Julia had dwelt on in a letter to Annie on 27 March (#484): "I had dreadful after pains for twelve hours after the child was born, and was not able to turn in bed without severe pain for two or three days, and when I first sat up, I felt a very great lameness in the hips—from all this, I infer that so very sudden a delivery is not so desirable as a more gentle one, it seems to wrench one so in pieces."

6. JWH to Louisa, 18 April 1848 (#485).

7. JWH to Louisa, 1 January 1847 (#464).

8. A comprehensive resource for information about the involvement of Americans in European revolutionary politics in the 1840s is Larry J. Reynolds's *European Revolutions and the American Literary Renaissance* (New Haven: Yale UP, 1988). Larry Reynolds and Susan Belasco Smith also provide an excellent overview of Italian politics of the day in their "Introduction" to Margaret Fuller's letters to Horace Greeley's *Tribune*. See *"These Sad But Glorious Days": Dispatches from Europe, 1846–1850* (New Haven: Yale UP, 1991), 18–35.

9. Fuller, *Dispatches*, 172.

10. In the letter published 27 November 1847, Fuller wrote: "I earnestly hope some expression of sympathy from my country toward Italy. Take a good chance and do something. . . . This cause is OURS, above all others; we ought to show that we feel it to be so" (*Dispatches*, 160). Two days later, Horace Greeley sponsored a meeting in New York to raise interest in and funds for the Italian cause, a moderately successful effort but far too little in Fuller's eyes. On 4 April 1849 she wrote, "How I wish my country would show some noble sympathy when an experience so like her own is going on" (*Dispatches*, 259), and on 11 August 1849:

I see you have meetings, where you speak of the Italians, the Hungarians. I pray you *do something*, let it not end in a mere cry of sentiment. That is better than to sneer at all that is liberal, like the English; than to talk of the holy victims of patriotism as "anarchists" and "brigands,"—but it is not enough. It ought not to content your consciences. Do you owe no tithe to Heaven for the privileges it has showered on you, for whose achievement so many here suffer and perish daily? Deserve to retain them, by helping your fellow-men to acquire them. Our Government must abstain from interference, but private action is practicable, is due. For Italy, it is in this moment too late, but all that helps Hungary helps her also, helps all who wish the freedom of men from an hereditary yoke now become intolerable. (*Dispatches*, 311)

11. *Passion-Flowers* (Boston: Ticknor, Reed, and Fields, 1854), 59–67. Although the poem bears the subtitle "1848," the internal reference to the French defeat of Roman revolutionaries testifies to a later date of composition. I am indebted to Jim Robinson for suggesting that the phrase "With fuller light" in the third-to-the-last stanza may obliquely acknowledge Margaret Fuller's role in sharpening Howe's sensitivity to Italian political issues.

12. This poem's striking gesture evidently had a basis in fact. A letter from Edward Twisleton (15 March 1855, #1697a) includes a paragraph tying this moment to an event involving Sir Robert Harry Inglis and his wife:

What an evening that must have been in the Ball-room at Newport, when Sir Harry Inglis's "charming" female acquaintance, whom he classed for her manners with lovely and wealthy ladies from Grosvenor Square, was suddenly transformed into an impassioned Cassandra, uttering shrill cries of woe as seeing sights and hearing sounds which the well-paid Band of Musicians, and the well-dressed dancers could not or would not hear and see! I wonder whether the late Member for Oxford knows what took place on that night, and whether he regards it as orthodox. I should like also to know whether Lady Inglis deems it to have been in accordance with the Thirty Nine Articles, and with those instructive unread Tracts which she showered in such abundance on her timid friend. There has been no such unexpected interference with revels, since the time when Ulysses, at the Banquet of the suitors, stripped of his rags, stood transfigured, holding his bow and his quiver full of arrows, and poured out his arrows before his feet, and addressed the suitors in bitter words, the precursors of winged death.

During their wedding trip the Howes had breakfasted with Inglis, a leading Conservative member of the House of Commons, and perhaps they reunited during the several weeks the Howes spent in England in the summer of 1850. No record exists (other than this letter) of attendance at a ball in either of the English Newports.

13. An extract from the letter, along with a "spirited poetical reply" by Maria Weston Chapman and other related documents, is printed in *History of Woman Suffrage*, 2 vols., ed. Elizabeth Cady Stanton, Susan B. Anthony, and Matilda Josyln Gage (New York: Fowler & Wells, 1881), 1:81–87. See also Jean Fagan Yellin's chapter on Angelina Grimke in *Women and Sisters: The Antislavery Feminists in American Culture* (New Haven, Yale UP, 1989), 29–52.

14. Stanton, Anthony, and Gage, *History of Woman Suffrage,* 1:69.

15. The moment occurred during a visit to Washington in 1861 (the same trip that produced "The Battle Hymn of the Republic"). The Howes were visiting the headquarters of Massachusetts Colonel William B. Greene, when he asked her to speak to his men. "Feeling my utter inability to do this, I ran away and tried to hide myself in one of the hospital tents. Colonel Greene twice found me and brought me back to his piazza, where at last I stood, and told as well as I could how glad I was to meet the brave defenders of our cause, and how constantly they were in my thoughts" (*Reminiscenses,* 271).

16. See *Reminiscences,* 57–58.

17. To Annie, probably early 1848 (#479).

18. JWH to Annie, 12 October 1848 (#336). In September three-year-old Florence was seriously ill. Longfellow had recently lost his infant daughter Fanny, and in writing to offer condolence Samuel Howe testified to his own fears for Florence's life and the aftermath should she have died: "it seemed to me that all the hours & days after that would be so blank & cheerless that nothing could enliven them. It seemed to me the most desirable thing would be to be buried with her, & next to that to live alone, separated from every one & to cherish her memory" (SGH to Longfellow, 23 September 1848 [bMS 1340.2(2867/2)]). In a letter to Annie three weeks later, Julia reported that Chev was dissatisfied because she gave time to her studies instead of teaching the children (JWH to Annie, 12 October 1848, #336). After weaning Henry in the fall, Julia was also again concerned about becoming pregnant; see JWH to Annie, 17 November 1848 (#489). This last letter is the one in which Julia expresses the hope that she will have "finished the wretched book" soon— perhaps a reference to the Laurence manuscript.

19. JWH to Louisa, 12 July 1849 (#499).

20. JWH to Annie, Fall 1849 (#495); 3 October 1849 (#497); 15 December 1849 (#500).

21. Fuller, *Dispatches,* 322.

22. JWH to Louisa, June 1850 (#531). Longfellow had recorded in his journal on 25 March his concern about Samuel Howe's restlessness and melancholy: "He thinks he has not long to live. He is fatigued with life; his nerves shattered; his pulse, he says, as low as forty-five!" Schwartz chronicles Samuel Howe's continually deepening involvement in Free-Soil party activities in the late 1840s (*Samuel Gridley Howe,* 156–70). On 7 April Longfellow noted that he had walked out to bid the Howes good bye, "who start tomorrow for New York, and thence perhaps for Europe." He observed that the doctor was quite ill, but that Julia after her confinement was "looking fresh as a rose."

23. See Richard Moody, *Edwin Forrest: First Star of the American Stage* (New York: Knopf, 1960), 245–94.

24. SGH to Sumner, 7 and 26 September 1850 (#1041 and #1042).

25. Quoted in Tharp, *Three Saints,* 169.

26. The Howes had learned of Fuller's death during a reunion with Florence

Nightingale's family, probably by letter from Sumner, whose brother Horace had been a passenger on the same ship and had also perished.

27. See Tharp, *Three Saints*, 173.

28. Annie to SGH (#52M-301 [565]); JWH to Louisa, 28 October 1851 (#533), 27 June 1852 (#52M-301 [384]), and 20 July 1852 (#537).

29. Information about Wallace's life comes from George Egon Hatvary, *Horace Binney Wallace* (Boston: Twayne, 1977), and an *Obituary* by Wallace's uncle Horace Binney (Philadelphia: C. Sherman, 1853). Chubbuck is quoted in Hatvary, *Wallace*, 25.

30. The poem as it appears in *Words for the Hour* (Boston: Ticknor and Fields, 1857; 52–56) is more than twice as long as this version. Howe's elisions may plausibly be read as an attempt to blur some of the particulars of her friendship with Wallace (see below), perhaps suggesting the degree to which, even fifty years later, the relationship could be viewed as volatile. The following stanzas appear as noted among the ten in *Reminiscences*:

Between the first and second:

> A marble God stands near it
> > That once deserved a shrine,
> And, veteran of the old world,
> > The Barberini pine.
>
> A very Roman is he
> > Whom Age makes not so wise
> But that each coming winter
> > Is still a new surprise.

Between the fourth and fifth:

> Those voices, illustrating
> > Their bargains, from the street,
> Shaming Thought's narrow meanness
> > With music infinite.
>
> Those men of stately stature,
> > Those women, fair of shape,
> That watched the chestnuts roasting,
> > The fig, and clustered grape;
>
> All this, my daily pleasure
> > That made none poor to give,
> Was near the Via Felice
> > Where Horace loved to live.

Between the seventh and eighth:

His work of consolation
    Abode when he was gone,
A tower of Beauty lifted
    From ruins widely strewn.

Our own inconstant heavens
    Were o'er us, when we met
Before a longer parting,
    Not seen, nor dreamed of, yet.

'T was when the Spring's soft breathing
    Restores the frozen sense,
And Patience, dull with Winter,
    Is glad in recompense.

There, in our pleasant converse,
    As by one thought, we said:
This is the Via Felice,
    Where friends together tread.

Again, my friend turned seaward,
    Again, athwart the wave
He flung the wayward fortune
    His fiery planet gave.

And, in that heart of Paris
    That hides distress and wrong
So cold, with show and splendor,
    So dumb, with dance and song;

Drawn, by some hidden current
    Of unknown agony,
To seek a throb responsive,
    Our Horace sank to die.

The first elision can probably be explained simply in terms of conserving space, the two stanzas describing the statue and pine contributing little beyond window dressing. The second elision, however, helps distinguish the poem's two environments from one another. Julia lives near the convent; its sounds call one to prayer, its Madonna to contemplation. The three elided stanzas describe the scenes in the Via Felice, where Horace lives—a lively, human place where handsomely built men and women vociferously advertise their market goods. That "music infinite" is contrasted to "Thought's narrow meanness." More significant, though, is that the omission causes us to assume that the window through which Julia watches Horace buy morning violets for her is *her* window, when in fact it is *his*. This "daily pleasure" takes place in his quarters, therefore.

The third elision tells us that besides being learned and knowing art well, he is also adept at the "work of consolation," capable of lifting a "tower of Beauty" out of widely strewn ruins. He was, then, evidently Howe's emotional resource during her period of misery. The "consolation" stanza and the subsequent three stanzas also seem to indicate that they met again after they left Rome. Wherever it was, they called it "Via Felice."

31. After his visit with Comte, Wallace went on to London, and from there back to the United States. George Hatvary suggests, without pinpointing the departure, that he left London some time late in May 1851 (*Wallace*, 30). Howe's return trip took her to London (these dates are exact) on 13–14 June; she did not linger there, but embarked immediately for home. If they were on the same boat, Howe would not necessarily have noted it in *Reminiscences*. Annie, it is clear from later correspondence, was Howe's confidante about the depth of her feelings for Wallace. See letters to Annie, one not dated but probably from May 1853, in which Julia mentions how much "dear Horace" will be in her mind when she next visits Annie (#318), and another from 27 December 1854, in which she recalls "that garden [in Bordentown] where I saw our dear Horace for the last time" (#560). In March 1852 Julia spent a week with Annie, and then in June she returned to Bordentown for an extended stay, nearly two months, to assist Annie during the birth of her second child. The February 1853 letter from Howe to Wallace is #52M-301 (401).

32. Howe wrote to Edward Twisleton that Wallace "used sometimes to address me as Glaukopis, and I have sometimes thought of 'Sybil Glauko' as a nom de plume" (20 April 1853; bMS Am 1408 [195]).

33. JWH to Louisa, 18 February 1853 (#542). The context is as follows:

Of course, Annie has written you all about poor Wallace. Was it not a fearful thing, his end? He, so precious, so full of help and comfort to many people, to fling away his life! surely, surely, he was insane. I believe it, and can almost fancy that I saw the elements of it in some of his ways— but that, one is apt to do. Oh! my poor, poor friend, to me at least you are dreadfully wanting. Really, Wevie, since Harry's death I have not had a loss more important, individually, to me. We were very sympathetic to each other—he helped me to my best thoughts, and knew which were my best. I do not wish you to understand that I have been exactly very wretched about him. My sensibilities are much exhausted—I shed few tears for him—it was rather like having had a limb amputated while under the influence of Chloroform, and then waking and feeling the loss in the *want*.

It could be argued that this account begins a good deal more warmly than it ends—perhaps a sign that Howe's attachment to Wallace in Rome was a point of discord between the sisters. Julia may have felt the indecorousness of proclaiming to Louisa that Horace's death affected her equally with that of their brother. At any rate, it is an abrupt transition from that sentiment to the avowal that she shed few tears. Compare JWH to Annie, 18[?] February 1853 (#544): "On Sunday last I wrote an endless letter in French to Auguste Comte, don't tell this to any one—it made my eyes very weak. . . . I shall sit with my hands crossed, in despair, if I do not cut my throat." The letter to Comte, dated 15 February 1853, is #543.

34. Parker to JWH, 2 September 1850 (#1575). I am grateful to Dean Grodzins for assistance in deciphering this letter and for conversations about Parker's relationship with the Howes. Grodzins's senior thesis at Williams College, "'Dear Chev . . . O, Julia': A Critical Edition of the Theodore Parker Letters in the Howe Papers at the Chapin Library" (1983), is a valuable resource for study of this relationship. See also Howe's "Parting from a New Friend," chapter 3, note 19, and the account of him in *Reminiscences,* 159–68. JWH to Annie, 1847 (#462): "After tea, I worked on the blue & red cushion, while Chev read an article on Swedenborg, of frightful length and stupidity—60 horrid pages, & the wicked Chev would not spare me one line of it—the essay was for Parker's Review, & as I am supposed to be familiar with Swedenborg, I was requested to give my opinion of it, wh[ich] was not highly favorable."

35. Written on the back of the last letter Howe received from him before his death in 1872.

36. JWH to Twisleton, 7 June 1851 (bMS Am 1408 [190]): "I should like to find out how Joshua contrived to make the sun stand still. So should my two days in London be each a week long, and include Panoramas, Libraries, Anthems in Westminster Abbey, an evening at the French Plays, and a quiet cup of tea at my ancient lodgings in Gower St, seasoned with endless philosophical dissertations, and the very last anecdotes about Mrs Lawrence. But alas! I shall have at best only a hasty glimpse of you. . . ."

37. Twisleton to JWH, 11 July 1851 (#1695).

38. *Passion-Flowers,* 122.

39. "I would substitute some forcible and melodious word for 'unproven', if I could. There is excellent authority for 'unproved' in the sense of 'untried,' 'which one does not know by experience'—but in those who know any thing of Scotland, 'unproven' is indissolubly connected in association with the cannie, cautious, and characteristick verdict of Scotch Juries, 'not proven', which they allow themselves, in order to avoid the necessity of saying either 'Guilty,' or Not Guilty."

40. JWH to Annie, 17 September 1851 (#513). JWH to Twisleton, October 1851 (bMS Am 1408 [198]): "I find a great difficulty in sending you my little (and very small) poems. I should like to give them to you in a state of completeness, but I am still at work upon them, and of those that are finished, I have but one copy. Had we spoken of this earlier, I could have lent them to you very easily, but in these last moments you could scarcely find a leisure moment for reading them. I think that it will be best for me to copy them, and send them to you, a little later. In coming to this conclusion, I am not in a hurry, you see—my heart really must confess a certain impatience to give them to you, and a very great

desire to hear from you that the conception and execution of them have deserved in some degree, your approbation. But I shall be all the more likely to labour in completing them, if I have before me the possibility of so high a reward." Twisleton responded on 14 October (#1696): "It will give me great pleasure to read your Poems, whenever it suits your convenience to favor me with a copy of any of them—but follow your own feelings as to *when* each Fruit is ripe for plucking." See also letters from 1853—Twisleton to JWH, 25 March (#1697); JWH to Twisleton, 20 April, 7 July, and August (bMS Am 1408 [195, 196, 197]).

41. Quoted in Tharp, *Three Saints,* 173–74.

42. JWH to Louisa, 28 October 1851 (#533).

43. JWH to Annie, September 1851 (#493). In later years Howe often felt that her two oldest daughters habitually took her husband's position during periods of family discord—a phenomenon that no doubt had its roots in this year of separation.

44. *Passion-Flowers,* 101–3.

45. JWH to Annie, Fall 1851 (#519).

46. Sumner to SGH, 15 November 1850. This letter concludes: "I must see you. There are many things I wish to speak of. Let us be a comfort to each other. Y[ou]r career is not ended; but the beautiful life you have led is to be continued to more beautiful things. Who has more than yourself to look back upon with satisfaction & delight?"

47. SGH to Longfellow after the death of Longfellow's daughter, 23 September 1848 (bMS 1340.2 [2867/2]). SGH to Sumner, 2 August 1850 (#1038). Longfellow recorded Sumner's response to *In Memoriam* in his journal for 30 June 1850. In later years Samuel Howe often emphasized to Sumner his affection for his children and his intense interest in their development. He took pride in organizing parties for them. See, e.g., SGH to Sumner, 30 May 1852 (#1090):

We had a party got up upon my plan. We had about fifty children who came early in the afternoon & frolicked to their heart's content. Afterwards came their parents to tea, & in the whole we had about eighty persons, whose pleasure & enjoyment it was pleasant to behold. We had swinging & dancing, & running, & tumbling: we had also music,—& a theatrical representation for the little folks: Altogether it was a good affair—a religious affair. I say religious for there is nothing which so calls forth my love & gratitude to God, as the sight of the happiness for which He has given the capacity, & provided the means; & this happiness no where is more striking than in the frolic of the young. It is true that the sight of *any* true happiness should call forth the same feeling; & if we only cultivated it, we should have a religion that all could enjoy,—instead of our own that is sad & repellant to all but a few minds of peculiar stamp.

Longfellow took his son Charlie to this event and later noted in his journal, "Howe has so much sympathy for children, that he manages all such matters admirably well" (28 May 1852).

48. The manuscript of this 1884 speech is in #51M-283 (320), Box 8.

49. SGH to Sumner, 6 December 1851 (#1063). This letter was a response to Sumner's of 26 November 1851, written from Delmonico's in New York: "Dearest Howe, Three times yesterday I wept, like a child; I could not help it. First, in parting with Longfellow, next in parting with you, & lastly as I left my mother & sister. I stand now on the edge of a great change. In the vicissitudes of life, I cannot see the future; but I know that I now move away from those who have been more than brothers to me, I feel pained by the thought that we may never more meet each other as in times past. My soul is wrung, & my eyes are bleared with tears. God bless you, ever & ever, my noble, well-tried, & eternally dear friend. Be happy, & think kindly of me."

50. SGH to Sumner, 20 April 1852 (#1086), for example: "I have made a rule lately to put in the *only safe* place such notes of yours as might be disagreeable to you to have seen by unfriendly eyes—on the *grate*. It cost me something to burn a piece of paper that has been hallowed to my eye by the impress of your hand, but I do it. I have no confidant for such things—no! not one."

51. The fullest account of Kossuth's impact on America is Donald L. Spencer's *Louis Kossuth and Young America: A Study of Sectionalism and Foreign Policy 1848–1852* (Columbia: U Missouri P, 1977).

52. Journal, 19 December 1851. The Samuel Howe/Sumner letters from this period are full of debate about the legitimacy of Kossuth's claims on American sympathy. From his Senate perspective Sumner opposed the prospect of formal U.S. intervention in European politics, but his friend was a rabid supporter. "My whole heart and soul is with this man & his noble cause," he wrote in April: "I hail him as prophet of good, a high priest of humanity, & I would cheerfully make any sacrifices in my power to aid him in his holy works" (#1082).

53. JWH to Annie, 1852 (#507); SGH to Sumner, 19 May 1852 (#1088).

54. Longfellow to Sumner, 24 August 1852: "The Hotel Rambouillet (so the envious outsiders call our house here by the sea) is a large white building on the Cliff, behind the Ocean House, and not very far from the beach. We have seclusion, no dust, and delightful walks. . . . a very pleasant place it is, and the inmates very merry." *Letters* 3:353.

55. SGH to Sumner, 22 July 1852 (#1094) and 25 August 1852 (#1097).

56. JWH to Annie, 1 October 1852 (#512). "[T]hese little artistic successes were the brightest touches in the picture—you can imagine that I paid dearly for them—Chev's sourness of disposition becomes so dreadfully aggravated by any success of mine. He was miserably sick every time he came to New Port, and fearfully cross—would not go out any where, and was strangely indignant at my enjoyment of society, wh[ich] was indeed very moderate."

57. JWH to Annie, 8 November 1852 (#534). This news came to her at a low moment: "Things do not promise very well for me, this winter. Having lost the

elasticity produced by my pleasant Roman life, I feel worn and weighed down just as I used to feel before I went away. I try to keep myself up as well as I can, but my evenings are most desolate. The children at least amuse me more than they did, a year ago, but my books are all that keep me alive."

58. *Reminiscences*, 184–85: "I had it in mind at this time to write a poem in classic rhythm. It was printed in my first volume, 'Passion Flowers'; and Mr. Sanborn, in an otherwise very friendly review of my work, characterized as 'pitiable hexameters' the lines which were really not hexameters at all, nor intended to pass for such. They were pentameters constructed according to my own ideas; I did not have in view any special school or rule." The poem is "Wherefore" (*Passion-Flowers*, 46–58). Clough evidently felt uneasy about accepting hospitality from the Howes because Samuel Howe's affiliation with abolitionism made Howe socially suspect from the point of view of the Ticknor circle. Clough regarded Julia as "the cleverest of the womenkind that I have met," but observed to his fiancée that "Mrs. Howe dresses so low that I'm always in terror lest she should come bodily up out of it, like a pencil out of a case." *The Correspondence of Arthur Hugh Clough*, ed. Frederick L. Mulhauser (Oxford: Clarendon, 1957), 2:333, 356.

59. The guests of honor on this occasion in October 1852 were Charles Lyell, the eminent English geologist, and his wife. Longfellow remarked on the absence of wine in a letter to Sumner on 27 October (*Letters*, 3:362).

60. JWH to Annie, 8 December 1853 (#540); JWH to Louisa, 18 February 1853 (#542); JWH to Annie, 18[?] February 1853 (#544).

5. "Ye Shall Listen Now"

1. Howe relayed this information to Annie (with whom she had been in close touch during the final stages) on 29 December 1853, a week after the book appeared. Emmanuel Scherb was a German literary man who first surfaced in the Boston area in May 1848; Sarah Freeman Clarke took him to meet Longfellow. The Longfellows offered him hospitality regularly during the next several years while he delivered occasional lectures on poetry and struggled to complete a tragedy on the Bauernkrieg. At one point Sumner reported him hospitalized in Charlestown for treatment of insanity. Longfellow found him "a sensitive, cultivated man, keenly alive to all that is beautiful in Art and Nature" (journal, 21 May 1848). Longfellow's journal places Scherb in almost daily contact with Julia Howe from 25 November through 11 December 1853. He carried poems to Longfellow for his last-minute advice before they were typeset.

2. L. H. Bailey, in *The Standard Cyclopedia of Horticulture* (New York: Macmillan, 1947), 3:2480–81, provides the following account (excerpted here) from Folkard's *Plant Lore, Legends and Lyrics*: "The passion-flower is a wild flower of the South American forests, and it is said that the Spaniards, when they first saw the lovely bloom of this plant, as it hung in rich festoons from the branches of the forest trees, regarded the magnificent blossom as a token that the Indians should be converted to Christianity, as they saw in its several parts

the emblems of the passion of our Lord." According to Bailey, the plant's emblematic qualities were first described in print by Jacomo Bosio, author of a seventeenth-century treatise on the Cross of Calvary, based on a drawing brought from Mexico. In Bosio's account the flower represents not so much the crucifixion as the "past mysteries of the Passion," designed to assist, in due time, in the conversion of the heathen.

3. "Laurence" manuscript, B99–100.

4. *Tribune*, 10 January 1854.

5. Emerson printed in Richards and Elliott, *Julia Ward Howe*, 1: 139–40, 30 December 1853; Holmes: from a typescript dated 1 January 1854 (#51M-283[208]); Hawthorne: *Works*, 17: 177. John Greenleaf Whittier's response passed over personal elements to praise the book's "noble aims," the bravery and beauty of Howe's grief at "the conditions of Europe"; the work, he said, "excited me like a war-trumpet" and would place her "at the head of us all" (#52M-283[208]). At the other end of the spectrum, Francis J. Child wrote to Arthur Hugh Clough: "The vanity of the woman is most amusing throughout her poems: she sets up to be a good dancer, to be a famous musician, a dab at theology, cooking, languages, and all the accomplishments. She hints at a time when she was a leading belle and gives you to understand that her beauty as well as her cleverness entitled her to that distinction. . . . She does *not* pretend to be a model wife and there are several obscure pieces addressed to different men unknown which might reasonably give offense to her husband, who by the way never saw the book until it was printed" (*Correspondence of Clough*, 2:475).

Wallace provides an insightful reading of the significance of *Passion-Flowers* to Hawthorne and of its "[i]mpulsive, transgressive, passionate" characteristics. He argues that the poems "rupture the decorum of English poetic diction and of American domestic ideology," representing "something untamed and revolutionary in American life" ("Hawthorne and the Scribbling Women," 221). Wallace also glances at the "ambiguity" of the Samuel Howe–Sumner relationship as a factor in the production of Howe's poems.

6. Although she took some occasional pride in pieces she produced, keeping a scrapbook of them for Annie, the work was not pleasurable. She wrote to Twisleton that she tried to avoid writing anything "trashy," but that it was "indeed grinding in the Mill" (20 April 1853; bMS Am 1408 [195]). In the spring of 1853 she was contributing twice or three times weekly, her assignments ranging from reviews of Oliver Wendell Holmes's lectures to defenses of the "anti-slavery Duchesses." To Annie she wrote that they had "obtained all the praise they can deserve, or I desire," adding that they "seem to me very inferior to what I have done and can do, with more time for deliberation" (JWH to Annie, May 1853, #318). She had, in addition, set herself the task of understanding Hegel and was making her way through the first volume of his collected works at the rate of about eight pages a day.

7. Fields to SGH, 5 May 1853. This letter is in the Chapin Library collection.

8. JWH to Annie, December 1853 (#555). It is unclear whether she followed

through with this intention. The book was published anonymously, but no one attempted to conceal its author's identity—the reverse, in fact. Howe urged her sister to "talk openly" of it in order to increase sales in New York (JWH to Annie, [29?] December 1853, #379).

9. JWH to Annie, [29?] December 1853 (#550).

10. SGH to Sumner, 16 January 1854 (#1132); Sumner to SGH, 18 January 1854. Longfellow's journal records two reactions to *Passion-Flowers*. The first is on 24 December 1853: "Julia Howe's 'Passion Flowers' published to-day. Poems full of genius; full of beauty; but what a sad tone! Another cry of discontent added to the *slogan* of the *femmes incomprises!* '¿Quien es ella?' say the polite Spaniards, when they hear of any mischief. 'Who is she?' as if there must be some woman at the bottom of it. And here is revolt enough, between these blue covers." Four days later, on 28 December 1853, he reported that Fanny had read some of Howe's "brilliant lamentations." He remarked, "There is a great deal of feeling, poetic and otherwise. I am sorry the tone is so sad." In June 1854 he wrote to Francis Lieber: "What of '*Passion Flowers*'? Are they not beautiful?" (*Letters*, 3:435).

11. JWH to Annie, December 1853 (#548): "This history of all these days, beloved, is comprised in one phrase, ie, the miseries of proof-reading. Oh! the endless, endless plague of looking over those proof-sheets—the doubts about phrases, rhymes, and expressions, the perplexity of names, especially, in which I have not been fortunate. Tomorrow, I get my last proofs. Then a fortnight must be allowed for drying and binding—then, I shall be out, fairly out, do you hear? So far, my secret has been pretty well kept. My book is to bear a simple title, without my name, according to Longfellow's advice. Longfellow has been reading a part of the volume, in sheets—he says, it will make a sensation. Chev knows nothing, as yet. I feel much excited, quite unsettled, sometimes a little frantic. If I succeed, I feel that I shall be humbled by my happiness, devoutly thankful to God."

12. Two more "editions" of the book were, in fact, printed. The first run had been one thousand copies; second and third runs of a thousand copies each were available on 18 February and 14 March. See Warren S. Tryon and William Charvat, eds., *The Cost Books of Ticknor and Fields and Their Predecessors, 1832–1858* (New York: Bibliographical Society of America, 1949), 267, 277.

13. JWH to Annie, [29?] December 1853 (#550).

14. *Tribune*, see note 4; *Harper's* 8 (February 1854): 426; *Putnam's* 3 (February 1854): 224. Francis Child, less kindly disposed, remarked to Clough that the poems "showed a sympathy with poetical feeling without being poetical," citing her "total want of ear" and calling the thoughts "crude in themselves and vaguely expressed" (*Correspondence of Clough*, 2:475).

15. As Susan Phinney Conrad, Emily Stipes Watts, Cheryl Walker, Mary Ryan, Mary Kelley, Alicia Ostriker, Susan Coultrap-McQuin, Nina Baym, Patricia Okker, Janet Gray, Karen L. Kilcup, and others have shown, in the 1850s abundant discouragement still faced women who wished to publish anything. The source was often their husbands. Lydia Sigourney's husband, for

example, wondered: "Who wants or would value a wife who is to be the public property of the whole community?" (quoted in Ann Douglas Wood, "Mrs. Sigourney and the Sensibility of the Inner Space," *New England Quarterly* 45 [1972]:166). Sigourney herself, despite her voluminous literary output, assured women in *Letters to Mothers* (1846) that in becoming mothers they had reached the climax of their happiness. Alicia Ostriker observes that the genteel tradition invited women to bare their hearts, but "gracefully and without making an unseemly spectacle." Women were "not to reveal that they had heads, let alone loins. They were not to demonstrate ambition. They were not to lecture on public issues or to speculate on philosophical or religious ones" (*Stealing the Language: The Emergence of Women's Poetry in America* [Boston: Beacon Press, 1986], 31). Susan Coultrap-McQuin notes that women writers were "stereotyped as 'bluestockings' and as 'strong-minded' women whose intelligence made them 'tough, aggressive, pedantic, vain, and ugly'" (*Doing Literary Business: American Women Writers in the Nineteenth Century* [Chapel Hill: U North Carolina P, 1990], 16). And as Baym has exhaustively illustrated, women who did find a means of expression through writing had an easier time of it if their work could be perceived as in furtherance of a patriotic agenda: it was "much easier to justify women who published for admirable civic purposes than those who published to display their supposedly inmost sensibilities" (*American Women Writers,* 67). See Conrad, *Perish the Thought;* Watts, *The Poetry of American Women from 1632 to 1945* (Austin: U Texas P, 1977); Walker, *Nightingale* and *American Women Poets of the Nineteenth Century;* Ryan, *The Empire of the Mother: American Writing about Domesticity 1830–1860* (New York: Haworth Press, 1982); Kelley, *Private Woman, Public Stage;* Okker, *Our Sister Editors;* Gray, *She Wields a Pen;* and Kilcup, *Nineteenth-Century American Women Writers.*

16. Although he seems to accept Deborah Pickman Clifford's judgment that "little true poetry" is to be found in Howe's first volume, Leonardo Buonomo has examined several of its poems as "examples of the American representation of Italy in the nineteenth century," finding them astute in their grasp of Italian politics and in their suggestive figurations of difference between Italy and America. Buonomo also argues (not very persuasively, for me) that *Passion-Flowers* was a source for Hawthorne's *Marble Faun.* See Buonomo's "Julia Ward Howe's 'Italian' Poems in *Passion-Flowers,*" 27–35.

17. *Poetry,* 64–65, 75. I am grateful to Paula Bennett for her insistence that Howe's work be firmly situated among that of other antebellum women writers who labored to find a personal voice. The struggle generated fascinating and ingenious strategies, yet, as Frances Osgood observed, despite her own efforts to speak frankly from the heart, "woman still / Must veil her shrine, Where feeling feeds the fire divine, / Nor sing at will / Untaught by art, / the music prison'd in her heart" ("A Reply [To One Who Said, 'Write from your Heart']," *Poems* [New York: Clark & Austin, 1846], 46).

18. The descriptors appear in a biographical sketch by Lucia Gilbert Calhoun published in *Eminent Women of the Age* (Hartford: S. M. Betts & Co.,

1868), 621–28. *Passion-Flowers*, Calhoun continues, proclaimed on every page: "Lo, this thing that God has made and called by my name! What is it? Why is it? Behold its passions and temptations; its triumphs and its agonies; its fervors and its doubts; its love and its scorn; its disappointment and its acquiescence!"

19. *Passion-Flowers*, 1–7.

20. Ibid., 8–25.

21. "Villa Massimo" is actually the Villa Negroni, as Howe revealed in two letters to Louisa: "You will find a mention of your villa in the long poem on Rome—only for the measure's sake, I had to call it Villa Massimo, instead of Negroni. I have also taken the liberty of introducing Crawford in a lever-like position, as it was *he* who was near me when I first heard the Nightingale" (20 December 1853, #549). Also, six months later: "Translate, for the sweet nightingales of Villa Negroni, my tribute to them" (23 July 1854; #52M-301 [385]). I suspect that Howe's assurance to her sister that Crawford was the "friend" alluded to was intended to deflect Louisa's thoughts from Horace Binney Wallace.

22. Ostriker notes that in most of the poetry she considers in *Stealing the Language*, "academic distinctions between the self and what we in the classroom call the 'persona' move to the vanishing point" (12). This phenomenon, common in twentieth-century women's poetry, is unusual in the nineteenth century, although as Walker rightly argues, the reason for women to write poetry was frequently to "convey autobiographical messages" and to be understood as doing so (see *Nightingale*, 29–32). Howe's distinction lies in her determination to lift the veil ostentatiously. I am not arguing here that the Whitman of *Leaves of Grass* is coterminus with the man Walt Whitman, only that both Howe and Whitman wished readers to feel this lifting of the veil.

23. Walker describes the use of the image of Philomela, the nightingale, by several women poets of the colonial period and suggests, on this basis, the existence of "a nightingale tradition, bound up with themes of aspiration and frustrated longing." The concept of tradition, she notes a few pages later, "does not imply that one woman was necessarily influenced by the others"; rather, it refers to "the existence of a larger body of poetry to which an individual's work makes reference, consciously or unconsciously. . . . A woman poet need not be consciously invoking this tradition to be operating within its bounds." It is hard to say whether Howe's association of the nightingale's song with the awakening of her vision is a conscious invocation of a tradition of women's poetic utterance; the letters quoted in note 21 suggest that a nightingale found its way into "Rome" because that is what she heard singing in Louisa's garden. But this poem and others in *Passion-Flowers* do, in a general way, exhibit the distinguishing marks of the tradition Walker analyzes. See Walker, *Nightingale*, 15, 18–19.

24. One such engirded being is "the hated Jew," confined to his ghetto, empathetically characterized as a listener to the music of David ("the poet-king"), still expecting "the Christ whom Christians show him not." Soon after her arrival in Rome, Howe engaged a rabbi to help her learn Hebrew (*Reminiscences*, 192). This passage commemorates the respect she felt for her instructor

by contrasting his purified, simple devotion with the "revelry" and "Fancy's masquerade" that Catholicism exhibited. The Jew is a surrogate for Howe, who explicitly identifies with his seriousness; in this identification she recalls Longfellow's compassionate attitude in "The Jewish Cemetery at Newport."

25. Larry Reynolds notes that in the fall of 1849, "accounts by Fuller and others of the defeat of the Roman revolutionaries made their way to the United States, where they were greeted by most with sadness or outrage" (*European Revolutions,* 81).

26. *Passion-Flowers,* 59–67. I do not mean to suggest that—in "Rome," for example—the prevailing *expressed* sentiment is anger. The emphasis rather falls on the city's (and through her identification, Howe's) martyrdom and suffering, as well as on the grief she felt at being compelled, eventually, to leave this site of gladness. The anger finds expression in her decision to suggest a personal analogy with the "piteous fugitive" forced back within gates, her light "quenched" by the "dim North." This "going public" about her domestic incarceration arises, I am proposing, from a need to identify and pillory her jailer. Looked at in this way, the poem seems congruent with the nightingale paradigm Walker describes: "What is significant about this myth . . . is the way it records the burden of woe the nightingale carries and the peculiarly autobiographical emphasis of her art" (*Nightingale,* 22).

27. *Passion Flowers,* 151–53.

28. Ibid., 93–98.

29. Early in 1853, this poem had provoked a striking illustration of the obstacles women writers faced in trying to speak even indirectly of intense feelings. Howe had submitted it to George Putnam, expecting that he would take it for his *Monthly.* But on 25 February she wrote to Annie that he had declined it:

> Now darling, don't be too much disappointed for me if I tell you that Putnam has sent me back my poem, with a short letter, saying that "people watch very narrowly the tone of his magazine," and that his editors thought there were "some lines in the poem wh made it inexpedient to use it." I couldn't help feeling very angry and indignant, but did not write a word in reply, though I have, oh! such a smart Newspaper squib to throw at him, if I chose to do it. The implication of some impropriety of thought or expression was what especially vexed me. (#545)

She did seriously consider drafting a satirical piece, to be called "How to Write for Putnam," and printing it in a New York newspaper. The "squib" evidently never materialized, but this confrontation would have given renewed energy to Howe's determination to be heard—and to express herself as vehemently as she pleased.

30. The quotation is from a letter to Louisa: "He must learn to understand those things which have entirely formed my character—I have come to him, have left my poetry, my music, my religion, have walked with him in his cold

world of actualities—there, I have learned much, but there, I can do nothing—he must come to me, must have ears for my music, must have a soul for my faith—my nature is to sing, to pray, to feel—" (15 February 1846, #450). See also the poem "Philosoph-Master and Poet-Aster" (*Passion-Flowers*, 128–31).

31. For example, Samuel Howe's response to *Evangeline* (8 Nov 1847 [bMS Am 1340.2 (2867)]):

> I thank you most heartily for the kind remembrance which you manifested by sending me your little book.
>
> Had it been a trifle, a straw, a word only which spared me of that remembrance it would have been most grateful to me,—how much more then such a book! It is not however for myself alone that I have to thank you, but as one of the many thousands who will read Evangeline.
>
> A book! a book that pleases, instructs & improves people, what a gift it is to the world!
>
> How much more useful miracle do you perform, my dear Longfellow, by turning your MS.S into a printed book than that of the loaves & fishes which merely filled five thousand maws that in five hours afterwards were empty again! You feed five times five thousand souls with spiritual food which makes them forever stronger & better.
>
> I have no scholarship, & cannot appreciate the literary merits of Evangeline. I cannot even say that I like the hybrid character of the measure; it would perhaps have pleased me better in ordinary verse or plain prose. But I can understand & admire the instructive story, the sublime moral, the true poetry which it contains.
>
> Patience, forebearance, long-suffering, love, faith,—these are the things that Evangeline teaches us,—and how much are these above the physical courage, the resistance, the passion, the strife, the victory,—the things of earth which poets deck out in the hues of heaven and make men believe to be truly glorious.
>
> But I meant only to send you my poor thanks for your kind remembrance & will not be so ungrateful as to impose upon you my stupid comments,—so I will only add that though I see so little of you I will try to have some of Evangeline's constancy in my hope of one day enjoying more of your society.

32. *Passion-Flowers*, 170–72.

33. Paula Bennett, in an important discussion of the means by which poetry afforded women a transgressive medium, suggests that Elizabeth Drew Stoddard's "Mercedes" (published in May 1858 in the *Atlantic Monthly*), in its appropriation of "literary, sexual, and emotional territories" generally reserved for men, was the first poem written by a woman in the United States to breach "the aesthetic and thematic limits sanctioned by domestic ideology." "Mercedes" is indeed a startling poem, but its (or Stoddard's) effrontery is not greater than that exhibited in "Handsome Harry" (or that of several other remarkable

poems by women of Howe's era; see, for example, Alice Cary's "The Window Just Over the Street" in *The Poetical Works of Alice and Phoebe Cary* [Boston: Houghton Mifflin, 1892], 53–54). See Bennett, " 'The Descent of the Angel': Interrogating Domestic Ideology in American Women's Poetry, 1858–1890," *American Literary History* 7 (1995): 591–610.

34. In addition to the five poems discussed here, this grouping includes two with fewer obvious autobiographical markers, but which seem to describe an interaction like Howe's with Wallace—"Coquette et Froide" (117–18) and "Coquette et Tendre" (119–21). Other pieces, too, may well be connected to her feelings for Wallace.

35. In an 1854 letter to the Twisletons, we find acknowledgment that someone specific did inspire at least one of these poems. Howe wrote: "Boston shook its head at some things, of course, but was tolerably civil. Would you believe it, I am constantly asked: 'who is the Master? Who is the Royal Guest?' Now *that* I will not tell, as Kossuth said at Faneuil Hall, apropos to his being asked, 'where he would land when he went back to the Continent.' " JWH to Edward and Ellen Twisleton, 17–25 April 1854; #51M-283 (164).

36. This fact might suggest that the sequence took shape in the late 1840s, when we know Howe began writing the Laurence narrative. In that case they would, of course, bear no reference to Wallace, whom she met in 1850. But it seems more likely that the association of these poems with the Laurence manuscript—if it is not the result of mere accident, a few loose pages arbitrarily stuck in the back of a large manuscript folder—rather suggests that Howe was still occasionally involved in work on her hermaphrodite narrative after her return from Rome. With the possible exception of Parker, no one in her life in the pre-Rome days is likely to have evoked the sentiments expressed in these poems.

37. *Passion-Flowers*, 104–12.

38. Except for the suggestion that the man addressed utters "holy words, that quicken and reprove" and brings "blessing," Parker is in fact an unlikely nominee. The relationship described is manifestly between an older woman and a younger man, and Parker was nine years older than Julia Howe.

39. *Passion-Flowers*, 157–58.

40. Perhaps I should say plainly that I do not mean to argue, here or elsewhere, that Howe's relationship with Wallace *was* physical. I have found no evidence to support such a claim, and indeed, reckless as she may have felt in Rome, for her to have taken that step seems improbable. I do, however, argue that the relationship's intensity was sufficient to be troubling to everyone involved, and that whether or not it became sexual, Samuel Howe found it deeply threatening.

41. JWH to Annie, February 1854 (#554).

42. *Passion-Flowers*, 80–85.

43. In this and in one other poem in the collection ("Philosoph-Master and Poet-Aster," 128–31), Howe adopts a satiric voice—the one strategy she could be sure would irritate her husband (see chapter 3, note 6). In "Philosoph-Master

and Poet-Aster," a poem expressing humorous exasperation at "Theologus" for his impatience with poetry and music, Samuel Howe is also the target.

44. I have in mind here her 13 June 1848 letter to Louisa regarding the former servant Clampit, discussed at the end of chapter 3. Clampit's loose-lipped behavior had prompted Howe to declare that marriage might be an unhappy state, but was nevertheless one in which "we assume grave obligations to other people, & it is quite as important that we should make them happy, as that we should be happy ourselves."

45. *Passion-Flowers*, 46–58.

46. The figure of Napoleon evoked deeply ambiguous responses from those sympathetic to republican causes. Carlyle's treatment in *Heroes and Hero-Worship* and Emerson's in *Representative Men* are typical: Napoleon's early commitment to the French Revolution and his indomitable will are admirable, but his imperialist impulses and egotism caused him to betray his promises. See Larry Reynolds's discussion of him as a model for Melville's Ahab (*European Revolutions*, 110–17). Louis Napoleon, the emperor's nephew and inheritor of his mantle of glory, had repudiated his socialist-republican sympathies when he was exalted to the presidency of France in 1848 and assisted Pope Pius IX in destroying the Roman Republic in 1849.

47. The personal subtext in this poem is significantly less pronounced than in others, but it is arguably there in Howe's association of the slow decline of Kossuth's heroic energy with the ritual breaking of the "nuptial cup"—"knowing too well that life brings us / Sordid and slow desecration of symbols most holy."

48. *Passion-Flowers*, 115–16.

49. Ibid., 154–56.

50. Other poems in the collection that sound this ameliorative note are "Behind the Veil" (86–87), "Ashes of Roses" (166–69), and "Mortal and Immortal" (176–78), the last including a stanza that typifies the cosmetic, unconvincing quality of this group of poems:

> A few short years of smiles and tears,
>   Of suffering, not in vain,
> And the weary smart of a wounded heart
>   I never shall know again.

51. *European Revolutions*, 50. Reynolds cites an Elizabeth Barrett Browning letter discussing Margaret Fuller's history of the Roman Republic. The book, Browning felt, was happily lost in the wreck that killed Fuller, for it could not "have been otherwise than deeply coloured by those blood-colours of Socialistic views, which would have drawn the wolves on her, with a still more howling enmity, both in England & America." See *European Revolutions*, 56.

52. *Passion-Flowers*, 68–79.

53. "Whit-Sunday in the Church" immediately precedes "Mind versus Mill-Stream," Howe's most pointed attack on her husband's controlling nature,

suggesting she associated the injustices Jesus speaks out against with the unequal distribution of power in marriage. Jesus acts from "righteous ire" in scourging hirelings from the temple and overturning the merchants' tables just as the stream with a mind of her own destroys the miller's confining structures.

54. Fuller, *Dispatches*, 119. This letter was published in the *Tribune* on 15 May 1847.

55. *Passion-Flowers*, 40–45. Fuller's association with Italian republicans brought her to a new view of the abolitionist movement. See Dispatch 18, published in the *Tribune* on 1 January 1848:

> How it pleases me to think of the Abolitionists! I could never endure to be with them at home, they were so tedious, often so narrow, always so rabid and exaggerated in their tone. But, after all, they had a high motive, something eternal in their desire and life; and, if it was not the only thing worth thinking of it really was something worth living and dying for to free a great nation from such a terrible blot, such a threatening plague. (Fuller, *Dispatches*, 166)

56. *Passion-Flowers*, 88–90.

57. Swedenborg was, in fact, closely connected with the genesis of these poems that became Howe's first book, as she notes in *Reminiscences:* "In the mornings [on board the ship home] I perused Swedenborg's 'Divine Love and Wisdom.' . . . [W]hen others had retired for the night, I often sat alone in the cabin, meditating upon the events and lessons of the last six months. These lucubrations took form in a number of poems, which were written with no thought of publication, but which saw the light a year or two later" (204). A few pages later she indicates that her interest, while substantial for a period, was not long lasting: "I read a good deal in Swedenborg, and was much fascinated by his theories of spiritual life. I remember 'Heaven and Hell,' 'Divine Love and Wisdom,' and 'Conjugal Love' as the writings which interested me most; but the cumbrous symbolism of his Bible interpretation finally shut my mind against further entertainment of so fanciful a guest" (209).

58. Audre Lorde, "Poetry is Not a Luxury," quoted in Rich, *What Is Found There*, 127.

59. *Passion-Flowers*, 183–87.

6. "Down the Bitter River She Dropped"

1. The phrase is Nathaniel Parker Willis's, part of a letter to Samuel Howe of 10 January 1854 (#1985), responding to his request for an opinion of *Passion-Flowers*. The tie between the two was evidently an old family one, Willis retaining memories from his boyhood of Samuel Howe's mother. The flamboyant Willis had for eight years been editor of the *Home Journal* and a prominent (if fatuous) literary personage, which perhaps explains the doctor's desire

to hear his reaction. Willis had not yet received the book, but had read the *Tribune's* review (and had, through a subeditor, published some excerpts in his own magazine). He wrote: "I am not in the least surprised at the revelation of power there is in the poems. Spite of being myself an aversion of Mrs. Howe's, I read her mind's shut leaves exactly as she has unfolded them, & could have written a general criticism of the tone & scope, without seeing the book. Her face was more legible than she represents it in her poem. She has volcanic resources, and may do what she pleases in the way of fame." Later in the year, Willis would find himself in a position very similar to Samuel Howe's, when his own obstructionist behavior toward his sister Sara's literary efforts would be mercilessly exposed in *Ruth Hall.*

2. JWH to Louisa, 23 July 1854 (#52M-301[385]).

3. Cheney's review appeared in John Sullivan Dwight's *Journal of Music* 28 (11 January 1854): 124–25. Although the review is not signed, Howe identified Cheney as the author (and in after years as a much-valued friend) in *Reminiscences,* 436. In her own autobiography, Cheney paid tribute to Howe's "great sympathy, tender love, and simple courage and faithfulness," adding, "The entire truthfulness which is so seldom united with graciousness of manner, has won my respect through all circumstances." See *Reminiscences of Ednah Dow Cheney* (Boston: Lee & Shepard, 1902), 160.

4. JWH to Annie, Thursday 27 [March 1854] (#552); JWH to SGH, 22 April 1854 (#317).

5. Draft of a letter to John Ward, 13 June 1854 (#1137).

6. JWH to Annie, 19 June 1854 (#316): "The Institution is sometimes mentioned, but I think he has renounced all intention of going thither, as much for his own sake, probably, as mine." In this same letter Howe reports: "Chev is as cold and indifferent to me as a man can well be—I sometimes suspect him of having relations with other women, and regret more bitterly than ever the sacrifice which entails upon me these months of fatigue and suffering."

7. JWH to Annie, 19 June 1854 (#316): "[W]hen I last wrote, I was suffering from recent illness, and from horrible depression. I have been better since. I had at that time one fit of raving hysterics, I was perfectly mad, and rushed from room to room like a wild creature. Chev happened to be at home, and was thoroughly frightened. I became calm at length, but had to go to bed, and finish the day there. I had been having these crises for some days—ever since then, he has treated me very kindly, and has not done any thing to plague me."

8. JWH to Edward and Ellen Twisleton, 17–25 April 1854 (#51M-283[164]). The letter suggests that a fair amount of time had passed since Howe had communicated with these friends—perhaps as much as two years. She excused herself by claiming not to know "in what enchanted region to pursue you," joking that "a letter directed to you at random in Paradise" might not reach them. The joke may conceal pain rising from the contemplation of people happier in marriage than she. Although Twisleton had encouraged her poetic

aspirations, she had evidently not written to tell him that her book was to become a reality.

About the book and her reactions to its appearance, she wrote:

> I feel that I have introduced my book to you in a very irregular manner— I meant, in the course of the letter, probably in the Post script, to have modestly hinted, ahem, that I had published a volume, small in size and pretensions, to which the public had been indulgent, and so on. Having been betrayed, however, into a somewhat jubilant burst of feeling, I might as well perhaps tell you honestly and at once that I consider "Passion Flowers" a clever production. Full of faults it is, certainly, and defective in many ways, but it will speak to the agglomerate Twisleton heart, and may even compel a tear or two respectively from the Twisleton eyes-es and noses. I have just been through a course of dining out, and general *treating* (yankee) in N.Y. At first I looked down and grew red whenever the book was mentioned, but gradually, I attained such a height of impudence, that when Geo[rge]. Ripley (of the Tribune) came up to me and told me that Passion Flowers had not been out of his mind since he first read it, I shook hands with him, saying: "I congratulate you, sir—if that is the case, you will never go wrong." (Please to understand that Ripley and I were already on terms of pleasantry.) Let me implore you, Ellen and Edward, not to read my book with critical wrinkles in the forehead—take it, as you accept me, with a certain tenderness of compassion, and even over the worst passages, say nothing harsher than: "poor child!["] I think I deserve nothing worse.

Almost a year passed before Edward Twisleton wrote in response to *Passion-Flowers* (15 March 1855, #1697a). He was complimentary, of course, praising the book as "the best which has appeared since the year when we were in London together" and adding, "one thing I feel certain of is that it is the production of a real Poetess—not of a mere cultivated writer who, being familiar with the poems of great Geniuses and with the laws of rhyme and metre, indites verses which seem wonderful to the many." Yet his appreciation focused on the comedic quality of the passionate interruption of festivities in "From Newport to Rome" and her satiric portrait of the convention-minded minister in "Whit-Sunday in the Church." He said little about the poems most clearly expressive of Howe's marital discontent, noting merely that some of the smaller pieces, though "nearly perfect in their kind" and "peculiarly powerful," seem to speak "to the initiated only, but, for the crowd, wanting interpreters." And although he praised "Entbehren," he emphasized that he could perceive its truth only from observation, not from experience—a perhaps too-pointed reminder of his own marital happiness.

I suspect that one of the poems in *Words for the Hour,* "A Letter" (99–100), expresses Howe's reaction to hearing from Twisleton during this period, or slightly later. The letter-writer's genial greetings, kind though they are, "touch not me," says the speaker: "We are too far apart, and you / Too closely wrapt in blessedness, / Pressing a cup whose brim allows / No rose-leaf, in its sweet excess." The two of them cannot connect; he is "destined . . . On Joy's wild impetus to soar," she to "rest prostrate, like the dead, / Who knows nor Love, nor longing, more."

9. SGH to Sumner, 30 November 1854 (#1143).

10. SGH to Sumner, 4 February 1855 (#1152).

11. In succeeding years Julia Romana's reciprocal deep devotion to her father became the central fact of her life. Howe's *Reminiscences* records her daughter's attendance on Chev—she was his "constant companion and faithful ally," as a young woman accompanying him every morning to the Institution, where she gave lessons. She regularly took blind students to musical events in Boston, and, at age twenty-five, married her father's assistant, Michael Anagnos. The couple had no children. When Dr. Howe died, Anagnos succeeded him as principal of the Institution, and thus in another way Julia Romana "became" her mother. The brief, disturbing glimpses provided by her parents' letters and diaries suggest that their battles took a toll on their eldest daughter's emotional health. On Julia Romana's twenty-first birthday, Howe recorded in her diary that her first child was "almost a stranger to me." See *Reminiscences,* 439–42 and Howe's journal for 12 March 1865 (#814).

12. JWH, *Words for the Hour,* (Boston: Ticknor and Fields, 1857).

13. Reviews cited below appeared in *Putnam's Monthly Magazine* 9 (February 1857): 219–20; *Harper's New Monthly Magazine* 14 (February 1857): 408; and *North American Review* 84 (April 1857): 567. Howe identified George Curtis as the author of the *Putnam's* review in *Reminiscences,* 230.

14. The book appeared late in December 1856 but bears an 1857 copyright date. A letter to Annie on 3 January 1857 (#571) records Howe's pleasure in it (it is "of course one of the first books of the Age, the country, and the race!!!!"), but observes that some will be displeased with its contents and that it will be, in any case, only a "little world that will take the trouble to read and discuss it." She admits to anxiety about its sales and projects a smaller audience—a problem, since "I want the money to help out the music lessons, and so on."

15. This fact was not lost on George Curtis, who applauded this "exquisite reminiscence of a friendship with one whose name is no longer a private name—Horace Binney Wallace."

16. *Words,* 52–56.

17. *Words,* 49–51. The following year, 1856, John Wallace published another collection of Horace's work, *Literary Criticisms.* Either of these books may have given rise to Howe's poem; in fact, the second may be the more likely, since the poem indicates that it has been two years since the author's death.

18. *Words,* 57–58.

19. Two other poems in *Words for the Hour*—"What I Have" and "What I Bear" (83–87)—may also be expressions of Howe's love for Wallace and grief at his death. If so, they reinscribe the hope voiced at the end of "Via Felice" that the two may be united after death. The second poem concludes:

So, thro' seas that swell to madness with the buffet of the storm,
In the arms that struggle onward, still I bear his lifeless form,
Till some wave, with swift uplifting, on the sands shall lay us both,
On the bosom of God's mercy, in the wholeness of our troth.

20. "The Poet's Wish" (101), for example, suggests that poets ought to be careful about leaving only records of grief and bitterness behind them. Better to die obscure and unloved than to leave "a seed / To harm the simplest soul that lives."

21. *Words*, 96–98.

22. Ibid., 105–7.

23. Ibid., 129–31.

24. Mary Grant describes the impact on Howe of reading, in her late teens, a packet of letters written by her mother:

> Julia could not miss the unhappy suggestion that marriage meant childbirth and that childbirth meant death as she pondered her mother's missives. "I cannot be resigned to her loss," she wrote her sisters. "I will not dwell on this topic any longer, but it has of late occupied my mind to the exclusion of everything else" [16 July 1838]. Nor could she ignore the religious tone of Julia Cutler Ward's writings, for, at the end of her life, Mrs. Ward had been in a perfect agony concerning the worthiness of her soul. Just as important, Julia saw clearly her mother's love of poetry and her fondness for writing it. . . . It was new to Julia, and it gave her the opportunity to develop her own, private image of her mother. The Julia Cutler Ward whom she now envisioned was certainly religious and virtuous, but she was also a poet who accepted publication. (*Private Woman*, 36)

25. Walker describes the image of the nineteenth-century "poetess": "intense, spontaneous, effusive, ethereal" and in particular, "melancholy." This self-definition, Walker argues, reformed the notion of what poetry was: "By defining the poet in terms of the capacity for pain, they implied that women had a special talent for verse. While men were out working in the marketplace, women, so the theory went, were at home suffering quietly and writing poems. Their feelings were more profound than men's; they were touched with tragic insight." See *Nightingale*, 88.

26. *Words*, 80–81.

27. Ibid., 38–44. Elaine Showalter's intriguing pairing of Nightingale and Margaret Fuller, intellectual women who did not like each other, reflects a tension similar to that Howe felt for both women. See Showalter, "Miranda and Cassandra: The Discourse of the Feminist Intellectual," in *Tradition and the Talents of Women*, ed. Florence Howe (Urbana: U Illinois P, 1991), 311–37.

28. See Donald, *Coming of the Civil War*, 298–304.

29. Those not discussed here are "Tremont Temple" (23–24), which com-

pliments Sumner's oratorical powers, and "The Senator's Return" (30–31), perhaps written to note Sumner's first visit to Boston after his beating.

30. *Words*, 7–22.

31. Ibid., 75–79.

32. Ibid., 108–10.

33. Ibid., 63–68. Parallels between the two women's lives are numerous. Kemble's love of her profession, like Howe's of her literary work, was a constant bone of contention. Against her husband's wishes, Kemble had published a high-spirited, candid account of her first year in America (*Journal of Frances Anne Butler*, 1835), which evoked much amused and outraged comment in the papers about both husband and wife. Both women, prior to marriage, expressed serious reservations about their fitness for it or motherhood, but took both steps anyway. Howe's knowledge of Kemble would have come through the Longfellows (Fanny was a close friend) and Sumner, who met her in the Berkshires in 1844 when he hastily abandoned Boston as the Howes returned from their wedding trip. A superbly readable biography of Kemble, and a useful if quirky picture of midcentury cultural life in America's chief cities, is J. C. Furnas's *Fanny Kemble, Leading Lady of the Nineteenth-Century Stage* (New York: Dial, 1982).

34. *Words*, 71–72. Richards reprinted the poem in her edition of her father's papers. See SGH, *Letters and Journals*, 2:123.

35. *John Milton: Complete Poems and Major Prose*, ed. Merritt Y. Hughes (New York: Odyssey, 1957), 96.

36. *Words*, 111–14.

37. Ibid., 119–20.

38. JWH to Annie, 1 October 1852 (#512).

39. *Words*, 155–58.

40. Howe was deeply influenced by both Brownings, as two poems in *Words for the Hour* attest. In "A Word with the Brownings" and "One Word More with E.B.B." (139–47), Howe makes clear the extent of her debt to their inspiration (and also registers her annoyance at them for having disparaged her first book).

41. *Words*, 159–63.

42. Ibid., 164–65.

43. One undated letter to Annie (#570) includes this brief note: "Working every day now on my Play—two first acts finished, very much shortened and, I think, improved. At work now on 3rd act, where there is less to do. Hope to finish this spring." This seems to be a comment about the revision process and thus may date from late 1856. Clifford (*Mine Eyes*, 126) is my source for the probable place and period of first composition, but as evidence she misleadingly cites page 239 of *Reminiscences;* there, Howe is clearly discussing a later work, *Hippolytus*, written for Edwin Booth.

44. See Arthur Hobson Quinn's introductory note to *The World's Own* in his *Representative American Plays* (New York: The Century Company, 1917),

388. Page references to the play's text are to the first edition (Boston: Ticknor and Fields, 1857) and are provided intertextually.

45. *New York Courier,* 17 March 1857. The "tempest of applause" phrase is from George Ripley's *Tribune* review (17 March 1857). Ripley, too, noted the distinction of the audience: "There was the historian, the poet, the novelist, the painter, the sculptor, the loafer, the beauty of the season, and her mamma, for whose addresses see the City Directory and the hotel books. Boston, too, had a delegation. A score or two of lions, forming a menagerie apart, came on thence. The auditorium, besides, contained the cream of society—the editors of the New-York papers." Howe evidently returned home immediately, for later in the week her brother Sam wrote to let her know that the play continued to draw capacity audiences, including some who attended twice (quoted in Quinn, *Plays,* 388).

46. The exact date of the second *Courier* essay is unknown; quotations are from an undated clipping in the Chapin Library. A letter from George Ripley suggests that the author of the *Courier* pieces may have been William Henry Hurlbert, a journalist who had begun writing for *Putnam's* in 1855 and who also wrote drama reviews for the *Albion* (see *Dictionary of American Biography,* 9 [424]). Ripley in any case urged Howe to ignore certain sharply critical notices, which seem to be those quoted here: "Hurlburt's [sic] articles are both flippant & foolish—& taste only of sour milk & water—." This letter to Howe is in Chapin Library, Williams College.

The two had become acquainted when Howe married and settled in Boston, but the relationship ripened into friendship when Ripley reviewed her first book. In her April 1854 letter to the Twisletons, Howe noted that she and Ripley were "on terms of pleasantry." His review of *Passion-Flowers* had delighted her, and she was gratified later to learn (as she also told the Twisletons) that the book "had not been out of his mind since he first read it." Later that year, when anxiety about Maud's birth had brought her to a low point, Howe asked Annie to be sure that, should she die in childbirth, Ripley receive her manuscripts (JWH to Annie, 8 November 1854, #559).

47. *The World's Own* was published on 12 April 1857. I have not discovered a second Ripley essay on the play.

48. McCabe, "Avenging Angel," 98–111.

49. Ibid., 108.

50. Ibid., 101.

51. To Louisa, for example, she wrote in November 1854 (#52M-301[385]): "I must not write further in this strain—it brings tears, and I never give way to these, lest I should lose the little eyesight I have left." In a letter to the Twisletons earlier in the year, she had portrayed herself as nearly desperate in the effort to avoid crying: "I am trying so hard, so hard, not to shed tears, for the sake of my poor corroded eyes—you shall help me. I will stand between you, taking a hand of each, and so we will go off into the pleasant fields of thought, away from the unkind and cruel things with which neither you nor I have any fellowship" (#51M-283[164]).

52. In this attitude, interestingly, Howe was of a mind with her husband. Samuel Howe wrote to Sumner on 30 November 1854 (#1143): "Why is it that we men are so shy about manifesting a natural feeling in a natural way, and letting down the flood gates of the eye to the flow of tears? I feared to go and bid you adieu on Wednesday, lest I should not be able to conceal my emotion, & hide my tears: I succeeded however & wept not until I was *alone!* Alone!—alas, what a word, what a feeling, for a loving heart! I am quite sure that, physically speaking, it is far better to weep when we feel prompted to do so than to refrain. Nature does every thing aright, & when we are *sure* we feel her real promptings we had better follow them. I ought to know, for I have swallowed in silence & with an exterior as calm as might be, bitter tears enough to turn my whole system into gall & wormwood."

53. Ripley to JWH, 14 April 1857 (Chapin Library). In this letter he also assured her that his high regard for the play owed nothing to his "love" for her, but was entirely a reaction to "[her] own merits & the force of truth."

A letter Howe received from Theodore Parker a few months later offers an illuminating contrast in how Ripley and Parker understood the idea of friendship. Beginning by observing that Howe could "have not many friends to whom your welfare is so dear as to me," Parker continued by lamenting the fact that she was so frequently at odds with her husband: "It grieves me sadly to see you both unhappy—each made so by the other. He has fine talents; Genius in some particulars, & a certain chivalry, & heroism of *Generosity,* which quite compensate for diverse failings." She, too, has many strengths, but Parker "need not say how rich" she is: "It seems to me you have all that mortal need ask. Health, talents, culture, competence, a distinguished success in your literary efforts, social position, five children, held gifted all in mind & body.—Surely the material of welfare abound." In light of this, he urged her to concentrate her efforts where they might do most good: "It seems to me not difficult for one so richly gifted as you to turn out such a silver lining in the house as shall fill it all with brightness, & charm it into love. Chev has his faults—some of them you bear with great sweetness,—but there is such a soul of *Generosity* in him that it seems to me you might make such music as would charm all the little household duties about him & so gladden & bless all the family,—making the seven into one." Doing this, he assured her, did not require the sacrifice of her literary "aspirations"; she should, by all means, "respect the individuality of [her] own nature." But, he added, "Nature has seldom blessed a woman with so many gifts of sense & skill; can't you turn these to the great purpose, the Art of Life? . . . Forgive me if I beg you to use great talents greatly, for this greatest end" (29 July 1857; see Grodzins, "Dear Chev . . . ", 110–12).

54. JWH to Annie, December 1857 (#578).

55. JWH, *A Trip to Cuba* (Boston: Ticknor and Fields, 1860). Schriber has examined Howe's accounts of her excursions in "Julia Ward Howe and the Travel Book," 264–79.

56. See chapter 4, note 15.

57. On the sources of the imagery, see Edward D. Snyder, "The Biblical

Background of the 'Battle Hymn of the Republic,' " *New England Quarterly* 24 (1951):231–38; and Edmund Wilson, *Patriotic Gore* (New York: Oxford UP, 1966), 92–96. Wilson finds Howe's treatment of Jesus "characteristic of Calvinism" and argues that his presence in the poem is a matter of obligation: "As is often the case with Calvinists, Mrs. Howe, though she feels she must bring Him in, gives Him a place which is merely peripheral. He is really irrelevant to her picture, for Christ died to make men holy; but this is not what God is having *us* do" (96). Deborah Clifford appears to accept this reading, seeing the depiction of Jesus (in the "lilies" stanza) as a sign of Howe's reversion to evangelicalism (*Mine Eyes,* 147). Yet it seems to be Christ's courage facing torture and excruciating death, rather than the emblematic redemptive aspect of the crucifixion, that the poem likens to the sacrifice readers are asked to make. The third stanza depicts a "Hero" born to crush the "serpent." This image of Christ is not necessarily Calvinistic or evangelical (and nothing at this point in Howe's life suggests a return to a mode of belief she had abandoned with relief twenty years earlier); instead, it may recall the militant, conviction-driven figure so compellingly limned in "Whit-Sunday in the Church."

58. *Reminiscences,* 268–69: "In his heart was written the music of the law of love. Before his eyes was the scroll of the great designs of Providence. And so, being at peace in himself, he promoted peace and harmony among those with whom he had to do; unanimity of action during the war, unanimity of consent and rejoicing when peace came. So beneficent a presence has rarely shown itself among us. I trust that something of its radiance will continue to enlighten our national counsels and to cheer our hearts with the great hope which made him great."

59. Tharp, discussing Howe's difficulty in finding a way to contribute to the war effort, notes another reason nursing was out of the question for her: "Miss Dorothea Dix, fearful lest the breath of scandal should touch her first corps of army nurses, was said to have decreed that no one need apply who was not plain almost to the point of being ill-favored. Julia Ward Howe was far too attractive ever to qualify." See *Three Saints,* 242.

60. Annie Dillard, introduction to *Modern American Memoirs,* ed. Dillard and Cort Conley (New York: HarperCollins, 1995), ix.

61. #814. See chapter 3, note 14.

62. Richards and Elliott, *Julia Ward Howe,* 1:75.

Index

References to poems by Julia Ward Howe are listed by title, in most cases followed by an indication of the source of the text. *PF* designates *Passion-Flowers; WH* designates *Words for the Hour;* MS designates an unpublished manuscript.